THE RIGHTS OF MY PEOPLE

THE RIGHTS OF MY PEOPLE

LILIUOKALANI'S ENDURING BATTLE
WITH THE UNITED STATES
1893–1917

Neil Thomas Proto

Algora Publishing
New York

Library of Congress Cataloging-in-Publication Data —

Proto, Neil Thomas.
    The rights of my people : Liliuokalani's enduring battle with the United States 1893–
1917/ Neil Thomas Proto.
        p. cm.
    Includes bibliographical references and index.
    ISBN 978-0-87586-720-5 (trade paper: alk. paper) — ISBN 978-0-87586-721-2 (hard
cover : alk. paper) 1. Liliuokalani, Queen of Hawaii, 1838–1917—Political and social views.
2. Liliuokalani, Queen of Hawaii, 1838–1917—Influence. 3. Hawaii—Kings and rulers—
Biography. 4. Sovereignty—Case studies. 5. Law—Hawaii—History. 6. Law—United
States—History. 7. Culture conflict—Hawaii—History. 8. Culture conflict—United
States—History. 9. Hawaii—Relations—United States. 10. United States—Relations—
Hawaii. I. Title.
    DU627.18.P766 2009
    996.9'027--dc22

                                    2009015486

Front Cover: Queen Liliuokalani (1838–1917), Hawaii's last queen.
Library of Congress LC_USZ62_27979

Printed in the United States

All throughout the long night the Queen lay in the Throne Room of the palace, the kahili-watches were made eloquent by the unforgettable Hawaiian wail for the dead.... [N]o other sound could possibly have within it the same wild, weird note of primitive grief, and the storming of outraged agony that refuses to submit to the onrushing ages and their ever-advancing changes.

— Wm. C. Hodges, Jr.
The Passing of Liliuokalani (1918)

TABLE OF CONTENTS

PROLOGUE. DUTY: WASHINGTON, DC, APRIL 7, 1910

On the day of the oral argument in *Liliuokalani v. United States of America* before the United States Court of Claims, the *Evening Star* described the weather as wet and unusually cool. It had been that way for more than a week. "In the lore of Hawaii," when such precipitation accompanied a fallen monarch it signified "that the spirit of the departing *ali'i* has found favor in the heavens." In Washington, DC, such precipitation in April signified the onslaught of discomfort; the impending humidity and stagnation that typified the spring and summer with no breeze to cleanse it.[1]

Liliuokalani, for the first time since the *coup d'état* in 1893, was seeking judicial review of her claim that the rents and proceeds from the Crown lands — upon which she lived in her former public life — had been improperly taken from her. From the moment of the *coup d'état* she had placed responsibility for the loss of Hawaii's constitutional monarchy and her sustenance on the United States of America.

Umbrellas and carriages mingled with trolleys and fashionable rain gear as the Queen's Counsel, Sidney Miller Ballou of Honolulu, left the subtle elegance of the Shoreham Hotel. His walk to the courthouse — a few blocks away — would take him through the dew-laden statues and green shrubbery of Lafayette Square. His task before the court of claims appeared formidable.

The court of claims, located on the corner of 17th Street and Pennsylvania Avenue, was not a house built for justice. It had been designed by James Renwick, Jr. to house and display William Corcoran's American and European collection of paintings. Renwick crafted the Corcoran Gallery's façade and interior in the French Second Empire style; in the manner of Napoleonic grandeur and a renewed commitment to a geopolitical empire. The building's ornate exterior gave way to a flowing and majestic interior staircase that opened into a 4,300-square foot grand salon with a forty-foot ceiling. In 1899, the United States purchased the building for a political and legal purpose. The grand salon was converted into a courtroom.[2]

The court of claims was located on the north side of Pennsylvania Avenue. On Pennsylvania Avenue's south side was the executive office building. It housed the Department of the Navy. The building also was designed in the Second French Empire style. Its interior motif was tempered by the nautical symbols that stood, triumphant, for America's geopolitical extension of military and commercial power to the Philippines, Puerto Rico, Cuba, the Isthmus of Panama, and the Islands of Hawaii.

In 1909, the Navy's sixteen new first class battleships — the "Great White Fleet" — had circumnavigated the world. A million people watched the Fleet depart from San Francisco on the Pacific portion of its voyage. The navigation was mostly for theater. But the message was plain: "The Pacific was as much our home waters as the Atlantic." The Fleet remained in its "home waters" when it docked in Hawaii. Battleships and their crews in dress whites occupied with a fledgling comfort the Crown lands once the province of Queen Liliuokalani.[3]

Since the annexation of Hawaii in 1898 and the passage of the Organic Act by the United States Congress in 1900, title to the Crown lands had been transferred to the United States of America. Those men who led the *coup d'état* in 1893 unilaterally declared that a million acres of such property no longer belonged to the Queen. They took, began to dispose, and then later transferred the remainder of the Crown lands without conditions or legal impediments and without providing any recourse in law or fairness to the Queen or the native Hawaiians for whom the land was held in trust. The resentment among native Hawaiians only seethed the more beneath the veneer of a governance arrangement that had largely and deliberately disenfranchised their otherwise dominant voting strength and historic presence.

The most prominent leaders who wrote, confirmed, and judicially and politically upheld the legality of that declaration and ultimate transfer included four lawyers. William O. Smith and Sanford Dole were the sons and Lorrin Thurston the grandson of Calvinist missionaries who colonized Hawaii in the early 1800s. Each man had been instrumental in Hawaii and the United States in denigrating the Queen's efforts in 1893 to add democratic elements to the Hawaii constitution. Each also had aided the coalescence of their private, exclusively Caucasian vigilante army into the timely, visible and decisive exercise of American military prowess plain enough for the Queen to witness from the veranda of the Iolani Palace as the *coup d'état* unfolded. The fourth lawyer was Sidney Miller Ballou, who, with a seemingly artful maneuver, now served as the Queen's Counsel.

Adjacent to the executive office building and separated by a courtyard is the White House. In April 1910, it was occupied by William Howard Taft. The Republican Party, led first by President William Henry Harrison, then President William McKinley, then President Theodore Roosevelt, and now President Taft had insisted on and supported the annexation of Hawaii with all the conventional means available in politics, law, and force. To many people in the executive office building acquiring Hawaii also was an integral part of our destiny as a nation. Within the fragile pretense of that "destiny" were the ubiquitous imperatives of racial and cultural condescension and the still rigorously displayed remnants of the Civil War. Such views were ensconced firmly in the minds and acts of war by four Presidents and leaders of the United States Congress. It had been that way in the corridors, social circles, and political culture of the nation's capital for almost four decades.

Only two months before the oral argument that Ballou had come to make, Liliuokalani left Washington, DC, for the last time to return to her Hawaii. Her efforts, engaged in personally and at considerable personal expense, to secure recognition of America's wrongdoing from the president and Congress had failed. She left "[d]iscouraged and broken down in health." To some individuals, the court of claims petition remained her singular hope for a broader vindication of principle and to stem the growing and disquieting effects of her personal financial fragility. Nonetheless, there was no unanimity among those close to her that such a claim was likely to prevail.[4]

Into the Grand Salon courtroom walked the attorney for the United States of America, Samuel S. Ashbaugh. Erudite and experienced, Ashbaugh had practiced frequently before the court of claims. He had sought the immediate dismissal of Ballou's petition and its legal arguments. Ashbaugh's reasoning was tempered by a defensive political as well as legal perspective. The real wrongdoing against the Queen, he had written, lay back in Hawaii among those who led the *coup d'état*. The United States, he contended further, had no related obligation.

Ashbaugh's office was located on Jackson Place in a Federalist style townhouse a block's walk from the court house and the White House and the Navy Department. The office was in a neighborhood of leafy streets and splendid townhouses. His neighbors included the homes of John Hay, the Secretary of State when Hawaii was annexed, and Henry Adams, the Boston Brahmin of both elite taste and intellectual stature. Both men entertained regularly the quintessential imperialist and cultural racist of this moment, Senator Henry Cabot Lodge of Massachusetts.[5]

Lodge was the personification of something quite more pervasive and disquieting than the imperatives that yielded the annexation of Hawaii. In his temperament and perspective were a "dauntless intolerance;" a recognition that no other culture or moral system or form of spiritual belief had the right or an enduring reason to impede the inexorable and righteous dominance of his own. The comfort that Lodge derived from the *coup d'état* in Hawaii was in the triumph of the

Anglo-Saxon and Christian missionary forces over the native Hawaiians. In *Liliuokalani v. United States of America* one problematic effect of that triumph remained alive. It was personified in the Queen.[6]

There was no threat by April 1910 that the constitutional monarchy would be restored or that the Queen sought restoration, except perhaps in her heart. To men like Lodge and William O. Smith, there was something deeper that lingered unresolved. It was found in Liliuokalani's seemingly quixotic persistence. She was seventy-one years old. What loomed large was the prospect of the legacy of such persistence.

The native Hawaiian in Liliuokalani — deep, subtle, recalcitrant even to her own adoption of Western mores — remained alive fully. She did not know her place; and her conduct since 1893 suggested she understood the exercise of political power in America. Worrisome, indeed, was that she was bolstered and defined by native Hawaiians throughout her former domain. Tens of thousands of men and women who formed the Hawaiian Patriotic League in 1893 in opposition to annexation retained, despite their failure, a steadfast commitment to their homeland and their Queen. They continued in that commitment undeterred by the missionary zeal of their adversaries in Hawaii and the Anglo-Saxon jurisprudence that had provided comfort in the nation's capital. The full, hoped-for effects of the *coup d'état* were not complete.

As the lawyers- Ballou and Ashbaugh — stood for the oral argument, the clerk announced the entrance of the judges who would hear the case. Chief among them was the Honorable Fenton W. Booth. He, too, was borne of the Republican Party. Within ten days of Theodore Roosevelt's inauguration, Booth was nominated by the president to the United States Court of Claims. When the attorneys for the United States and Liliuokalani entered the court room, Judge Booth's ambition for elevation by President Taft already may have manifested itself.[7]

In the solitude of Washington Place, the Queen's classically-crafted home in Honolulu, seated perhaps on the simple, splendid white lanai that surrounds it, Liliuokalani awaited the outcome of the first judicial clash between her native Hawaiian culture and the United States of America. No doubt she had much on her mind. On that day, in that court room, the Queen had no one who truly believed in her position.

Her once flowing dark hair was, by now, a dignified gray, often coiffed neatly behind her head which she held stately in place for photographs and by habit. She often wore black when, as in this moment, she was visible to the public. To some people the dark hue in her clothing was a mournful reflection of the loss of her husband, John. To others, the unadorned black also reflected the loss of Hawaii, not in the inevitability of it but in the unprincipled taking. Black was dissonance; a rejoinder to those people and nations seeking an easy comfort.

In the shadowed quietude of the evening, she would have viewed the flow-ered lushness of her home's gardens and the expansive grasses that melded into the storied structure that lay only a few hundred yards away. Iolani Palace, where she once resided and governed, was now the office of the Territorial Governor. High atop its standard, still in the evening's calm, was the reason for his succes-sion: the flag of the United States of America. Perhaps she found solace in the future; in a memory it was still her duty to create.

PART I. WHERE THE SUN RISES: THE FIRST BATTLE FOR SOVEREIGNTY

CHAPTER 1. THE PRESCIENCE TO DRAW LINES

In the anticipated calm of dusk slowly forming a sharp gray clarity to the grounds and nearby government buildings, Queen Liliuokalani moved forthrightly onto the verandah of the Iolani Palace. From a distance her Victorian dress with its formed bodice, accented by the black laced shawl that accompanied her inner mourning, easily distinguished her to each passersby watching in awe along King Street. When summoned to the verandah by aides and the incongruous sounds of men marching and equipment handled and pulled she already knew what to expect: the United States Marines. It was January 16, 1893.

There had been time to think through a response. In November 1892, the Queen was made aware that "it was the intention of the American Minister [John Stevens], with the aid of some of our residents, to perfect a scheme of annexation, and that [the] Cabinet had knowledge of the fact." In mid-December, "the perfect correctness" of that intention was confirmed in terms that were global but not surprising to her in their geopolitical and ideological reach. "Some American official," she was informed further and reliably, had been given "to understand that he had instructions to press and hurry up the annexation scheme...with the help and assistance of the present Cabinet."[8]

President Benjamin Harrison and his secretaries of state, James Blaine and John Foster — their diplomatic pretense to neutrality aside — had been easily discernable advocates for the annexation of Hawaii. Harrison's loss in the November 1892 election to Grover Cleveland was well known to the Queen. She welcomed it immediately. She had met Cleveland during her first visit to Washington, DC, in 1887. Harrison, a Republican, would remain president only until March 4 when Cleveland would be inaugurated. The United States was in a hurry. So, too, were the leaders of the long brewing, now imminent *coup d'état*.

Members of the cabinet already had distinguished themselves to the Queen as disingenuous, unprincipled pawns in service to the *coup's* leaders. With accuracy she recognized one of them as unabashedly "a traitor."[9]

In that moment, on the verandah, a warm breeze of normally melodic memories of her nation's islands and people — harshly disrupted by the distaff sounds and malevolent motives unfolding elsewhere — embraced Liliuokalani's intellect and wisdom and duty as queen. In critical respects she was prepared for this moment. She already had moved methodically to seek political strength among native Hawaiians and, when appropriate, was prepared to draw her own lines in order to preserve the integrity of the Hawaiian kingdom and the culture that had defined her and nourished its people. She had no illusions about the formidable power, including the now obvious control of the means of violence, possessed and displayed by her adversaries. She also knew she had resources and skills and the need to take the long view. The unfolding confrontation would not be — and she could not allow it to be — resolved quickly or easily.

On two occasions she had assumed the responsibilities of regent when her brother, King Kalakaua, had left Hawaii during his reign; in 1881 for nine months, and in 1890, when he left to visit San Francisco for his health and returned draped in the black crape of death. Cabinet ministers had insisted they share equally in the responsibilities of governance. She refused any such limitation. She embraced singular accountability. To the discomfort and enduring recognition of the cabinet's members and those men who controlled them, her choices were prudent, decisively made, and largely praised. It did not endear her to them or how they thought about the future or the place of women in governance. She directed executive agencies with clarity including through an unexpected emergence of small pox. She understood daily the meaning of controlling government; the depth of its reach into people's lives and the fate of the nation.[10]

She also was aware acutely, including within her own family and ancestry, that death — through disease, neglect, depression, imposed hard labor, and the missionary and business community's often callous disregard and racial condescension for the "heathen" — had disseminated with cruelty the native Hawaiian people. She had experienced their warmth, self-reliance, broadly-formed literacy, their manifest commitment to family and neighbors, and her commitment to them for the preservation of their lives and culture and the Hawaiian meaning of justice and *aloha* each time she traveled the islands to touch and be touched and to learn. From the moment of her early teenage participation in discussions of the affairs of state until she took the throne at age fifty-two, she came to understand the depth of her commitment to what began rhetorically during the reign of Kamehameha IV and V but emerged concretely during the reign of her brother and blossomed fully during her own: the ideological and practical imperative of "Hawaii for the Hawaiians."[11]

Only days earlier, Liliuokalani had sat in the Palace's Blue Room with her cabinet. All men. None was her first choice to hold the constitutionally-recognized responsibility they now did. Under a constitution she deplored but, with a recognized reluctance, had sworn to uphold, each of these men had been forced on her by the legislature. There were few decisions she could make without the cabinet's collective approval. It was a system reflective of neither the British nor American order of governance. Hawaii had a council of elders through proxy. The nation's order of governance was founded in seventeenth-century New England.

Liliuokalani had crafted a new constitution. The council of elders would be abolished. She could appoint her own cabinet without legislative approval and the influence of those men who had often captured the nation's government. The appointment authority gave her more direct control of the executive departments in a nation where the legislature was not in constant session and where the disposition of valuable swathes of property and resources, the granting of licenses and franchises, and the conduct of foreign affairs were engaged in daily.

Other proposed changes to the constitution also were dramatic; none so disquieting to the leaders of the imminent *coup d'état* than her proposed abolition of the life tenure of Supreme Court judges. Here, too, was a source of power and a branch of government that — from the early days of the Supreme Court's establishment in 1840 — the forces now moving inexorable toward the *coup d'état* had solidly and knowingly controlled. At stake that morning in the Blue Room was the fate of precisely the land tenure, hereditary, property, and contract labor laws that, in the end, the judiciary determined. Preeminent among those men whose tenure and power and communal prestige of office were at risk was 48 year old Justice Sanford Dole.

Dole was a lawyer, the son of missionary parents. He was tall and lanky, with neatly trimmed white hair and a plainly untrimmed, double-pointed beard. He appeared frequently in the dark suits and stiff-collared shirts that marked his parent's origins: New England. He had been appointed to the Supreme Court in 1887 by King Kalakaua under a constitution imposed on the king under threat of violence and assassination and in the presence of an armed Caucasian paramilitary force. No comparable disregard for an orderly transition in governance had occurred in Hawaii since a constitutional monarchy and a form of popular elections had been instituted in 1840.[12]

Dole was part of the leadership that had crafted the 1887 constitution. Without any specific allegation that the King had violated the existing constitution, and in the absence of any principled adherence to the law, Dole was part of the arrangement that yielded his appointment and further secured control of the judiciary. It is unclear that in the absence of coercion the King would have considered Dole qualified. The constitution imposed on Kalakaua had one underlying purpose: Ensure that a council of elders, whether formally part of the government or not, controlled the two branches of government that mattered, the executive departments and the judiciary.

In what was effectively a palace *coup d'état*, Dole exposed himself for what he was: A man perfectly capable of the expediencies necessary to take by force what was essential for power under guise or pretense. In 1887, the pretense was the king's formal acquiescence to a new constitution. It was precisely this imposed constitution that Liliuokalani — away at the time in England but already the designated heir to the throne — vowed to change in accordance with established law and precedent. She had made her intention plain when she hurriedly took the oath of office following the untimely death of her brother in 1891; standing in her black embroidered holoku dress; disquieted in this radical alteration of her fate but in full control of her duty and sense of history. Her proposed revision to the 1887 constitution was now before the cabinet.

She also knew that one revision bore piercingly into the soul of Hawaii's past: changes to the law on who could vote. In 1874, when full manhood suffrage was restored in Hawaii through 1887 (when the Dole imposed constitution eliminated it in favor of severely restrictive property requirements and race-based prohibitions against naturalized Asian voters), Hawaii's population was nearly sixty thousand people. Forty-four thousand were pure native Hawaiian and another three thousand five hundred were part Hawaiian ancestry. Fewer than three thousand were Caucasian and only thirteen hundred were of American ancestry. Hawaiians elected by the popular vote dominated the House of Representatives. That domination was no longer the reality. The property restrictions on the franchise and control of the executive and judicial branches of government had corroded artificially native Hawaiian participation in the land they called home and dominated numerically.[13]

Almost immediately after the coerced imposition of the 1887 constitution, native Hawaiians came together to form the *Hui Kalaiaina* — the "Political Association" — to protest substantively and actively the diminishment of native voting rights and a place in governance. They and others informally petitioned Liliuokalani to revise the 1887 constitution; a proposition she began to examine as early as 1889. With her ascendancy to the throne, formal petitions arrived. Almost seventy percent of the registered voters, in a severely constrained voter list, signed the petitions. They were endorsed by the *Hui Kalaiaina*. The Queen moved politically and with a deep moral and historical imperative to gain the *Hui's* support. "To have ignored or disregarded so general a request," she wrote later, "I must have been deaf to the voice of the people, which tradition tells us is the voice of God." Herein lay her strength politically and geopolitically. She knew it. In the United States, numbers — in enduring principles and in practical politics — also mattered.[14]

*

Dole and the other *coup d'état* leaders, especially William O. Smith and Lorrin Thurston, had found this change to the franchise and the other revisions Liliuokalani proposed anathema to what they believed was just and righteous. It was an attitude Dole and his colleagues had ingrained deeply in their experience and upbringing. Having native Hawaiians exercise broadly the franchise in order to govern the nation was antithetical to the wisdom that, even with the passage of decades and orderly governance, the children of the missionary's believed they alone possessed.

Dole, Smith, and Thurston's grasp of governance — how it should be done and who should do it -was founded in the theological pronouncements of the quintessential Calvinist, Cotton Mather. In Mather's "common provincialism" was "an egocentric universe...no larger than the narrow bounds of a Puritan Commonwealth, whereof Boston was the capital." The form of governance was defined further through the spiritual compulsion and anointed words of Mather's successor, Jonathan Edwards. God, Edwards believed, had separated and specially elected individuals to determine the cultural and social rules — and the law — of those people who needed to be governed. It had been that way in the dwarfed world of the seventeenth-century Massachusetts village the Calvinist missionaries idealized. Both ministers had bestirred men — many unsettled and looking elsewhere — to embrace conduct that, like Edwards,' was little more than "an abundance of small ends, many cloaked in a high pretense of religion;... and blown up by a pretended zeal, yet really and truly by nothing more divine than interest or ill nature."[15]

In the early nineteenth century, a refinement of Jonathan Edwards' theology emerged with fullness: the "New Divinity." It added two tenets to Edwards' theology. First, "Christ died for everyone, for Negroes, Indians, and the disinherited generally, as well as for the godly and substantial classes;" a tenet that was global in its reach. Second, for the elect of God the duty was to ensure the conversion to God's commands with unselfishness, a disinterestedness which — by its nature — would ensure that the elect's actions were without sin. It was this second tenet — disinterestedness — that the political and cultural imperative of the theology derived its most frightening and militant determination. The purpose of the effort was to displace the indigenous culture. To the elect, only those people prepared by grace and through the deed of heartfelt, visible conversion to God's commands, that is, by taking "the Kingdom by violence," could be saved. It was "the church as a radical new kind of community at odds with the world."[16]

In 1806, Samuel Mills, Jr. — later considered the "father of American foreign missions" — went to Williams College already under New Divinity influence. At Williams, Mills "created a secret missionary society of 'the Brethren,' comprising students who pledged themselves to the missions to the 'heathen.'" Mills' efforts also reflected his canny skill as a publicist. Periodicals — the *Massachusetts Mis-*

sionary Magazine, the *Panoplist* ("the whole armor of God") — represented a grasp of how to communicate; how to create the perception of the theology's successes, including for raising money and framing debates in America. If a righteous success was said to be occurring in an impenetrable wilderness or in a distant island, who could reasonably question the legitimacy of the claim? Nothing discouraging, critical of the missionary effort or reflecting failure would be published.[17]

The New Divinity found its home in Boston in 1810, with the formation of the American Board of Commissioners for Foreign Missions (ABCFM). The leading founders of the ABCFM also had the entrepreneurial outlook and values of an expanding economy embraced by Adam Smith, especially the individual imperative of acquisitiveness. To Elihu Root, who less than a generation later would embrace the virtue of acquiring foreign cultures to serve America's interests as Secretary of War for President William McKinley, "God means us to be ambitious." The "Protestant religion," he continued, "encourages success in capitalist endeavor.... [B]usiness was virtuous, and success was blessed."[18]

The missionary zeal also melded easily with the people and institutions that provided support: The banking and trading companies of Boston, Providence, New Bedford, New London, and New Haven and the ship building and whaling industry operating out of the same ports. People in the trading and shipbuilding industry also provided the means for trade in another form of early nineteenth-century commerce: Slavery. The meaning of slavery remained only dormant amid the enthusiasm and visible exercise of theological and political power by the ABCFM.[19]

Many among the young married missionary couples were from small villages and rural areas, in search of the stable financial subsidy — salary, stipends for children, tools, utensils, prefabricated homes, books, land fees and costs, livestock, and more — the ABCFM and its donors could provide. The theological risk among the missionaries was subtle and pervasive. Acquisitiveness, when engaged in by "God's chosen people," would easily correlate grace with avarice. The believers would not know the difference, especially when the acquisition was "cloaked in a high pretense of religion." In the winter of 1819, the Calvinists were "providentially favored to carry the gospel overseas...." To those people ordained and elected by the Divine, Hawaii had one essential and salient characteristic. It was not Christian.[20]

The missionaries who left for Hawaii were men and women who knew only three worlds: New England and sections of the Ohio Valley as they narrowly conceived both places at the time of their departure, and Hawaii. Their directive from the ABCFM: Create a commonwealth of the elect that ensured conversion to the word of God that did not exist in their land of birth. The missionaries did not receive even the most rudimentary forms of cross-cultural training. They also brought no vows of poverty. On the contrary, they believed that "[I]f God had blessed one with His grace, He surely would not permit one to suffer unduly on earth.... [T]hose who did well economically could take their success as an indication they were among God's chosen people." [21]

The missionaries who arrived in Hawaii between 1820 and 1848 — for all their claims about disliking a monarchy — had no fundamental reverence for democracy as the alternative. Neither did their children.

*

King Kalakaua's and now Liliuokalani's commitment to "Hawaii for the Hawaiians" was still alive. Liliuokalani had drawn a line essential to her people and their nation. The line was reflected in her proposed revision to the constitution. Dole's commitment to principle and allegiance to a constitutional process and law he had sworn to uphold as a Supreme Court justice had reached his theological limit. The Mather-Edwards effect also was still alive. Compromise with the Queen was never sought by Dole or the other *coup* leaders. Dole committed to resign to become the provisional government's president.[22]

The Blue Room where the cabinet had been seated was used for informal receptions and meetings. The room was located on the palace's first floor. Indigenous and elegantly carved koa wood formed its entrance off the Grand Hall. Electric lighting illuminated its interior. The Queen took her place with, no doubt, her normal countenance of firmness and with a disquieted foreboding of what precisely was to come and whether she grasped fully the small and bold choices she might need to take.

The Queen already had presented the new constitution to the cabinet for its review. A few had shared it immediately with the leaders of the *coup d'état*. Minister Stevens already knew its contents and purpose. So, too, did some of the *coup*'s leaders. One of them — William O. Smith — had secured the services of a spy deeply ensconced in the Queen's sphere of conduct and, through him, had secured a copy.[23]

Smith, like Dole, was the son of missionaries. Like many of the missionary couples, Smith's parents made a successful transition from the financial protections and subsidies against privation provided by the ABCFM to becoming landed gentry and entrepreneurs. Their son moved seamlessly into the same milieu, invested successfully in sugar, and was an insistent advocate for the exploitive system of contract labor to serve the sugar plantations. The exploitation involved race and poverty — substituting Asians for Hawaiians — in ensuring largely Caucasian material comfort. Liliuokalani "thought the 'slave labor' on the plantations was 'inhuman.'" How she might act to move her country away from the human exploitation that had plagued it was an intolerable risk to Smith and the interests and values he represented.[24]

Smith was 45 years old. He was a skilled lawyer in a legal system developed largely on a New England model with whatever modifications were necessary to protect property and in a bar of lawyers dominated almost exclusively by Caucasians, relatives, and friends into the late nineteenth century. Control of the legal system honed and expanded his power perhaps more than did his skills. His office was the primary center for the *coup*'s planners. He helped craft the basic documents, had a solid grasp of words and tactical maneuvers, "and often seemed possessed by the clearest mind." When word of the Queen's proposed revisions to the constitution emerged, Smith's friends and clients comfortably expressed their views to him "that her actions were arrogantly autocratic and intentionally provocative. It may have further aggravated them that in such a male-dominated era... a member of the 'weaker sex,' and a dark-skinned one at that, had dared to defy them in a shocking show of unladylike audacity." At no time did Smith fail to get support from the pulpit of churches throughout the nation or exploit the tenets long advocated by the early missionaries to serve a political purpose. Smith and Dole were childhood friends. Smith had agreed to serve as the provisional government's attorney general.[25]

Within moments of the cabinet's deliberations and in the ensuing hours, Liliuokalani observed the formal effort to undermine her from the inside unfold. The cabinet balked. Its members claimed ignorance of the proposed constitution's content and the need for more study. The cabinet had begun to constitutionally and politically separate itself from the Queen. They anticipated, once the *coup d'état* came to fruition, they would be the only remaining constitutional head of government. It was an illusion. They were irrelevant to the enduring purpose of the *coup d'état* and the intentions of the United States. Her response: She denounced the pretense of ignorance, had the new constitution read aloud, and, in doing so, she began effectively to separate herself from the constraint of the cabinet.[26]

The Queen also acted the historian and the canny prognosticator of the long view. She recognized that the collaboration among her cabinet, the leaders of the *coup d'état*, and the United States had taken on a concrete form. She withdrew the constitution. In doing so she eliminated the ostensible reason for the *coup d'état* but not the rationale for the constitutional changes she advocated. She created the likelihood that in time and with diligence Dole, Smith, Thurston, and Stevens could be exposed as lesser persons to a broader historical and political judgment as their intentions were laid bare. She also created an additional basis for the arguments she likely would need to make during and after the *coup d'état* was effectuated.

*

The United States Navy cruiser USS *Boston* under the command of Captain Gilbert Wiltse had been waiting in Honolulu harbor. Wiltse had received Minister Stevens' directive to land American forces following Stevens' agreement with Lorrin Thurston, the *coup d'état*'s leader.

The pretense that landing troops was related to protecting American interests and citizens was pierced on King Street. No American interests of consequence existed near, on, or even proximate to it. Wiltse's objective was the immediate display of military prowess to quell any notion of a police or military action by the Hawaii government, or to provoke a confrontation and casualties. He knew the *coup d'état* would occur the next day. He was there to protect the *coup's* leaders regardless of nationality and to allow time for the re-formation of a Caucasian vigilante force. Liliuokalani already had directed there be no armed resistance. She would not engage the fully armed marines with force or acquiesce in Wiltse's potentially deadly maneuver. The loss of an American life would alter dramatically her fate and separate Hawaii from the United States.[27]

In the early nineteenth century the Navy's Pacific Squadron sailed and docked frequently along the coast of South America, Mexico, California, the Oregon Territories, and Hawaii. The Navy's duties included protecting America's interests from the colonial and trade interests of the British, the French, the Mexicans, and the Russians. In Hawaii, where the United States maintained only a commercial attaché, the Navy's conduct on the front line was often diplomatic. In an era of limited communication, especially from distant Washington, DC, the Navy settled nuanced disputes, made the judgment about the use and threat of force, brought dispatches from presidents and State Department officials, and determined the form of protocol with foreign nationals and leaders. The Navy hierarchy at sea had been tempered by a corps mission and an independence of action with only infrequent and delayed accountability from the nation's capital.[28]

The Navy's Pacific Squadron, however, never received the resources or prestige accorded its counterpart in the Atlantic. This disparity was evident during the Civil War. It was in the Pacific that the Confederacy was able to attack and destroy American commercial and whaling vessels with little risk as part of its naval strategy to weaken the north. It was apparent, especially to those who had made the Navy a career, that the Pacific Squadron lacked "fleet concentration"; the number and range of vessels and stations to control the ocean and protect American interests.[29]

When Captain Alfred Thayer Mahan began his literary advocacy for naval expansion in the Pacific, asking if the United States "would...acquiesce in a foreign protectorate over [Hawaii], that great central state of the Pacific," he did so as an officer who served in the Pacific and understood the squadron's cultural discomfort within the Navy. On January 31, 1893 — only a few weeks after Liliuokalani witnessed from the verandah of Iolani Palace the exercise of power by the Navy — Mahan informed the *New York Times* that Hawaii was "unrivalled by that of any other position in the North Pacific" in its strategic value that otherwise could be "reached only by the long and perilous voyage around Cape Horn." In an unnecessary and perverse justification for fleet concentration, Mahan posited further that the Pacific Squadron would certainly have to protect America from the "barbarism of China."[30]

Captain Wiltse's move into King Street echoed triumphantly within the Navy's Pacific culture. His actions were a reflection of a confident career maneuver for which the United States would be held unequivocally and correctly responsible and the Navy's disquieting place in Hawaii's history would be set permanently. Wiltse needed little impetus from Minister Stevens or the legal and political authorization Stevens' received from the Harrison Administration.

Long before this moment of American troops with bayoneted rifles and gatlin guns, Liliuokalani knew the geopolitical breath of the Navy's imperatives and the method of thinking imbued in its commanders. She had listened intently as a child in the line of succession to the throne when visiting admirals, commodores, and captains spoke at the Royal School she attended; later, when the royal families or sometimes she alone was entertained or consulted by naval attaches; yet again in her lifelong, sometimes formally tutored, study of Hawaii's history and the meaning of its place in the Pacific; throughout much of her life in dealing with United States' resident ministers, including through the stories about Anthony Ten Eyck who exercised his authority from a rented room in what was now her home, Washington Place; and, during the time she was the designated heir apparent, through her experience and informed insight into the Navy's decades long preoccupation with fulfilling its own cultural needs and America's purpose in acquiring exclusive control over the Pearl River harbor.[31]

The military move by Wiltse and Stevens of January 16 was disquieting and its purpose in support of annexation was plain. Liliuokalani had something in mind, however, that Wiltse may have believed had been settled and that Stevens hoped was settled: the American Constitutional principle and deeply engrained tradition of civilian control over the military. Stevens spoke for Harrison. He did not speak for President-elect Cleveland.

*

Two broad, painfully nagging realities also had emerged for Liliuokalani and those people who would lend her support as the breath and complexity of the task before them took form: the insidious use of race and cultural condescension, and the fate of the Crown lands. Dealing with both would take mastery of perceptions and politics and law in the United States. Her adversaries had skill and comfort in attaining such mastery in the land of their roots and, for some, a land in which they still held citizenship. Both realities also would require the long view as only a queen could do.

In the United States, Senator John Morgan of Alabama, one of the south's most vehement defenders of racial and religious superiority and the resurgence of a distinct, Caucasian southern identity had insisted on America's control of Pearl Harbor. Race and cultural condescension were on the table. Morgan and

Cleveland also were from the same political party. They were, potentially, on a collision course with respect to race and annexation and the still unsettled extension of American values when imposed outside the United States.[32]

In Hawaii, Smith, Dole, and Thurston had crafted the 1887 constitution deliberately to exclude Asians who were naturalized Hawaiian citizens from voting. Asians generally had supported the king. In 1892, when the explicitly racial exclusion was challenged in the Hawaii Supreme Court, Justice Dole — who shared responsibility for drafting the exclusion — recognized no ethical discomfort in writing the opinion that upheld the exclusion's legality. Now Smith, Dole, and Thurston had called upon the United States to uphold by force the same exclusion already applicable to native Hawaiians under the guise of property restrictions. It was an easy sell. The insidious forces of race and cultural condescension reflected in the Mather–Edwards imperative of the elect continued unabated in Hawaii and with a stunning and only latent boldness in the United States. Liliuokalani's unease must have been palpable. In her lifetime, a Hawaiian monarch had experienced racism in America. Her brother had met President Ulysses S. Grant. The generation of Americans that fought the Civil War and suffered its deaths and dislocations and shame may have changed only venues and methods. They now held positions of influence in Washington, DC.[33]

Resting alone in her private quarters on the palace's second floor while her advisors were at work, or perhaps in a contemplative moment, worn bible in her lap, she also knew the *coup d'état's* leaders coveted the Crown lands. How and when should she tell the story of the Crown lands in America? Understanding would take a knowledge of Hawaii history and culture few in America would be willing or capable of embracing. Anglo-Saxon jurisprudence — in a court of law — could not accommodate easily such complexity.

"Originally," as she sought later to describe the Crown lands' history, "all territory belonged to the king, by whom it was apportioned for use only, not for sale, to the chiefs [the *ali'i*], who in turn assigned tracts, small or large, to the people; an excellent system for us, by which the poorest native had all the land he needed and yet it could not be taken from him by any designing foreigner." The missionaries had encouraged a change. It was consistent with their religious views and conduct, especially with respect to enhancing the financial posture of their children and those not constrained by a contract with the ABCFM. The monarchy had a different intention: to protect as much property as it could in the event of a foreign acquisition of the kingdom. In 1848, the king divided the "territory of the Islands into three parts," nearly equal in size. "One third was devoted to the use or expenses of government [government lands]; one third was apportioned [for sale] to the people; and the remainder — [now 915,000 acres] — continued, as from all ages, the private property of...the reigning monarch [Crown lands]." The

Queen believed that by legislative act, recognized practice, and the rulings of the Hawaii Supreme Court, the Crown lands still remained her property.[34]

The common people had found "private property for sale" an alien concept. The rules that governed its use and disposition and hereditary constructs were Anglo-Saxon, drawn largely from New England and the ancient practice of the English gentry. The rules also were pronounced by judges and land commissioners (who often were not Hawaiian) with multiple agendas and in the absence of an ethic that prohibited conflicts of interest. In short order the consequence emerged: "That part of Hawaii given by the king [for sale] to the people had [by 1893] almost entirely left them, and now belong[ed] to the missionaries and their friends and successors."[35]

The purpose of the Crown lands weighed heavily on the Queen. It was the only land with a special trust and public purpose she controlled. The land and its proceeds — some $50,000 a year — were used to aid and protect the common people, the poor among native Hawaiians, and to supplement her own needs. That income would be lost to her. Also underpinning her unease and the depth of her determination was patriotism. To preserve "the love of the very soil on which our ancestors have lived and died," was the *sine qua non* of Hawaiian identity. What arrogance among these men, she later pondered openly, had accumulated into a certainty and a right that the nation — and the land — was theirs to give away? "[I]f we manifested any incompetence," she added, "it was in not foreseeing that *they* would be bound by no obligations, by honor, or by oath of allegiance." A line in law and history and the meaning of patriotism had to be drawn.[36]

The argument was forming. Perhaps unwittingly, Dole, Smith, and Thurston had given her two vehicles to mold and define — substantively and with respect to timing — the ensuing dialogue and action. The fate of the constitutional monarchy she headed and her ownership and control of the Crown lands were intimately entwined. She believed both elements of sovereignty shared a compelling principle for their preservation: The *coup d'état* now in progress was illegal, immoral, and unjustified and what followed from it was tainted indelibly in history and in law. Her goal was plain. She needed to regain the nation.

*

Lorrin Thurston had not anticipated this moment with precision. He had a different scenario in mind. The scenario was formed during and after his spring 1892 visit to Washington, DC.

Within the seemingly detached and cramped quarters of 1509 Pennsylvania Avenue was the United States Court of Claims. It was located on the southeast corner of Lafayette Square across from the Treasury Building and only moments away from the White House. This location was the court's third home since its creation by Congress in 1855. The court's chief clerk was Archibald Hopkins.

Thurston was introduced to Hopkins by the descendant of one of Hawaii's original missionary families, who were Thurston's most reliable ideological and political framework for relationships in the United States. Thurston needed access to decision-makers. He wanted to assess the practical prospects for annexation and to ensure he would have intelligence and an advocate he could control in the nation's capital. He found both in Hopkins.[37]

Hopkins was born in Williamstown, Massachusetts. He was an 1862 graduate of Williams College, where his father was president. Williams — largely through Hopkins' father — was the intellectual home for a renewed Calvinist and Edwards' theology that also provided the practical and theological rationale to the missionary purpose of the ABCFM when it was founded in 1810. Sanford Dole had graduated from Williams in 1867. He was mentored by Hopkins' father.[38]

Hopkins entered the Civil War after graduation, led troops under Generals Sheridan and Grant including at Appomattox, was cited for gallantry, and retired as a full colonel. His reputation was enhanced by his New England lineage and his marriage. His grandfather commanded the First Massachusetts in the Revolutionary War. His wife was the granddaughter of Edward Everett, former secretary of state. Among her relatives were members of the Adams, Frothingham, and Hale families. Her father was a captain in the United States Navy. After completing military service, Hopkins studied law at Columbia, graduating in 1867.[39]

In 1874, Hopkins was appointed chief clerk to the court of claims during the administration of his former commander, President Ulysses Grant. The court had an elevated status in Washington, DC, because of the visibility and political sensitivity of the enormous financial claims Congress had entrusted it with resolving. There was nothing "lowly" in his position. On the contrary, given the importance of what the court did and how claims against the government often originated in Congress, having a politically wise and discrete person in the clerk's office was essential to Washington insiders. There also was patronage to be distributed.

Hopkins was the quintessential model for the exercise of influence by stealth. He was financially comfortable, socially and culturally enmeshed, and had a recognized literary skill in poetry and prose called upon frequently by cabinet officials, Senators, and others. He defied the stereotypical, visible rise to authority and power, except for those who understood how to attain and exercise power over time. He moved flawlessly through Washington society and entertained regularly at his residence on Massachusetts Avenue.[40]

There were no meaningful constraints within the civil service on engaging in private ventures. Concerns about conflicts of interest in Washington, DC — excepting scandals too odious to be ignored- were rhetorically expressed at most. Hopkins understood power in the executive branch of government. He also understood how to convey impressions among the judges and lawyers of the court of claims.

Hopkins was retained by Thurston to represent the annexationists on a monthly fee. Thurston got his access. He came away from Washington with confidence and a plan to effectuate annexation that assumed the Queen would falter politically and his own influence with her cabinet would remain impenetrably strong. Annexation — once Hawaiians were properly educated — would follow readily. Hopkins made his own contribution to Thurston's approach. From his experience on the court of claims, some strategically placed inquiries, and his knowledge of Washington politics he assured Thurston the United States would be prepared to compensate Liliuokalani two hundred and fifty thousand dollars for "her rights as sovereign."[41]

Hopkins continued to provide Thurston with intelligence and strategic advice and provide guidance and quiet but penetrating forms of advocacy. His role meant that from the outset a formidable person with knowledge, political sensitivities, and an opinion adverse to the Queen had seeped permanently into the culture of the court of claims. Hopkins' view — acknowledged by Thurston — was that something of value was taken personally from the Queen. He also set its worth.

Thurston returned to Honolulu, but, as events unfolded, the Queen did not act the pliant woman or the intimidated monarch. Liliuokalani had used properly and had pierced skillfully the constraint of the 1887 constitution. She also acted under the constitution when she sought the approval of the cabinet for revisions to its terms. Her political support among her people was solid; and she engaged in no formal overt actions that were illegal or unprecedented. She had no fear of Smith, Dole, or Thurston's skill, only their lack of constraint in securing "their own personal benefit." They could not depose her alone, not then. She had outmaneuvered them politically and legally. The *coup d'état* could only occur with the military support of the United States.[42]

*

Late into the evening of January 16, an uneasy calm had taken hold among Iolani's retainers and cooks and the normal preparation for meals and slumber. Hibiscus petals — yellow was the Queen's favorite color — turned brown and broke free. The Pacific's subtle breezes may have brushed against vases of Hawaii's red ohio or Molokai's white kukui blossom and against the weathered and vigilant faces of palace guards. In the quietude of her bedroom, thought and reflection displaced Liliuokalani's routine of noting her diary. Into the early morning of January 17 and with further consultation, her reflection yielded tactical and strategic decisions that soon would need words and actions and further refinement. It was her last full day in Iolani Palace.

In the early afternoon of the January 17, on the steps of Aliiolani Hale, the government building across from the palace that also housed the Supreme Court, one Henry Cooper — in Hawaii less than a year — read a proclamation to no one in particular. He "had walked unarmed and unnoticed through the streets to take possession of an almost deserted building. In the offices, a few subordinates were at their desks. The proclamation declared the monarchy was at an end and the provisional government established "to exist until terms of union with the United States of America have been...agreed upon." Caucasian men — armed, passionate, lurking in the shadows and reflective of a clannish gathering in the American South — emerged to protect the building. Knowing the failure of the *coup d'état's* leaders to gain control in fact of important buildings — the military barracks and the police station — and their failure to make a demand on the Queen that she surrender, Minister Stevens recognized the provisional government immediately.[43]

The Queen was informed of the *coup d'état's* seeming finality. Her thinking needed words and a formal response. She sent for seven men. For most of her adult life but especially since being designated heir apparent at age 39, she was engaged in testing her allies in and outside the government: Whom could she trust? Who had experience and skill in Hawaii? She was about to lose the benefit of Hawaii's diplomatic corps, especially in San Francisco and Washington, DC. Who had experience in the United States? Who had experience for the tumult and uncertainties she would confront and the tactics and strategies that needed to be implemented? Testing the temperament of men had not been a neat process, certainly not in the past few days. In the chaos that surrounded her, enhanced by the military presence of the United States and the rush to take sides in an apparent future controlled by the coercion of the gatlin gun and armed Caucasian vigilantes, men moved cautiously, some erratically, others foolishly, still others with duplicity.

Into the Blue Room walked Paul Neumann, a lawyer from San Francisco whom she had sought to include in her cabinet but who was excluded by the legislature; Edward C. Macfarlane, a former cabinet minister who had spoken forcefully and publicly against Minister Stevens; Herman Widemann, also a former cabinet minister; Joseph Owen [J.O.] Carter, considered a councilor to the Queen; Archibald Cleghorn, her brother-in-law and the father of Princess Kaiulani who was next in line for the throne; and the young princes, David Kawananakoa and Jonah Kuhio Kalanianaole, both also in line for the throne.[44]

The men took their seats. She entered. "[S]he seemed calm and relaxed [and] a little weary." She may have longed for a respite amid the subtle breeze and painted evening skies of her occasional retreat near the beach in Waikiki. She remained, however, as she had some months earlier, "'every inch a queen' ... with noble grace and...the lonely honors of her rank." She also still remained "distinctly handsome"; with a countenance that was "a coffee color... surrounded by thick black hair." The discussion began.[45]

The Queen and her advisors had no plainly obvious precedent or analogue to guide them. The "Paulet Incident" in 1843 — when an errant British captain named Paulet took Hawaii in the name of the Crown without authority and was later rebuked — was of little relevance. No large contingent of foreign troops had landed, no indigenous uprising occurred to depose the king or support the British, and the British monarch had no plans for colonial expansion. The circumstances confronting Liliuokalani were quite different in time, the gravity and complexity of the conditions, and in the meaning of the long view. Other possible antecedents where "protests" were filed that might provide guidance were equally unavailing for the same reasons.[46]

That afternoon her judgment reflected her analytical skills honed over decades. Foremost, her judgment showed an insight into herself. She was free from constraints. She could set new rules of conduct. She was not bound by the conventional wisdom or the rules set by the *coup* leaders and the United States through Minister Stevens and the Navy. What they thought was settled and stable and secure with military prowess, she would soon undo with a form of ordered chaos. She could focus on her own subjectivity about being Hawaiian and would define what that meant to her, to those who looked to her, and to those who would now judge her and the culture she embraced. It was the beginning or fulfillment of a new era.

She knew the effort to regain the nation would be an arduous, contentious, and dangerous battle. She could be killed. She had the confidence to manage the uncertainties in men's foibles and the forces and people she could bring together. It also would be expensive. She intended to finance her efforts and those who represented her entirely though her own resources.[47]

She had drawn lines where she needed to. The approach and the form of her statement were agreed upon. The analytical and historical judgment was hers. She would yield nothing with respect to God or who was in compliance with the constitution. Into "the early lamplight of January 17," perhaps alone in the Blue Room, Paul Neumann crafted her judgment into words:[48]

> I, Liliuokalani, by the grace of God and under the constitution of the Hawaii kingdom Queen, do hereby solemnly protest against any and all acts done against myself and the constitutional government of the Hawaiian kingdom by certain persons claiming to have established a provisional government of and for this kingdom.
>
> That I yield to the superior force of the United States of America, whose Minister Plenipotentiary, His Excellency John L. Stevens, has caused United States troops to be landed at Honolulu, and declared that he would support the said provisional government.
>
> Now, to avoid any collision of armed forces, and perhaps the loss of life, I do, under protest and impelled by said forces, yield my authority until such time as the Government of the United States shall, upon the facts

being presented to it, undo the actions of its representatives, and reinstate me in the authority which I claim as the constitutional sovereign of the Hawaiian Islands.

Neumann, it has been said, provided words "more potent, possibly, than he could foresee." They were words the Queen approved before they were made public. They reflected the formal opening move in a strategy. Some critical elements she already had put in place, including perhaps some trusted and skilled allies. More allies and good fortune would be necessary. In her diary entry made at the end of the evening, she wrote, perhaps with more modesty than warranted: "Things turned out better than I expected."[49]

Liliuokalani moved to Washington Place at ten a.m. on January 18. Her carriage and belongings and a few retainers joined her. On January 19, she began the process and the exercise of judgment necessary to regain the sovereignty of Hawaii.

Chapter 2. Allies: The Constitutionalists

Washington Place had become, finally, Liliuokalani's home.

It was constructed between 1842 and 1847 by John Dominis, a Boston émigré and commercial ship captain, quite worldly in business acumen and travel, especially along America's northwest coast and the Far East. He was lost at sea in 1847. Dominis' wife, Mary Jones Dominis, also was from Boston. They had one son, John Owen Dominis. He married Liliu Paki — later Queen Liliuokalani — in 1862. She moved into the house, bringing her royal lineage and her financial resources. Mary Dominis had survived her husband's death by taking in boarders, almost exclusively American and British. Among them was Anthony Ten Eyck, the resident commissioner of the United States. His rooms were the official United States legation in Honolulu. It was Ten Eyck, with Mary Dominis' imprimatur, who provided the appellation, "Washington Place." The American flag was flown. It remained that way until Mary Dominis' death in 1889. Liliuokalani had the American flag taken down.

The house was set back from the wide expanse of Beretania Street "far enough to avoid the dust and noise" but close enough so that visitors to the house and any diplomatic visitor to the nation would recognize immediately the social importance of its proximity to Iolani Palace. The political meaning of the house's location had reverberated daily when, in 1877, Liliuokalani was designated heir apparent. On January 18, 1893, Washington Place took on a new meaning. It was the capitol of an emerging parallel government. Liliuokalani was still the Queen.[50]

Washington Place "is a large, square, white house," two floors in height, elevated slightly off the ground, "with pillars and porticoes on all sides." Its Greek revival character was modified architecturally through its coral stone exterior for coolness and multiple louvered doors for ventilation. The architect drew thoughtfully on the Vetruvius, Palladium, and English to colonial America continuity and the pattern books that embodied Greek revival's essential elements and acceptable variations. The house also was surrounded by "shaded trees and ample lawns," with imported and indigenous flowers and lush fruit trees that Liliuokalani cultivated herself; a source of simple aesthetic and sensory joy, contemplative moments, and a prism into her intellectual imperative to understand and imagine daily the Hawaii culture. With the exception of the vernacular adjustments for climate, the house — viewed from the exterior — could be in New Bedford, Massachusetts or the British colony in Singapore. Washington Place projected a cosmopolitan image to the world consistent with the Queen's intellect and political stature. The house was a tool to be used as well as a home to be lived in.

Embedded in this setting — the house's interior architecture and her historic relationship to it — also were elements of Liliuokalani's learned skill at integrating cultures, the meaning of Hawaiian aspiration, and the formation of the long view. The interior reflected a "Polynesian character under an American disguise." The central hallway had a koa wood staircase up to the second floor. There were two rooms on either side of the hallway. The first floor had a koa wood interior that "united the elegance of the curled maple and black walnut" molding and furniture used throughout with the "mixing of Hawaiian symbols, like the kahilis, among the western settees, upholstered arm chairs, indigenously crafted wood tables, piano, and Chinese" made cabinetry reflective of John Dominis' travels and Liliuokalani's tastes. In the spacious, comfortably arrayed study she established on the first floor, textured by worn books and official papers, the Queen moved methodically to protect the fate of the nation.[51]

On January 19, Liliuokalani crafted and approved for transmission letters to President William Henry Harrison and President-elect Grover Cleveland. Timing was critical. She no longer had control of the apparatus of state. Thurston, Dole, and Smith did. A delegation led by Thurston took passage immediately on the steamer *Claudine* bound for San Francisco. They denied passage to the Queen's delegation. The next ship would not leave until February 2. The USS *Boston* was still docked in Honolulu harbor. American troops were only a few blocks from her home. She could not leave safely.

Her goal was to ensure that an investigation would occur before the *coup* leaders — now referred to as the provisional government — negotiated the contours of a treaty for annexation to the United States and convinced the senate to ratify it. Paul Neumann and J. O. Carter provided her thoughts and words. She effectively began two processes: Separate, with a pragmatic care, the two political parties in the United States and begin to define the story of the *coup d'état*, to project it abroad into a political and cultural setting where she had an uncertain sympathy and no infrastructure. Primarily, however, she was using her stature and compelling story to move a president of the United States.

To President Harrison, she made plain she was acting within the framework of the constitution. The *coup d'état*, she wrote, was "against the constitutional government of my kingdom"; and the establishment of "a Provisional Government in direct conflict with [Hawaii's] organic law." She still exercised the only legitimate legal authority. The *coup* leaders, she explained, had only "attempted to depose me." Based on "incontestable proof," Minister Stevens "had caused troops to be landed for that purpose." His scheme had not succeeded. It forced her only to restrain any enforcement action against the *coup* leaders. The blame and the fate for the *coup* rested with the United States. "[Y]our Government," she wrote with a solid tenor of confidence, "will right whatever wrongs may have been inflicted upon us in the premises.... I now ask you, in justice to myself and to my people, that no steps be taken by the Government of the United States until my cause can be heard by you."[52]

The contours of Liliuokalani's argument remained essentially unchanged. Everything that flowed from the illegality of the *coup d'état* was itself immoral and illegal, including any formal determination by Harrison to give credence to the *coup* or its leaders. From a distance she was elevating Harrison to the judgment of history. He would be acting on his own no matter who was around him. This letter was sent on the steamer *Claudine*.

Her letter to Cleveland was more intimate. "I have the boon of your personal friendship and good will," she wrote. She wanted him to use his power to stop annexation before he had the authority of the president. She parsed her request in a classic political manner: "I do not veil under this request to you anything the fulfillment of which could in the slightest degree be contrary to your position; and I leave our grievance in your hands."

On January 31, Liliuokalani appointed Paul Neumann her Envoy Extraordinaire and Minister Plenipotentiary to Washington, DC. She informed Cleveland: "I have instructed the Hon. Paul Neumann ... to submit to you a *précis* of the facts and circumstances."[53]

*

Paul Neumann was the most sophisticated intellect and practitioner among Liliuokalani's advisors. He was fifty-four years old. He had a solid build, a distinguished, natty manner of dress, and a full, closely-cropped mustache. Due to a series of accidents, he had a leg amputated early in life. He regretted that "this [loss] incapacitated [him] from serving his adopted country during the Civil War."[54]

Neumann was born in Bavaria. He immigrated to California at fifteen years old, when the gold rush altered dramatically the state's evolution and, in 1850, its entrance into the Union enhanced its stature. He knew the grit and tumult of the mining camps where he labored when he first arrived. He also was an early member of San Francisco's Bohemian Club, chartered in 1872. He moved comfortably among its distinguished literary and artistic members such as Ambrose Bierce, Henry George and, later, Mark Twain, Jack London, and Frank Norris. He supported the club's commitment to enhance San Francisco's operatic, symphonic, and theatric offerings at a time when, flush with wealth, it sought character in a way Chicago later sought to emulate New York.

Neumann had political savvy. He had been a financially successful lawyer representing industrialists in California that had major real estate and sugar interests in Hawaii. He had been elected to the California statehouse in Sacramento and made an unsuccessful bid for Congress. He moved to Hawaii and was appointed attorney general by King Kalakaua and, later, won a seat in the House of Nobles. He also engaged in various diplomatic missions for Kalakaua, including in Japan. He had observed and challenged Minister Stevens' criticism of the Queen long before the *coup d'état*. In private practice he "was perhaps the best trial lawyer of his day in the Islands." When Liliuokalani appointed him and Edward C. Macfarlane to her cabinet, she believed that they were "men in whom I had reason to know the community had confidence that their transactions would be straightforward and honest."[55]

It is unclear whether Neumann's experience included any political machinations in the nation's capital. Much of his history was in San Francisco; so, too, was one of his benefactors in law and in his public career, Claus Spreckels. Spreckels had sugar and financial interests in Hawaii and a watchful eye on its statecraft. Neumann's experience did, however, reflect something more: the ease of travel, proximity to a cosmopolitan city, a deeply skilled medical profession, financial opportunity, money for investment, and the political interaction that existed between San Francisco and Honolulu.

Neumann, like any good advocate and negotiator, needed to prepare for alternative courses of action including the possibility of failure or the seemingly unexpected turn of events. He had prepared the précis. It was written in an orderly, succinct manner and with a lawyer's skilled objectivity and proper reliance on correspondence written by Thurston, Stevens, the Queen, and the cabinet. He began with the coerced imposition of the 1887 constitution and its deprivation of Hawaiian voting rights. The précis ended with the comfortably crafted assertion that an investigation would reveal the illegal and improper role played by Stevens and the Navy and the opposition of native Hawaiians to annexation. The précis made no reference to the Crown lands or compensation. In the privacy of the Queen's study at Washington Place, Neumann also discussed the meaning of America's movement west, and the growing ambitions of the Navy. There should be no illusions about what was at risk and the depth of commitment necessary to attain the Queen's goal. He also wanted the full benefit of the Queen's experience, especially with President-elect Cleveland.[56]

The Queen also understood the still reverberating remnants of the Civil War and what that might mean for Neumann's journey. She had traveled across the United States via Chicago in 1887 and stayed in Washington, DC. She already was the designated heir apparent; preparing to meet with President Grover Cleveland, visit relatives and dignitaries in Boston, and move in social and political circles in New York and Washington. Given her insight and penchant for observation and learning, she was paying attention. Less than a decade earlier, the contested election of 1877 between Rutherford B. Hayes and Samuel J. Tilden was resolved at Wormley's Hotel in the nation's capital in part with a deal: The withdrawal of United States forces from South Carolina and Louisiana. It was the end of Reconstruction; a formal recognition that the Ku Klux Klan, the denial of voting rights, and lynching would be denounced only rhetorically. When she began her travel eastward via rail, discrimination in the northeast and the Ohio Valley already was rampant against people with dark skin. They were now citizens and possible voters. The United States Supreme Court had found forms of discrimination in public transportation in Louisiana and Mississippi constitutionally acceptable and discrimination in private, commercial activity beyond constitutional challenge.[57]

Liliuokalani knew as well that in Washington race would underpin all discussions. Senator Morgan had set the tone with Pearl Harbor. He now was even more deeply ensconced in the Senate Foreign Relations Committee. She would not have been surprised to learn that one of the arguments later made personally to Cleveland by a well-informed Caucasian supporter of the *coup d'état* was: "[H]ow ... would [he] like to have Washington city governed by the negro population of the District," even though they had more property and education than native Hawaiians; or, perhaps, that Lorrin Thurston already may have found comfort in telling *sotto voce* to his acquaintances in the United States the tale of Kalakaua being a "coon" and the illegitimate son of a black barber that Thurston reiterated later in writing.[58]

Neumann had demonstrated a consistent loyalty that warranted an appropriate degree of trust. Distance, the uncertain evolution and duration of events, and the difficulty in communications, however, made assumptions about his skill and trustworthiness inherently problematic. The Queen gave him, as he properly requested, a broad portfolio and power of attorney, including authority to negotiate, if necessary, forms of compensation for her and Princess Kaiulani. She made clear she neither expected nor wanted it. In addition to doing what was necessary to stop annexation and encourage an investigation, Neumann was explicitly directed to claim the Crown lands were illegally confiscated by the *coup* leaders. She financed his expenses with her own money.[59]

Two other men joined Neumann at the Queen's request. The young Prince David, perhaps to reflect the relationship of the monarchy to the constitutionalism the Queen symbolized and embraced in her letter to President Harrison, and Edward C. Macfarlane, who, at thirty-nine years old, was a persistent and informed opponent of annexation as a legislator, minister in her cabinet, and in public statements during a private visit to San Francisco. Macfarlane's expenses were being paid by Archibald Cleghorn. Cleghorn wanted to ensure that the interests of his daughter, Kaiulani, were protected fully. Foremost, however, he directed Macfarlane to work diligently to ensure the attainment of the Queen's goal. Macfarlane also was a successful businessman and, as matters were about to demonstrate, had a solid acumen in understanding how to influence the media with respect to the singular, narrow but critical task the three emissaries were to accomplish: to ensure the preservation of the constitutional monarchy and, through it, the proper exercise of the people's voice.

As Neumann, Macfarlane, and Prince David set sail from Honolulu, no doubt weighing on Liliuokalani was whether her absence in America would make a difference. She had the most solid grasp of Hawaii's history and how to tell its story. She could not leave now. She was the personification of resistance to any violence from the vigilante army that organized and roamed at will. She also was the head of the parallel government. But a broader issue was at play that, perhaps, she alone could address that Thurston and the missionary structure he called upon in the United States already began to define: The role of the monarch.

Throughout the history of constitutionalism in Hawaii the monarch had four sources of power: Continuity through family and tradition, a characteristic unique to monarchy; forms of legal immunity for his actions, a characteristic generally applicable to all forms of constitutionalism including in England and the United States; the prerogatives and constraints identified in the words and provisions of the constitution; and the conventional political maneuvering with the public and within the legislature necessary to effectuate the monarch's agenda for the nation. It was the third source of power — the words and provisions of the constitution — that Thurston and others imposed on King Kalakaua in 1887 to constrain severely his prerogatives. Constitutional changes — when Liliuokalani sought to regain monarchial prerogatives — were the expedient pretext Thurston relied upon to rationalize the *coup d'état.*

In the United States, however, it was the meaning of the fourth source of power that implicated values, personality, race, culture, status, democracy, and duty that would form the dialogue invoked by Thurston and others: Who is Liliuokalani? Who are native Hawaiians? Who should control the one million acres of Crown lands and for what purpose? And who should control the nation and for what purpose? Liliuokalani had exercised this source of power with a skill that exceeded Kalakaua's even before her reign began. She had discerned, cajoled, encouraged, and given practical meaning to the voice and needs of the people including through their vote even when it was severely restricted. Both monarchs could work a room and discern and actively affect the mood and direction of political parties and the nation. Liliuokalani now had taken away the seeming certainty of the *coup's* success and converted it into a battle for sovereignty on a global scale based on democratic and constitutional principles.

Neumann and Macfarlane were not equipped culturally or as historians or in their relation to the land to engage in that dialogue or to set the contours or premise for an alternative way of viewing the questions or establishing different ones. Their argument as Caucasian representatives, however, was essential in the short run: Hawaii was being treated illegally and unfairly.

*

In the chill of early February, amid the gray soot and the locomotive's unfettered noise, Lorrin Thurston arrived at the snow-dusted Baltimore and Potomac railroad station, west of the Capitol building on the Mall. Thurston would have sat only among Caucasians on his train ride. The discrimination and ill manners experienced by the young Hawaiian Prince Alexander Liholiho in the same Washington train station in 1850 had not altered for anyone with dark pigmented skin forty years later. Thurston was walking into a Southern city, heavily segregated and operated under the subtle tutelage of Caucasians. Maryland and Virginia, although on different sides of the Civil War, differed only marginally in their treatment of African Americans. Reconstruction in the South had failed and, in practical terms, so too had various civil rights acts and the fourteenth, fifteenth, and sixteenth amendments to the constitution. Both Maryland and Virginia had chapters of the Klan, its force directed against anyone, African American and eastern and southern European immigrant, with dark skin. The national government was tolerating lynching with respect to both groups. Thurston had nothing to fear from Washington's culture.[60]

In its urban design, the city was struggling with the meaning and intent of Pierre L'Enfant's original plan. The location of the railroad station reflected the distance it still needed to travel. Fetid, ice-crusted waterways still lined some walkways. Horse-drawn buggies still moved along the city's streets. Within the northwest section, however, new apartment houses and period revival hotels flourished: The Portland Flats, The Everett, and the Richmond Flats along Massachusetts Avenue, 16th Street, and New Hampshire Avenue, and the Shoreham, Ebbitt House, and Arlington hotels, and the Romanesque and Moorish revival Cairo Hotel then under construction.[61]

Thurston and his colleagues had arrived in the midst of the "brilliant winter social season." Parties and dinners were held in elegant, still holiday-laden residential enclaves of political power, like the Slidell House, the Corcoran House, and the John Hay and Henry Adams homes with their shared facades and "soaring chimneys," and in the homes of the slowly emerging capitalists of the Ohio Valley.[62]

Thurston had met the secretary of state and naval officials on his previous journey and, no doubt, was pleased to be welcomed by Archibald Hopkins on this visit. Perhaps Thurston took a private carriage to the court of claims and, together, they walked easily across wind-swept Pennsylvania Avenue to the White House or the executive office building. They also agreed that Hopkins would join Thurston and his colleagues again toward the negotiation's conclusion for a meeting at Wormley's Hotel, where the reconstruction of the south and the fate of African American political rights and freedom from fear had been politely negotiated away. President Harrison had been one of its beneficiaries.[63]

Thurston's first meeting with Secretary of State John Foster was scheduled for the next day, February 4, at the executive building. Thurston's task was formidable but he had the endorsement to negotiate a treaty from a Republican president already expressed through the exercise of military force. Democrats, however, effectively controlled the senate where the treaty needed to be ratified by two-thirds of its members.

Thurston submitted the provisional government's written proposal for a treaty one day after arriving. The proposal was formulated on the two week journey from Hawaii with direction and guidance from Dole and Smith before departure. In addition to wanting a "full, complete and perpetual union between the United States and Hawaii," and proposing the obvious political inducement for the Navy's support, that is, "to establish a coaling and naval station at Pearl Harbor," the proposal also required that none of the officials who would administer the government would be subject to election except under very circumscribed limitations. The proposal also reflected Dole and Smith's interest in insuring the unimpeded continuation of contact labor — what American Federation of Labor President Samuel Gompers had characterized as "slave labor."[64]

The provisional government's clearest disclosure was its unequivocal intention to own and control the Crown lands. "That the lands located at the said Hawaiian Islands heretofore known as... [the]Crown Lands," the proposal stated, "shall continue to be the property of the local government of the said Islands ... and all the proceeds thereof devoted to the purposes and uses of such local Government." The Queen's interests and the historical beneficial purpose of the Crown lands for native Hawaiians were disconnected from the land.[65]

Thurston later asserted that in the Queen's surrender to the superior forces of the United States and appeal to the president she "gave to the provisional Government a written release of the possession and control of government property and jurisdiction." Thurston seemed to assume this so-called "release" — nowhere evident — also included the Crown lands.[66]

Dole always had sought the Crown lands. They were "almost a million acres of fertile farmland, rolling pasture, forest tracts," and coastal shoreline. They had not been properly used, he contended, toward "a higher civilization than our dusky predecessors [one commonly used euphemism for racial denigration-] could boast." He believed the lands "should be broken up and granted or sold as small homesteads. Either to heretofore landless Hawaiians or to immigrants." Dole later sought to revise the historically documented communal nature and purpose of Hawaii's land. He molded and boxed that history neatly into an Anglo-Saxon framework of private property — with "market value" and "land tenure" — that would make the lands readily accessible for private ventures and use.[67]

His concern for the landless native Hawaiian was hardly credible given the missionary history he embraced. He also would have little incentive — even if he wanted to exercise it — to withstand the historically-documented, now affirmed Caucasian need for larger sugar plantations, including those represented by or invested in by Smith and Thurston. Sugar cultivation required the channeling, piping, and usage of remote sources of water, the destruction of native fishponds and taro fields that did not serve a commercial purpose or stood in the way of other ventures, and the easy acquisition of rights of way for roads, communications facilities, and commercial development. Entrepreneurship, as Dole and Thurston defined it, and the need to manage politically the participation of native Hawaiian and immigrants brought in to work the plantations, required the provisional government's control of the land.

*

There was a disquieting parallel to Dole's intention concerning the Crown lands already evident in the United States. Senator Henry Dawes of Massachusetts, motivated by the compulsive need of eastern missionaries to save, mold, and vocationally train the heathen Indians into farmers, spawned the General Allotment Act of 1887. Reservations would be opened for non-Indian settlement. Indians and settlers each would be given one hundred and sixty acres so the Caucasian could help civilize the Indians. The missionary would open schools, attendance would be compulsory, the protestant religion would displace the native culture, and elementary vocational skills — and English — would displace any other native skill, custom, or aspiration. The act would give government sanction to what already was occurring, sometimes with violence. Dawes received support from western senators who embraced his idea for an entirely different reason: control of the land. The process did not take long. Reservation boundary lines and jurisdiction over millions of acres of land changed from native control to Caucasian control with missionary acquiescence and participation. Rights of way for railroads, pipelines, and mineral exploitation occurred. The checker board pattern of the allotment isolated Indian families in a venture they knew little about. Their land was purchased, stolen, or abandoned.

Dawes was supported in his efforts, at times critically, by Senator John Morgan. Alabama's Mount Vernon Barracks, controlled by the Confederacy during the Civil War, served as a concentration camp for four hundred Apache warriors including Geronimo. Dawes' and Morgan's intentions were not likely the same except in one respect. The ABCFM, which endorsed Dawes' effort, already had agreed that the Cherokee Indians, among whom missionaries lived, could own black slaves. Morgan did not disagree.[68]

In early 1887, when the Queen was making her way across the United States via Denver and northwest toward Chicago, Indians were being moved at will, herded, and hunted down and their culture and family structure emasculated. In 1891, in the early days of the Queen's reign, the United States Army had massacred unarmed, Sioux Indians — mostly women, children, and elderly, at Wounded Knee. Liliuokalani understood the imprecise but nonetheless coercive analogue of allotments upon Hawaiians as well as Dole and Morgan did. Expressing her concern about the effect of annexation and the harm it would continue to do to the Hawaiian people — Dole's intention for the Crown lands would ensure it — she wrote that, "The conspirators, having actually gained possession of the machinery of government...refused to surrender their conquest. So it happens that, overawed by the power of the United States to the extent that they can neither themselves throw off the usurpers, not obtain assistance from other friendly states, the people of the Islands have no voice in determining their future, but are virtually relegated to the condition of the aborigines of the American continent." Dole deluded no one; certainly not the Queen. Unabashedly, Lorrin Thurston wanted the Crown lands.[69]

*

Wormley's Hotel, where the delegation from Hawaii apparently stayed, was only a few blocks from the White House and executive office. Bundled against the harsh morning cold, pedestrians made their way to work including to the nearby court of claims as the negotiators prepared their papers and positions. Secretary Foster and his entourage had their own agenda. Patience was required first. Perhaps, however, Archibald Hopkins served a useful Washington purpose: Ensure both sides were familiar with the content of each other's proposal so that, in effect, negotiations already had begun.

In Thurston's proposal, the Queen was relegated to an unspecified form of pay-off disconnected from the Crown lands or with any rationale other than to ensure she declared her loyalty to the provisional government. Thurston always believed she could be had for "the coin" disconnected from a principle other than what he wanted: The end of native Hawaiian resistance. Minister John Stevens had made a similar, failed effort at "offering money." Perhaps as well the unsettled amount was a form of posturing in a negotiation not only with Foster but with the Queen and the constitutionalists led by Neumann. Thurston's proposal provided that an "appropriate financial provision be made for the support of the ex-Queen Liliuokalani and the ex-heir presumptive Kaiulani so long as they shall in good faith submit to the authority and abide by the laws of the Government established by virtue of this treaty."[70]

The Harrison Administration had a different proposal. Secretary Foster had his eye on how to ensure ratification in an unfriendly United States Senate of limited duration. The president recognized that a plebiscite concerning annexation would be the most effective argument in support of ratification. The Queen's letter may have caused him discomfort. Foster did ask Thurston to provide him with an explanation of her position. Foster needed a political if not an historical cover for the seemingly abrupt, obviously dramatic departure he wanted to make from America's foreign policy without the benefit of careful congressional hearings or a national dialogue. When assured a plebiscite would guarantee annexation's defeat and pierce any pretense Thurston represented the Island's people, Harrison sought a different, seemingly unassailable rationale to substantiate the provisional government's legitimacy: Religion and property.

In the treaty's preamble, Foster made Christianity the righteous purpose of the treaty and Hawaii a nation devoid of native people. His draft treaty began: "[I]n view...of the intimate part taken by citizens of the United States in their implanting the seeds of Christian civilization... [and] of the preponderant and paramount share thus acquired by the United States and the citizens in the productions, industries and trade of said Islands," the acquisition of Hawaii was warranted and the legitimacy of the provisional government established. A plebiscite was unnecessary in Hawaii. The rules of conduct were founded not in the principles of John Locke or Jean Jacques Rousseau or Thomas Paine or Thomas Jefferson but in the commands of God, John Calvin, and the control of property.

In a manner customary to the admission of states into the union, Foster's draft treaty required that title to the Crown lands — title in "absolute fee", the clearest form of unencumbered ownership — along with all other government owned lands be transferred to the United States "together with every right and appurtenance thereunto appertaining." Whether those "rights" included Liliuokalani's or native Hawaiian interests was not articulated formally. But Thurston got what he wanted: A degree, still unspecified, of local control over the Crown lands. In a manner that was not customary, the proposed treaty provided that "The existing laws of the United States shall not apply to such lands in Hawaii, but the Congress of the United States shall enact special laws for their management and disposition." In the meantime, the lands could be disposed of by the provisional government. Revenues from the Crown lands also could be used, for the first time, for the military and naval purposes of the United States and for local government. Beyond those uses, revenues "shall be used solely for the benefit of the inhabitants of the Hawaiian Islands for education and other public purposes." Whatever those terms meant precisely they altered the clarity of the historic purpose the Crown lands had served for native Hawaiians.[71]

The continued use of contract labor was not rejected affirmatively by the United States. During the negotiations every effort was made to preserve the freedom of the planters if not the Hawaii government to continue its use unimpeded, including by scrutiny from the Supreme Court of the United States. Thurston already was looking to encourage additional Portuguese immigration with government financial support to satisfy the demand for labor and to further dilute the voting power of the Hawaiian majority. To satisfy domestic prejudice in the United States, however, Chinese laborers were explicitly excluded from entering Hawaii or from entering the United States through Hawaii. Manipulating race, cultural prejudice, and a form of human chattel were central to gaining senate approval.[72]

Secretary Foster also had a different view of Liliuokalani. He recognized, as the provisional government did, that deposing her warranted some form of compensation or payment. His goal also was plain: Stop Hawaiian resistance from the top down. Unlike the provisional government, the United States proposed a considerable sum to the Queen with critical political and legal limitations. "The Government of the United States," the treaty read, "agrees to pay Liliuokalani, within one year from the date of the exchange of this Treaty the sum of twenty thousand dollars, and annually thereafter a like sum of twenty thousand dollars during the term of her natural life...." It was a substantial amount of money.[73]

The annuity was conditioned on three requirements. First, the money had to be appropriated by the Senate *and* the House of Representatives which may or may not be amenable to providing it over the lifetime of the obligation. The first payment would not be due until a year after the treaty was approved under a different administration and Congress. Although the value of the Crown lands had not been calculated, the value of their income was approximately $50,000 a year or easily two and one-half times what Foster proposed. Second, Liliuokalani was fifty-five years old. Royalty had not lived long in Hawaii. Her brother Kalakaua died at age fifty-four. Her sister Bernice had died at age fifty-two. Her sister Miriam Likeliki had died at age thirty-six. The United States had done its actuarial calculations both theoretical and in her family. Finally, accepting the payment would have ensured the end of Hawaiian sovereignty and the acceptance of the *coup d'état's* illegality and everything that flowed from it. Thurston and his colleagues proposed that the annuity would cease if the Queen took part in "any proceeding in opposition to the Government of the United States," or engaged "upon any revolutionary act." The former limitation suggested that Thurston was concerned she would sue the United States and, absent a monetary penalty to stop her, such a lawsuit would be filed legitimately. The reason for the second limitation was explained explicitly: Because any revolutionary act on her part would be against the United States and subject to its laws, Thurston's colleague said, "It may induce her to go to some other country to live." In taking the long view, the Queen would never accept such terms. At this juncture, however, she was unaware of the precise form of the offer.[74]

The negotiated draft treaty was considered by Thurston and the other commissioners on February 14 at Wormley's. The draft also was discussed with William Kinney, Thurston's law partner, who was asked to accompany the provisional government's representatives. Archibald Hopkins also reviewed the draft treaty and participated in the discussions about its content, what it meant politically in Hawaii, what to anticipate in the Senate, why Dole, Thurston, and Smith wanted it, and why both the United States and the provisional government separated the Crown lands from Liliuokalani and its beneficiaries — native Hawaiians. Hopkins and Kinney endorsed acceptance of the treaty. Thurston informed Secretary of State Foster of the delegation's agreement.[75]

The treaty was submitted to the Senate on February 15. Another disquieting deal had been struck at Wormley's Hotel.

*

Lorrin Thurston was thirty-five years old when the *coup d'état* occurred. He had "read" the law in order to begin practicing; a common experience in Hawaii. He also left the islands to attend Columbia Law School for two years. He returned in 1881. He was included in the deal that imposed the 1887 constitution on Kalakaua. Thurston became the minister of interior, which gave him control over the nation's resources and lands. In 1893, he was practicing law a few blocks from the Iolani Palace with William Kinney and William O. Smith, when he and Smith secretly coached members of the Queen's cabinet into forms of dishonesty and the pretense necessary to rationalize the intervention of the United States.

Thurston bore some resemblance to his missionary grandfather, Asa Thurston: He was solidly built, pugnacious in temperament, bearded, and filled with rhetorical skills and a sense of the bravado. He was not academically inclined or, it appears, easily taken by subtle intellectual pursuits. He never finished high school and was expelled from Punahou, the academic school established by the mission exclusively for their own children. He was gifted in terms of his ability to cultivate and use relationships, in pursuing his agenda, and in the know-how to coalesce that agenda with the agenda of others. Before and after the *coup d'état*, Thurston was a committed capitalist and investor. During this visit to the United States, he devoted considerable time to his private concession and cyclorama display of a volcano at the Chicago Exposition.[76]

Thurston's missionary heritage was undiluted, intimate, and unique in its character. Lucy Goodale — Lorrin Thurston's grandmother — married Asa Thurston within three weeks of their first meeting. Her idea of the marriage was, she wrote, "pledging themselves to each other as close companions in the race of life, consecrating themselves and their all to a life work among the heathen." It was an acknowledged marriage of opportunity. The form of arrangement also was not exceptional. Dr. James Smith, the father of Attorney General William O. Smith, sought out "a fine girl who, he had reason to believe, might leave her home for him and the career of a missionary at the Sandwich Islands. She was out. But her younger sister, Millicent Knapp, was in, and within a week after he had transferred his affections to her she accepted him." Emily Ballard, who married the Reverend Daniel Dole, believed that "a sudden light shone over her and her heart cried, This...is the awaited call!" Wives were encouraged to do whatever was essential to help their husbands.[77]

Lucy Thurston had five children, including Asa Goodale Thurston, Lorrin Thurston's father. Her experience as a mother, however, was both powerful and prophetic of a deeper tension. "[B]urdened by the need to protect her children from 'heathenism,'" Lucy Thurston began what evolved into a "missionary theory that centered on the Christian home."[78]

"Throughout their childhood the Thurston children were virtually prisoners in their children's quarters closely supervised and educated by their mother, kept separate from the indigenous people and forbidden to learn the Hawaiian language." A prefabricated wooden house, donated by the ABCFM, was placed in the Thurston's "large retired yard of three acres, and ... especially devoted to the accommodation of [their] children." Lucy Thurston wrote in 1830 that "No intercourse should exist between the children and the heathen." She said it again in 1835, describing the broader use of fences and regulations to ensure the separation of cultures. "We are willing to come and live among you," as she described her conversations with Hawaiian parents, "that you may be taught the good way, but it would break our hearts to see our children rise up and be like the children of Hawaii." The missionaries established Punahou only for their own children. "Native influence," their experience led them to conclude, "is very bad for children."[79]

"Exemplifying the Christian home" was sufficient. "The [natives] could at once behold order and application," Lucy Thurston wrote, "and though ignorant of the English language, they shrewdly judged that our children were prodigies of obedience compared with their own degenerate offspring." This approach — recognized and affirmed by the ABCFM — had practical consequences: In some families, the missionaries deliberately (or perhaps with a more subtle indirection) instilled condescension into their children toward the nation's native people. When it came to defining power and sustaining a hierarchy in governance, Lorrin Thurston remained solidly within his culture.[80]

Thurston was, in fact, still the unrepentant missionary wanting to fulfill his grandfather's parting pronouncement to his colleagues as they left the Boston Harbor in 1819 to embrace "the miseries of a world lying in wickedness."[81] The Reverend Asa Thurston, his wife Lucy standing dutifully nearby, took to the podium in the Park Avenue Church and spoke in a manner his grandson Lorrin intended to make prophecy: "In a few days we expect to leave this loved land of our nativity, for the far distant isles of the sea, there to plant this little vine, and nourish it, till it shall extend through all the islands, till it shall shoot its branches across to the American coast, and its precious fruit shall be gathered at the foot of her mountain."[82]

Thurston wanted to be the victor in Washington, DC, the triumphant Cauca-sian revolutionary that brought Hawaii into the American fold. It did not work. The pretense was pierced readily. The *raison d'être* of the *coup* — that the Queen had abrogated the constitution by preparing a revised one — was given little credence in the United States. One *coup* leader, once confronting the *realpolitik* judgment of members of Congress and the nation's newspapers, recognized that "It is not admitted that we can be honest or patriotic." The view of Thurston, Dole, Smith, and Minister Stevens remained fairly consistent: "If we are," one member of Congress said, "ever to step from the shores of this continent out upon a career of empire and colonization, let it be with head erect and above even the suspicion of dishonor, intrigue, or low dealing." The four men served one useful purpose. They presented the United States with an opportunity to acquire Hawaii.[83]

When Paul Neumann, Prince David, and Edward Macfarlane arrived a few days after the treaty's submission to the Senate, Macfarlane reported, with "con-sternation," that there was "general satisfaction with...the Annexation question... with the people and the press."[84]

Lorrin Thurston was in command of the field.

CHAPTER 3. ALLIES: WOMEN AND THE RENAISSANCE OF THE *ALI'I*

The splendidly expansive bay at Hilo is framed by Mauna Keo and Mauna Loa. Their geologic strength is grand in stature. Though the molten lava and eruptive power of their volcanoes plied the imaginative vigor of Hilo's residents, both mountains provided a predictable solace; a protective warmth to those who entered the bay by canoe or small steamship through the churning and precarious currents that surrounded, clashed, and renewed daily the island of Hawaii.

Nearly ten thousand people lived in Hilo in 1893. Most were native Hawaiian. Through Hilo's boundary runs the Wailuku River; its origins ten thousand feet above sea level, moving through the harsh strength of Rainbow Falls and the rough, unpredictable tumult of Boiling Pot's descending plateaus. The bay at Hilo turned "somewhat yellowish when the waters of the Wailuku River are high," recalled Joseph Nawahi, during a visit outside Hawaii in more tranquil times in his life. He knew. He had swum and fished and canoed in the Wailuku and luaued and talked and walked along its shore and the shores of the bay with his family and friends since childhood. His sojourns throughout the island also would have included walks and horse rides across Crown lands, which touched the Hawaii coastline and expanded deep into its interior. He had represented the Puna District near Hilo in the national legislature since 1872. Nine victories. Twenty years. His deep sadness and steadfast commitment to his people and the constitutional monarchy ensured he would never again attend a session of the Hawaii legislature.

Nawahi was born on Hawaii in 1842, less than four years after the birth of Liliuokalani on Oahu. Like her, he was raised in a generation that still felt the meaning and memory of Kamehameha's unification of the islands into a nation. Hilo was the place where Kamehameha formed and launched his armada of eight hundred warships. Also like Liliuokalani, Nawahi understood intuitively how islands separated by water and oceanic currents and terrifying wind and swells can be unified and preserved as a nation. Unlike Liliuokalani, Nawahi was not an *ali'i* in origin or lineage.

Nawahi's skill at oratory and analysis and law, including his knowledge of foreign affairs and global history, were recognized by his constituents and his adversaries in Hilo and in Honolulu. He had spoken eloquently about the "negro people [of Haiti]" who, "because of the love of their country," stopped their ministers from acting improperly "through the power of the common people in the legislature," and, later, about the experience of the French in Mexico and the risks of not being responsive to the needs of the local citizens. He was considered the "Gladstone of the Pacific" and compared by one of his admirers to America's Washington and Germany's Bismarck. He had witnessed and opposed the treaty in 1876 that transferred authority over Pearl Harbor to the United States. He had met with other native Hawaiian leaders in July of 1890 to support a new constitution and had come to Liliuokalani's residence in Waikiki to provide her counsel on their thinking. She had asked him during her reign to be the minister of foreign affairs. His skill and knowledge and potential at diplomacy had overshadowed the fact he had left Hawaii only once to visit San Francisco. She had made a prudent and farsighted choice.[85]

Hawaiian resistance to the *coup d'état* and annexation formed immediately as the people of the nation — outside of Honolulu and Oahu — came to understand fully what had happened on January 17. The *Hui Kalaiaina* — the Hawaiian Political Association — already was in existence. The *Hui's* purpose was primarily to seek a new constitution. Its composition and political strength was in Honolulu. The culture and governance of the nation was now in peril. The struggle was both local and global. Unity needed to be displayed and projected concretely in a form and manner recognizable, persuasive, and unassailable in its origins. With an organizational skill that easily surpassed Kamehameha's coercive success at organizing and defeating warriors, native Hawaiians on Oahu, Molokai, Lanai, Kauai, Nihau, and Hawaii formed the *Hui Aloha Aina*. The name reflected a cultural purpose embedded deeply in the Hawaiian experience. However westerners characterized native Hawaiians, they referred to themselves as "the people who loved the land" — *Aloha Aina*. The English translation — losing, as it did often, the more profound meaning — was "the Patriotic League." Its president was Joseph Nawahi of Hilo. Simultaneously, a "sister organization" was formed, the *Hui Aloha Aina o Na Wahine* — the Patriotic League of Women. Its president was Ms. Abigail Kuaihelani Maipinepine Campbell of Honolulu. Its leader on Hilo was Emma Aima Nawahi, Joseph's wife.[86]

Emma Nawahi was tall and poised, her manner a "simple directness" expressed with the same empathy that characterized her husband. She was born in Kukuau, Hilo, a rural part of the island. Her origins were seemingly common and of the land. Her maturity and intellect were recognized early. She became a teaching assistant at the United Hilo School. She also inspired poetry. Joseph Nawahi, then a legislator, wrote to her: "Oh dainty lehua blossom there with Hopoe, You beautify our relationship, love will always be with you, like the fine rains that adorn the uplands." They were married in February 1881. Emma embraced both the motherhood of three children and, with a discerning skill, the form of civic service embraced and learned by her husband. She later became a lady-in-waiting to Queen Liliuokalani.[87]

Abigail Campbell was "a very tall women, a full commanding figure" with an "exquisitely low and full voice....Her manner gracious." She had married into financial comfort. Joseph Campbell was Irish. He had come to Hawaii in 1850. His wealth was derived from early investment in sugar refining and, later, in real estate development. Although Joseph Campbell supported her effort, she made plain that if he or any other women's husband had not, "Oh that would be very hard. But — if I were the woman — yes, I should work for my people anyway.... You see, they are so poor, so helpless. They need help so badly."[88]

Abigail Campbell's and Emma Nawahi's origins and experiences were different. Both women now would draw on their intuitive and learned skills in the context of a grave public matter: how to discern motives, recognize emerging political forces, report on events, and prognosticate the future in order to provide leadership and counsel to others.

The purpose of the men's League was informed by the value of participation in governance lost since 1887 and the need for equality of treatment denied by the *coup*'s leaders and sanctioned by the United States. "The object of this association," the men's constitution read, "is to preserve and maintain, by all legal and peaceful means and measures, the independent autonomy of the islands of Hawaii nei; and, if the preservation of our independence be rendered impossible, our object shall be to exert all peaceful and legal efforts to secure for the Hawaiian people and citizens the continuance of their civil rights." The men's League represented "over 7,500 native-born Hawaiian qualified voters throughout the islands (out of a total of 13,000 electors), and ... a woman's branch of 11,000 members." The Patriotic Leagues' purpose represented a principled fealty to the historic evolution of the constitutional monarchy and to the Queen. No one was content with the *ali'i* or the monarchy acting alone or on their behalf.[89]

Within a few months of the *coup d'état* both organizations held elections throughout the islands to select representatives for a formal assembly in Honolulu. Interest was intense. "[T]the Hawaiian people had developed as an active political force regardless of their ranking at birth." The assembly's purpose: To debate and approve continued actions to support independence and the individual civil rights of all Hawaii's citizens. The Patriotic Leagues' leaders, perhaps at Joseph Nawahi's suggestion, later sought diplomatic intercession from France, Portugal, England, Japan, and Germany. The effort was unavailing. But it reflected an attitude about the Patriotic Leagues' legitimacy and the boldness of its strategic thinking. The assembly in Honolulu was a parallel legislature. [90]

With Liliuokalani at Washington Place, native Hawaiians had reconstituted a discernable, responsive semblance of representative governance. They sought to occupy and command the field in their own nation.

*

There had been no reigning female monarch of Hawaii until Liliuokalani ascended to the throne in 1891. She was a woman in a governance history that had been dominated almost exclusively by men. She also was the oldest reigning monarch when she ascended. She had the longest period of time to understand her nation's dramatic transformation.

Two elements of that transformation were incontestable. First, the missionaries came to Hawaii to colonize and prosper materially. They had done both. They and their children did all they could within Hawaii and in defining Hawaiians to the people of the United States to engender a "shame of [Hawaii's] past." They brought a form of civilization but not civility. In a twentieth-century incarnation, their conduct would be characterized as "a terrorism of the mind." Second, the ideological forces essential for an enduring struggle for Hawaii's identity — especially the identity of women — were present from the outset of the missionary arrival. The Lucy Thurston model was only one element among those forces. The use of Christian values to justify Caucasian material comfort or to explain the demise of the Hawaiian people, the condemnatory message in newspapers and sermons from the pulpit to justify the *status quo* in class and race and with respect to who could enter God's kingdom, and the missionary's vocational rather than academic approach to native education confirmed the legitimate basis for critical ferment. As a practical matter, the Hawaiian communal, land, and ancestral values integral to their identity and the spiritual character of their Polynesian history ensured a deeply rooted ideological tension with the Adam Smith, Calvinist, and largely New England values embraced by the missionary and their children. [91]

Polynesian families had settled Hawaii proximate to the time Jesus emerged from the arid hillsides of Nazareth. In a second migration, Tahitians had brought with them the *ali'i* system of governance. A chief acted as steward of the land, and managed and directed the commoners to ensure the land's productivity and preservation and the commoners' well-being. The stratification in class grafted onto this civic order a critical element of separateness. It took two forms. The continuity of the Hawaiian culture was held in the common people. The *ali'i* "could be ousted for failing [to keep] their religious duties... [and] by extension to care" for the land and the common people. Second, the effectiveness of an *ali'i* in fulfilling his obligations was judged by the people. When English and American traders entered Hawaii's port communities in the late eighteenth century, many of the ruling *ali'i* embraced the benefits of trade to enhance their station in life. The harsh burden of western contact felt over time by the common people was attributed directly to mistakes in judgment on the part of the *ali'i*. The mutuality of obligation of the *ali'i* system had begun to lose its core. [92]

In 1819, Kamehameha grew ill. He left to Kaahumanu, his second wife, the responsibility of serving as chief counselor to his son, Kamehameha II. She was not satisfied. She declared that she "would share the rule over the land." To consolidate her power, she abolished the religious rules and elevated the importance of the *ali'i* in civil governance. It also was the *ali'i*, especially Kaahumanu, who embraced the Calvinist religion and the missionary role in government when they arrived in the 1820s. The missionary never relinquished it. Common Hawaiians continued to persevere in their religious practices at considerable risk of harm.[93]

In 1827, a French-based Catholic mission came to Hawaii. The Calvinists, led by Reverends Asa Thurston and Hiram Bingham, resolved that the Catholics "are a danger to the civil government of these islands [and] enemies of sound morality." Freedom of religion or the enactment of the First Amendment to the United States Constitution in 1791 was irrelevant to the missionary from Boston. Kaahumanu ordered common Hawaiians "who attended the Roman Catholic services" to hard labor. The commoners were forced to build miles of stone walls with few tools and regardless of age, and to clean excrement. They were denied food. She expelled the priests. The *ali'i* had imposed vengeful, horrific punishment on defiant Hawaiians who refused to join Reverend Bingham's church. It was another moment of separation. Hawaii's government and Calvinist theology were indecipherable. It was the intolerance of a seventeenth-century New England village. Kaahumanu had ingratiated herself further into the missionary model of woman. Native Hawaiian men and women endured the consequences.[94]

The missionary embrace of materialism also caused discomfort among its members with further problematic consequences for native Hawaiians. In 1832, the missionary, Dr. Dwight Baldwin, wrote to the ABCFM in Boston that, "The resources which missionaries have in these Islands, for placing themselves in easy and comfortable circumstances, not to say of getting rich, are far greater than the Christian public generally suppose." The entrepreneurial impulse, Baldwin continued, had pierced the pretense of piety the missionaries continued to profess publicly and from the pulpit. Dr. Alonzo Chapin also noted in 1833, that, "*The large houses, numerous domestics,* and *extensive tenanted domains,* possessed by individuals of this mission [are] ... at variance with [our] ... disinterested motives." The greed suppressed under the cloak of piety emerged as a reality in short order.[95]

The ABCFM recognized the greed as well. In 1848, it reprimanded the mission. The "Grand Crisis" that warranted the ABCFM to begin withdrawing its support in tools, building materials, goods, and books was not because the mission had succeeded but that it was a financial and ethical embarrassment. The ABCFM had "sent out supplies in bulk to its secular agents in Hawaii to be held as a common fund, and to be distributed by the secular agents to the individual missionaries...as needed." The exploitation — which its agents Samuel Castle and Amos Cooke recognized and fostered — was draining the ABCFM's resources. Both men were using the ABCFM to distribute wealth, support private financial gain, and ensure gratitude to Castle and Cooke through loose credit and delayed accounting. When combined with the expansive growth of privately-held livestock, homes, and land, the destruction of irrigation systems that denied their availability for native Hawaiian sustenance, and missionary acquiescence in the use of servants and contract labor, the ABCFM decided to declare victory over the heathen and to handle the financial scandal — unique to Hawaii — quietly, so as not to discourage financial contributions to other missions.[96]

The practical and ideological foundation for a deeper social critique and colloquy between and among missionary and native Hawaiian values was set. By the 1850's, however, "the true reins of government were not in the hands of the Hawaiian *ali'i*, but in those of the foreigners, primarily the Americans." Missionary and their descendants, who had inter-married into the wealthy commercial class, also were in "the teaching corps, in the pulpit, in the press, and in what was to become all powerful — the economy." The danger to native Hawaiians was exacerbated further by the difference in language. Hawaiian embrace of the poetic metaphor and its political subtext defined, in part, the people's articulation of facts and opinions. Hawaiian, as Hawaiians used it in oral and in written form and as the missionary imbued its words with their own narrow meaning, was not interchangeable. The danger was founded in who held positions of power when the translation mattered to the commonweal in law, commerce, and education. Those positions were not held by native Hawaiians. The *ali'i* — as that class was once understood in the Hawaiian culture — was dead. One additional, very practical fact also was incontestable and heightened the importance of a timely critique: Native Hawaiians continued to die in disquieting numbers. By 1866, leprosy had begun to take its sadly measurable toll in human life.[97]

Hawaii's fate bore deeper and with a more insidious swath into the fabric of the nation than the long reign of the Kamehameha family could absorb and resolve. Was there enough resilience in the common people and the monarchy to reclaim the culture and law of their nation? If so, what form would it take? And, in accordance with whose values?

*

In 1845, commoners protested in a formal petition to King Kamehameha III "the presence of powerful foreigners in government and foreigners' ability to own land." The people sought the appointment of Hawaiians and restrictions on foreign land ownership, both of which the commoners believed would bolster the kingdom's independence and fundamental Hawaiian values and identity. The petition was an implicit critique of the king's judgment and the materialism and values Hawaiians witnessed among the foreigners and the *ali'i*. The petition was signed by sixteen hundred people and reprinted in Hawaiian and in English for a broader audience. The boldness and confidence of the commoners' action — now in the form of the printed word — reflected the continuity in their capacity and willingness to judge the *ali'i* and their duty to preserve the cultural values of the kingdom. The king's advisers, with the familiar ambivalence of skilled politicians seeking to preserve the *status quo*, rejected the plea. The petitioners' prescience was remarkable. In 1848, at the same time the ABCFM was reprimanding the mission for its acquisitive greed, the king, under the guidance of Caucasian advisors, divided the land and opened it to foreign acquisition and, ultimately, foreign domination.[98]

Hawaiians also developed a weekly native language newspaper, *Star of the Pacific*. The newspaper, read widely throughout the islands, unabashedly was a forceful, informed critique of the seventeenth-century-New England village and the Calvinist embrace of materialism. The newspaper contained for the first time in a printed form songs, chants, poetry, and stories of a communal cultural tradition previously confined to oral transmittal the missionary's had discouraged. They included a "song of affection for education/civilization" and other writings that challenged the missionary proscriptions for native Hawaiian moral and family conduct, vocational education, and Hawaiian subservience in the civic and economic order especially on sugar plantations. Women wrote articles in a manner reflective of Hawaiian cultural history and a valued, independent voice that the missionary coda, the Lucy Thurston model, and the ambivalent journey of Kamehameha's wife, Kaahumanu, did not condone.

The *Star of the Pacific* was in the nature of a manifesto, "a fundamental critique of the materialism which was to become the central characteristic of nineteenth-century society," a roughly-hewed collection of a theory of history that suggested a plausible future centered on Hawaiian values with a cosmopolitan intellectual core. Those values provided a Hawaiian definition of civility and patriotic thought. In its manner of organization and purpose the *Star of the Pacific* was yet another call to the king and *ali'i* that a social contract existed with reasoned, historically embedded purpose. In a constitutional monarchy, such a call was the closest approximation Hawaii had to incorporating the will of the people — and the voice of God — into governance. In the absence of responsive government, democratically active, highly literate Hawaiians could make and act on their own reasoned choices. A new definition of civic leader was emerging.[99]

Liliuokalani was in her teens when this colloquy was occurring. Her birth had been commemorated with a name song titled "O Liliu-lani." The song embraced a deep civic and political meaning and the continuity of duty with respect to the land. "[I]t could never be hers entirely, for it was shared by all." She had learned early and it was reflected in her own poetry and use of "exquisite imagery" a tenet fundamental to her identity: The native Hawaiian belief that they "first held the lands of Hawaii in trust for the gods of our nature" and their "descendants [continued] to have a vested responsibility and right to hold those lands in trust."[100]

Liliuokalani's appreciation of the generational and political communicative purpose of music and the poetic verse remained central to her identity. The proximate Western analogue in this use of poetry could be found in the work of Percy Bysshe Shelley. He had argued that poetry is "more than a display of verbal ingenuity... It has the most serious aim of prophecy, law and knowledge. Social progress can be achieved only if it is guided by ethical sensibility." In the intellectual and aesthetic exercise of selecting the words, "the achievement of poetry is to push forward the moral progress of civilization." There also was evolving within Liliuokalani the intuitive and learned meaning — the ideology — of "Hawaii for Hawaiians." The evolution of that meaning was formed, in part, through the critique and colloquy manifested in the emerging Renaissance of ideas and perspective reflected in the *Star of the Pacific*.[101]

The entire journalistic effort was viewed as a threat to the then thirty-year long missionary intention to shame Hawaii's past. The effort also was directed to the decayed conduct and definition of the *ali'i*. The content of the *Star* was a self-evident violation of the imperative of subservience and God's command. Missionary took to the podium and pulpit to denounce the newspaper. Abraham Fornander, editor of the *Polynesian*, a Honolulu based English-language paper, wrote that, "The greatest opposition comes from the Protestant Missionaries, who...use every endeavor to crush the [newspaper] and stop its circulation...The editors...are defending themselves valiantly, and the contest has led to some very plain talk about the limits of clerical interference with the economic and political relations of the people.... The truth is that there is a mental revolution going on among the native population, which the Missionaries are equally incompetent to comprehend, to master or to avert."[102]

Among the *Star's* more prominent editors was young David Kalakaua, Liliuokalani's brother. It is not hard to imagine the quiet conversations he and his sister would have had alone, about governance or the meaning of the "people's voice" or the harsh reality that was enveloping Hawaii. Missionary religious and economic imperatives and the earlier choices of the *ali'i* had imposed plainly evident limitations on the exercise and full attainment of Hawaiian nationalism. The limitations had to be removed.

*

Liliuokalani awaited the efficacy of Paul Neumann's efforts in the United States. With the exception of an occasional visitor, like J.O. Carter or the careful reportage of intelligence and the daily machinations with her retainers, she was often alone at Washington Place. She arose early and read the bible daily. She had changed churches when the minister at the famed Kawaiahao Church supported the *coup d'état*. On Sundays she was welcomed warmly at the Episcopalian Church closer to her home. In the quietude of her study or amidst the sounds and fragrance of her gardens she had time and further reason to contemplate the evolution of Hawaii's history and the meaning of the long view, which included forces she had not started and could not control.

The harsh conundrum of monarchy in the complexity of a constitutional setting was that succession occurred after death. Learning the realities, culture, and politics of governance comes in part by learning from each other during life. Liliuokalani had shared with her brother much of the tumult of his reign, including in personal ways. He was no longer available to her. One lesson she learned: He could not satisfy the *coup* leaders and what they represented.

Kalakaua was "a handsome, largely self-educated but knowledgeable, quick-witted and shrewd young man of immeasurable charm and personality, qualities he never lost." He had served in various positions of government, including the House of Nobles and the military, traveled the islands widely, visited Vancouver and San Francisco on official business, and engaged in the substantive task of editing the *Star of the Pacific*. He studied law and became a member of the bar. He also engaged in the gritty politics of elections and the legislature when he was elected monarch in 1874. In 1888, during his reign, he published a thorough, engaging book on the history, culture, and mythology of Hawaii and the Kamehameha dynasty, *Legends and Myths of Hawaii*.[103]

No one understood the ideological and practical tension and the need it presented for a Renaissance of the Hawaiian culture better than Kalakaua and his sister Liliuokalani. They needed allies and the intellectual resources to define and govern the nation. To accomplish a Renaissance also required a redefinition of the *ali'i*, based on education or civic accomplishment, not mere genealogy, heredity, or royal edit. Both monarchs also required a renewed and more pervasive role for women in Hawaii's governance and fate. Women represented a force in intellect and the "voice of the people" not expressed fully in decades. The burden on Kalakaua and Liliuokalani was enormous. What needed to be done was given the formal sanction of government. Both monarchs had thought and acted on the need for change before their reign began.[104]

Kalakaua understood the latent nature of Hawaiian nationalism. He invoked it symbolically, practically, and politically from the outset of his reign. It was contentiously done. He was the first monarch that was not a direct descendant of Kamehameha. Native Hawaiians were, at first, uneasy.

He undertook crucially important ventures to encourage Hawaiian identity and culture and the formation of law. He traveled around the world with a deliberateness of purpose and with a diplomatic and intellectual skill not previously exercised by a Hawaiian monarch. His entourage of advisors supported but did not lead him. He traveled to the Far East. He met with dignitaries in Burma, China, Egypt, and India. In his meeting with the emperor of Japan he discussed trade and immigration and the possibility of an alliance through marriage. He met with Pope Leo XIII in Rome. The meeting occurred at a time the Catholic Church and Europe were struggling to respond to massive social ferment, and the emergence of socialist ideologies that challenged the economic *status quo* and the belief that church teachings were irrelevant to the harsh daily lives of its members. Within his reign, Pope Leo would issue his encyclical on Catholic social teaching that deeply embedded the church on the side of workers and peasants and the affirmative duty of government to protect the elderly and children. Italy also was in its own nascent form of parliamentary democracy. In the United States, Kalakaua met with President Grant. Both were witnessing the effects of Reconstruction and the meaning of government affirmatively ensuring former slaves could vote, run for office, and travel with, at least, legal freedom. Kalakaua also addressed Congress.[105]

Kalakaua reflected a disquieting departure from the past. He was an intellectually sophisticated and culturally independent native Hawaiian with an increasingly informed geopolitical vision and confidence. During his reign, he also sought to establish solid relationships with other island nations in the Pacific. He signaled to the Europeans — Germany, France, and England — that despite their size and stature and imperialist or colonial designs he held to the principled belief of nationhood for all the small nations of the Pacific. His attempt, albeit short lived, to establish a naval presence in Hawaii's waters reflected the same principled belief: Hawaiians could define their own nation.[106]

He also recognized the symbolic value of a permanent seat of government. Previous monarchs had conducted business from what were lovely homes. He authorized and received legislative funding to build a new palace on the site of an ancient place of worship, the Iolani Palace: *Io*, the Hawaiian hawk; *Lani*, the heavenly, the royal, and the exulted. Construction began in 1879 and was completed in 1882. The palace was stunningly attractive; Italianate in architectural style with its Palladian loggias and modified campanile tower. It was characterized — appropriately for Kalakaua's purpose — as "neo-Renaissance." It had a global appeal. Distinctive elements of it could be seen in Melbourne, Florence, and New Orleans. Hawaiians walking through it could see indigenous woods, moldings, art work, furniture, and the feathered elegance of the royal robes. They also had access to the palace grounds for ceremonies and to plead their cause. The king's coronation deliberately included the revival of chants and the hula; practices the missionaries had prohibited with the tacit agreement of previous monarchs.

Kalakaua was an informed skeptic of Calvinist religious beliefs. He had seen too much. The traditionalists in the missionary community and those among them looking for a rationale to discredit the king were discomforted by his irreverence. Spiritually, Kalakaua had never taken God's "Kingdom by violence" as the New Divinity creed required. In contrast, "[n]o other member of the Royal School [where she was educated] took early Christianity as seriously as Liliuokalani did, nor stayed with its religion." She also was imbued with the Hawaiian culture from birth and personified its resilient memory and persistence. She, like many other Hawaiians, had melded aspects of their Hawaiian and protestant religious belief into a coherent whole and thoughtful way of living. It was plain early in her life, however, that when the duty of governance evolved to her in 1891, she would not succumb either to the natural order of the commands of God's elect or the exercise of their temporal power. Her duty was to engage in the epical fight to secure Hawaii's identity as a nation.

Kalakaua also appointed native Hawaiians to cabinet positions; supported and campaigned for native candidates for the legislature; and contributed and supported native Hawaiian scientific societies. In his success he provoked a prescient debate led largely by the Caucasians: What was the role of the monarch? Did he merely "reign" in deference to the cabinet and the elders? Or did he "rule" in deference to the voice of the people? Kalakaua knew when and how to do both.[107]

Kalakaua also sent Hawaiians abroad for an education. Among those was Robert Wilcox. Wilcox had a modest claim to a genealogical lineage that was still considered a sign of distinction; a reflection, it was presumed often without more, of the *ali'i's* foresight in governance and duty toward a social order that embraced the entwined values of custom and fairness. In turn the *ali'i* insisted on respectful treatment and deference. Wilcox's distinction had different origins and reflected a commitment to duty borne of his education and civic service.[108]

He was recognized and selected by King Kalakaua to be educated abroad for two purposes. Wilcox could help Kalakaua to re-invent — with a European orientation — an indigenous counterpoise to the Caucasian militia and a broader role and image for Hawaii in the Polynesian Pacific. Wilcox's study in Italy during the *Risorgimento* also exposed him to two forces: The nationalism that ensured the independence of modern Italy with the related formation of democratic institutions under Giuseppe Mazzini and Camille de Cavour and the remarkable courage, successful guerilla warfare, and commitment to principle of Giuseppe Garibaldi.

Wilcox was forced to leave Italy because of the changes wrought by the 1887 constitution imposed on Kalakaua. Hawaiian nationalism and the sophisticated military and diplomatic vision Kalakaua sought were antithetical to Thurston and the missionary heritage. Shortly after Wilcox's return and with the acquiescence of Kalakaua and Liliuokalani, Wilcox gathered a force of Hawaiians "all of whom were dressed in red Garibaldi shirts while he wore his Italian uniform" and assaulted and occupied a portion of the palace grounds. He demanded a new constitution that elevated Hawaiian nationalism. The effort failed. Wilcox was later tried for conspiracy and acquitted. He garnered respect and a place in the commoners' heart and Hawaii's history. He had, through his education, civic commitment, and risk to his life contributed to the formulation of a model or distinctive characteristics that redefined the origins and *raison d'être* of an *ali'i*. His subsequent election and tenure in the Hawaii legislature affirmed that definition.[109]

Wilcox was not alone. Other Hawaiians who made similar civic commitments to public service, elective office, civic organizations, education, law, and medicine did the same. Joseph Nawahi of Hilo solidified the definition of the new *ali'i*. In addition to his legislative service, Nawahi also was a musician, surveyor, painter, and, for many years, served as tax collector. He became a member of the bar through a rigorous oral examination by a skeptical Supreme Court. His skill was all self-taught.

In the early 1880s, Kalakaua's wife Queen Kapiolani, with Liliuokalani's support, began the creation of a maternity home to care for newborns from Hawaiian mothers in order to impede the decimation of the Hawaiian people. In 1882, Liliuokalani also brought together a broad range of women to begin the creation of "a school for young girls — Liliuokalani College — where they would learn not how to be domestics alone ... but to be ladies and scholars....The women would also be taught the Hawaiian language, music, tradition, customs and history." It was a deliberate affront to the missionary intention to ensure Hawaiian women would remain in a largely class or vocational framework. She also sought to create a bank exclusively for women. Money from the sale and inheritance of Hawaiian land was in the hands of Hawaiian women who had married Caucasian men. A bank in which the women were allowed to "'conduct their own affairs'" would encourage the money's retention in the Hawaiian culture.[110]

During Liliuokalani's visit to Washington, in 1887, she went to Mount Vernon to visit the home of George Washington. She paused in Martha Washington's bedroom "to listen to the story of her constancy to the memory of her husband." The story, she later wrote, "spoke to me of the sister women who sat and reflected over the loss of that heroic life.... Why is it, by the way, that she is now 'Martha Washington,' when even in that day she was always remembered as 'Lady Washington'? Is it part of the etiquette of the new women's era, or of the advancing democratic idea?" As always, Liliuokalani was astutely aware of the historical and cultural implications and relevance of what was unsaid. She also had no discomfort with the relationship between women and the "advancing democratic idea."[111]

Other experiences during and after her journey affirmed and reflected the same attitude. She had stopped in Boston to meet her husband's family and visited Deer Island, Massachusetts' notorious maximum security prison. Along with Queen Kapiolani, she visited the quarters assigned to the women and spoke with one of the inmates. While in England, during the jubilee for Queen Victoria, she witnessed a "scrambling in the water" among small boats trying to get through a lock before it closed. She witnessed the unfairness and "indifference of the men, who lounged in the stern..., while the poor girls with poles exerted their strength to the utmost to shove their boats into the waters of the lock....Taking their ease, while from those called the weaker sex came the exertions necessary to get the boat into her place among the crowd of others." One of her earliest decisions after assuming the monarchy was to select a woman, Princess Kaiulani, as the heir apparent. Liliuokalani encouraged her to develop her skills in literature, music, poetry, and history to govern wisely. In 1892, when native Hawaiian men — as "qualified voters" — submitted petitions to Liliuokalani in support of a change to the constitution, she also received petitions from women. They had "crossed out the references to qualified voters, substituting their own wording so that the petition read, in part, 'we humbly, the people of your own Lahui [Nation] to whom the names below belong...are Hawaii's own Native women.'"[112]

In the end, the imposition of the 1887 constitution and, in 1893, the *coup d'état* had little to do with Kalakaua's or Liliuokalani's lack of adherence to constitutional norms or to profligate spending. The imposition had to do with their skill at evoking Hawaiian nationalism in a way that now seemed permanent, and in exercising an ability to govern politically. Their sin: Both monarchs challenged the seventeenth-century New England model that Thurston, Dole, and Smith insisted upon.

The intellectual ferment and cultural tension occurring in Hawaii, soon to be recognized abroad in the singular form of the *coup d'état*, reflected strains of thought that would intersect and conflict with the no less contentious and divisive dialogue occurring in America. These included the debate over race, immigration, and the recognized failure of Reconstruction; the post-Civil War critique of civil and voting rights led by Cady Stanton, Susan B. Anthony, and Victoria Woodhull; the concern for post natal care, health, and social obligation at Hull House and the work of Jane Addams; and the harsh critique of capitalism and its influence on government voiced by William Jennings Bryan, Senator Richard Pettigrew of South Dakota, and the literary realists Frank Norris and Theodore Dreiser.

*

In 1893, when Joseph Nawahi of Hilo assumed the presidency of the Men's Patriotic League and Emma Nawahi and Abigail Campbell assumed responsibility for the Women's Patriotic League, Liliuokalani had witnessed and, with her brother, had helped foster another dramatic transformation in Hawaii: The re-definition of the *ali'i* and the reemergence of women in what she knew — when taking the long view — was an enduring struggle for Hawaii's identity imbued deeply in the fate of the land. The Queen had allies. The political question that loomed unanswered in the shorter term was whether, after Kalakaua lost his spirit in the 1887 *putsch* and the United States ensured the *coup d'état*, Liliuokalani and native Hawaiians could bring the Renaissance to fruition in a way that en-sured continuation of the constitutional monarchy.

Chapter 4. The Long Echo of the Civil War: James Blount

The Capitol building was described by Mark Twain as "a long snowy palace projecting above a grove of trees, and a tall, graceful white dome with a statute on it surmounting the palace and pleasantly contrasting with the background of blue sky." The statute is the allegorical female figure of *Freedom Triumphant in War and Peace*. Her helmet is composed of an eagle's head, feathers, and talons, reflecting the costume of Native Americans. She stands atop a globe encircled with the national motto, *E Pluribus Unum*. The original drawing, however, had her wearing a liberty cap, the symbol of freed slaves. The drawing was objected to by Secretary of War Jefferson Davis. Davis departed the government to lead the Confederacy. *Freedom* was raised atop the dome in December 1863. Echoing loudly was the sound of a thirty-five gun salute followed by the guns of the twelve forts protecting Washington, DC.[113]

Beneath the dome and encircling the rim of the Rotunda is a frieze panorama depicting significant events in American history. In 1893, the panorama was incomplete. The exacting work of Italian émigrés Constantine Brumindi and Filippo Costaggini, painted in grisaille, a monochrome of white and browns that resembles sculpture, starts sixty feet above the floor. The fresco traced the nation's history from the arrival of Columbus through the discovery of gold in California. What remained undone was the depiction of the single most horrific and transformative event of the nineteenth century: The Civil War. The fresco would not be conceived fully, painted, and displayed for another sixty years. The war's meaning in 1893 was painfully unsettled.

Among those who walked toward the Senate chambers to debate the fate of the proposed treaty with Hawaii was Richard Franklin Pettigrew of South Dakota. Pettigrew was forty-five years old. He was born in Vermont, moved with his family to Wisconsin, studied law in Iowa, and taught law at the University of Wisconsin at Madison. He settled in Sioux Falls, South Dakota. He lived within the still extant Fort Sill, designed by the United States army and fortified to engage and quell the Sioux Indians.[114]

Pettigrew did not have the inherited wealth or social cachet or family rootedness central to the identity of Republican George Hoar of Massachusetts or Hoar's newly elected senate colleague, Henry Cabot Lodge. Pettigrew had, however, an unassailable pedigree. His ancestors fought in the Revolutionary War. His father was an abolitionist who, as Pettigrew witnessed as a child, helped southern slaves escape to freedom. Pettigrew became a Republican because the party had opposed slavery and supported Reconstruction.

Pettigrew also was a populist, a Midwestern antecedent to George Norris of Nebraska and Robert LaFollette of Wisconsin. Here, too, he diverged from his party. He distrusted corporate accumulation of wealth and its insidious, increasingly welcomed influence on both political parties. With an "eloquent, firmly-knit, well-informed, and keenly perceptive mind," he argued that having naval stations or securing better trade relations outside the United States was an easily pierced pretext for exploiting native labor in order to keep American wages low and working conditions dismal.

In the social circles of Washington, perhaps in the grand parties held at the home of Henry Adams, Adams' neighbor and friend, Republican John Hay, had described Richard Pettigrew as a "howling lunatic." It is easy to imagine who Pettigrew had in mind when he said, "The early years of the century marked the progress of the race toward individual freedom and permanent victory over the tyranny of hereditary aristocracy, but the closing decades of the century have witnessed the surrender of all that was gained to the more heartless tyranny of accumulated wealth." Within a few years Pettigrew would revolt from his party and support William Jennings Bryan for President.[115]

When Paul Neumann, Edward Macfarlane, and Prince David reached Washington, DC, on February 17, they learned there was no unanimity among the president's party. George Hoar and Henry Cabot Lodge were for the annexation treaty. Richard Pettigrew was against it. Neumann met immediately with individual senators and other American officials. He presented them with arguments against the treaty: Native Hawaiians had not been consulted and events warranted a proper hearing before any action was taken. Neumann delivered the précis to Senator Morgan and fifteen other members of the Senate. Morgan already had orchestrated the treaty's approval in the Foreign Relations Committee and its readiness for a Senate vote.[116]

Neumann met with Secretary of State Foster on February 21. He gave Foster the précis. Substantively, Neumann made essentially the argument agreed upon with the Queen: Were it not for Minister Stevens' actions the *coup d'état* would not have occurred; a plebiscite would ensure the restoration of the constitutional monarchy, precisely the exercise the secretary most feared; and, the Crown lands could not be bartered away because they were owned by the Queen. Neumann also made arguments consistent with the exercise of the discretion the Queen gave him and the need to thwart the president's effort. Hawaiians were not unfriendly toward an appropriate form of American presence, Neumann said. The Queen and Kaiulani had a right to be compensated, the amount or reasons left vague. Neumann highlighted the embarrassment to the president of going forward without more facts. Foster did his best to keep the content of the précis quiet.[117]

Armed with Neumann's précis, Macfarlane left Washington for New York City. He stayed at the elegantly furbished Victoria Hotel. He was welcomed by editors of newspapers with broad readership. The *New York World* reprinted the précis in full on February 24. The front page headline set the tone: *Liliuokalani's Brief, Why Didn't Secretary of State Foster Give this Out? Was it because of the Light Thrown on Minister Stevens' Acts?* Editorial opinion moved toward the side of caution. Macfarlane characterized the editorials as "fighting the treaty on the grounds that any attempt to rush it through the Senate at this time would be hasty, ill-advised and piratical."[118]

Three elements of the debate indicated the difficult reality the constitutionalists confronted. Morgan had power. He had no difficulty getting the treaty reported favorably to the Senate floor. Second, the fact the United States had an interest in Hawaii was not questioned seriously. The notion of Hawaii independence would not be acceptable without some conditions. Third, the discomfort of most opponents was largely with the inappropriate influence exercised by Minister Stevens and the Navy, the absence of native Hawaiian support, a dislike of Thurston and the motives of the *coup* leaders, and annexation's departure from the way America expanded its borders. Members also expressed the concern that native Hawaiians, Asians, and those inhabitants of mixed non-Caucasian heritage were not worthy of inclusion among the American electorate. It was an argument alluded to by the treaty's opponent as well as supporters. Race and culture mattered.

The Queen's absence made a difference. The précis set out, in summary form, Hawaii's constitutional history since Kalakaua. The deeper threads of that history — almost universal literacy, constitutional governance since 1840, Hawaiian embrace of the franchise, domestic tranquility in terms of lawfulness — were not a part of the dialogue. Members and treaty advocates, including Thurston, characterized the monarchy and the Queen with only modest constraint. The fate of the Crown lands or the government lands was not part of the dialogue except in one way. An appropriation would be required for Liliuokalani. Appropriations start in the House of Representatives under the constitution. Members of the House may have recognized another reason for their role. By the late nineteenth century, Congress had stopped considering agreements with Indian tribes as "treaties" solely within the province of the Senate. The Indians had been conquered. They were now a "dependent" nation. It was a portentous sign, another factor to be weighed in formulating strategy for the constitutionalists and the president.

Newspapers became the forum for counting votes and engaging in public debate. Senator Hoar had been asked to draft the Massachusetts' Republican Party platform for the next election. He criticized publicly any attempt to take down the American flag in Hawaii. Richard Pettigrew's opposition came, in part, from his populism. "This whole matter, " he was reported as saying," is not much more than an attempt on the part of the great sugar planters of [Hawaii] to share in the bounty now paid by this Government on domestic sugars." The benefits of annexation would accrue only to corporate interests[119]

The précis was delivered to President-elect Cleveland at his retreat in Lakewood, New Jersey. He examined the matter with Secretary of State designate, Walter Q. Gresham, a Republican, and Treasury Secretary designate, John G. Carlisle. The strategy was set: to inform Democrats that the president-elect did not want a vote on the treaty. He wanted an investigation of the conditions that gave rise to the *coup d'état*.[120]

*

Liliuokalani waited. Iolani Palace, only yards away, remained largely abandoned except for the militia. The fragrance of freshly cut flowers had faded, the sounds in its hall ways were different, Hawaiian access to the palace grounds prohibited. She needed money to support her family and friends, finance living expenses, and drive the still uncertain effort to regain the kingdom. She mortgaged property and sold bonds. She borrowed money from Abigail Campbell's husband James. She also needed detachment and the long view. Properly protected by guards, she visited her estate in Waikiki. It was property she had inherited from her mother. It did not have the grandeur of the homes owned by others in the royal family or the homes being built by financiers and plantation owners. There were two cottages, each one story, simply framed, with large inviting living rooms decorated with "things Hawaiian [and] a feathered *kahili*." There was a two-sided screened porch to keep the flies and mosquitoes at a distance but not the sounds and smells of nature. The property had access to the beach and the sound of the Pacific. It was the closest place to being her own "home" that she possessed and could seek a respite. She did it often. She shared a meal with her retainers and reviewed the maintenance of the grounds and gardens. Her dress became more casual; her countenance relaxed; her meals simpler and shared with others. Within this singular culture and family memories, she could be Hawaiian.[121]

The provisional government had moved awkwardly. Dole's legitimacy came from Minister Stevens. There was no assembly or voice of the people from whom Dole could seek affirmation. Dole also could not ensure elementary public safety or protect the permanence of the provisional government except through the vigilante army. He requested Stevens to intercede. Stevens' declared an American Protectorate. The flag of the United States was unfurled atop the government building that housed the Supreme Court.

On March 9 (a few days after Cleveland's inauguration) the treaty was withdrawn. Two days later, James Blount, a former congressman from Georgia, was appointed to undertake an investigation. Blount had been the chairman of the House Committee on Foreign Affairs. His task was defined publicly by the Secretary of State Walter Gresham: "You will investigate and fully report to the President all the facts you can learn respecting the condition of affairs in the Hawaiian Islands, the causes of the revolution by which the Queen's Government was overthrown, the sentiment of the people toward existing authority, and, in general, all that can fully enlighten the President touching the subjects of your mission." Blount also was vested with "full discretion...to determine when the [naval] forces should be landed or withdrawn." Gresham also conveyed to Blount and, through Stevens, to the provisional government that Blount had "authority in all matters touching the relations of this Government to the existing *or other government of the islands....*" Perhaps Gresham hoped a confrontation would occur that Blount would have to resolve.[122]

In the opening foray into global politics, Liliuokalani had matched and then out-maneuvered her adversaries. She had denied Lorrin Thurston his pretense as a revolutionary. Members of the provisional government were uneasy about her persistence. "[P]ersons backing it came to her telling her she could abdicate and accept the money from the provisional government. She replied she would rather be 'poor with [my] people' than sell the country." She had set the structure and the tone of the ensuing response by President Cleveland. He responded to the diplomatic and moral vehicle — and the line drawing — she had created in her declaration following the *coup d'état*. Nonetheless, the United States had recognized the provisional government since January 17. The Marines still occupied the nation. The American flag flew over Hawaii. The son of a missionary was in control of the provisional government. The fate of the Crown lands and all other government property were still held in suspense.

The Queen awaited the arrival of James Henderson Blount.[123]

*

James Blount was fifty-six years old; stocky in stature, handsome and distinctive in the white suit that often was his trademark in Congress. When appointed by President Cleveland, Blount had just retired. Because Cleveland saw his mission as an extension of a presidential inquiry, Blount's appointment was not submitted to the Senate for approval. Embracing the prospect of spending more time with his family, he accepted the appointment with unease. Blount had met Lorrin Thurston during Thurston's 1892 visit to Washington, DC. Blount found Thurston unlikable but he was indifferent to a cause that, he thought, would no longer be his responsibility.

Blount was raised in relative comfort on a large cotton plantation by relatives. His parents had died early in his childhood. He attended private school and graduated with honors from the University of Georgia in 1857. He read the law and joined a prestigious Macon firm. He was "[w]ell-connected..., a thoroughly self-confident young man." He also was preparing for marriage. Eugenia Wiley was from Macon. She was the daughter of a prominent, financially comfortable family. She was traveled and classically-educated in literature and theater. She attended Miss Spangler's School in New York. Her clothes were as likely to come from Europe as from Atlanta. Her family entertained men active in the secessionist movement and Eugenia participated in those discussions. She was prepared to be an active, informed participant in her husband's professional and political choices. Many an evening, their daughter later recounted, they would go into the parlor alone to quietly discuss the events of the day.[124]

Blount was twenty-three years old when he volunteered to fight against the United States. It was 1861. Two months earlier, the Georgia legislature voted to secede from the Union. The gray and blue flag — the "Stars and Bars" — was "stirringly beautiful" when displayed atop the armory in Macon. Blount expected the war to be short in duration. He volunteered for a year. He departed for Virginia to engage the Union forces at the front line of battle.[125]

Eugenia joined her husband in Virginia. She stayed in Portsmouth. He began training in Norfolk while rumors and anecdotes flowed down from the battles that ensued at Manassas. He also was joined by his man servant, Booz, who remained with him long after emancipation. The war intensified. General Lee sought to outmaneuver and destroy General George B. McClennan's Army of the Potomac as it moved toward Richmond. Blount contracted typhoid. He remained to fight. His troop defended a fort on Drury's Bluff on the James River that was attacked by the Union ship *Monitor*. He was ordered to the Chickahominy River to fight the Union forces, part of the Virginia Peninsula Campaign. He was wounded severely. In 1862, he returned to Macon to recover from his illness and injury. He had been elected a Lieutenant Colonel.

The war went badly. Blount organized and trained a group of volunteers. Refugees, new workers frantically trying to make cannon balls, shells, and guns, and wounded, disoriented soldiers moved to Macon. Union soldiers, with a rough, harsh vindictiveness, occupied towns, took what they wanted, and burned factories, slave quarters, and homes. The Blount plantation was among them.

Southern perspective on the consequences of Reconstruction was not diverse. Caucasians resented it deeply and at their peril. It was not just a loss of privilege and wealth. There was a dramatic alteration in real property rights, business development, and forms of governance. Ulysses Grant became president. Soldiers from the North occupied towns to preserve the new order. Former slaves became legislators, congressmen, councilmen, and proprietors of business. The Ku Klux Klan and other nativist groups emerged in the Midwest and South. They engaged in horrific acts of vandalism, murder, and lynching against blacks, Catholics, and dark-skinned immigrants. A mentality emerged: anger, insidious disquiet, and unalterable suspicion. The Blount family's expectation of the rural country life was over. Blount practiced law in Macon. He entered politics. He was a Democrat.

In the early 1870s, northerners began to question the oppression that pervaded a majority of the south's population. In 1871, John Quincy Adams set a tone Caucasians in the south embraced cautiously. The Union, he wrote, "is now held together by force...the North is to rule the South." He advised the South to accept voluntarily "revolutionary changes forced on the Constitution... [in] the new relation toward the emancipated class." Caucasians in the south had a choice.[126]

The Republican Party split apart in its view of the South and Reconstruction. Grant was re-nominated by the Radicals. Horace Greeley of New York was nominated for president by the Liberals. Greeley sought reconciliation in the form Blount found acceptable: A respect for "the people;" a return to the local control Reconstruction had thwarted. The Democratic Party endorsed Greeley. Blount campaigned for Congress. Greeley lost to Grant badly. Blount was elected. He was forty years old. He never lost again.

"Reconciliation" between the North and South was formalized at Wormley's Hotel in 1877. The harm to the civil rights and lives of blacks was blatant, harsh, viciously employed, and permanent by 1893. Only modest-sized pockets of men within both parties retained a civility — a kind of gray form of civic restraint — with respect to race and culture. In Washington, DC, Blount and Grover Cleveland, albeit in different ways, were among those men. They were on the closing cusp of an era.

*

The intellectual and cultural battle over slavery was not confined to America. The abolitionist movement — vociferous in New England — recognized the global nature of slavery and how that related to the ABCFM and the mission in Hawaii.

In 1837, the Reverend Thomas Lafon, M.D., arrived in Hawaii. "He was a product of ... [the] Anti-Slavery movement...and had himself set free his inherited slaves. He found much fault with [the] missionaries for not paying fixed wages to their [native] servants. He denounced it as a form of slavery." Some among the mission had argued that "Domestic assistants, to assist our females...are exceedingly necessary... [and] that the strength of the Missionary [must] be maintained." Lafon wrote to anti-slavery newspapers in the United States "that the majority of Sandwich Islanders lived in a condition not far removed from that of Negro chattels in the South." He was focused on missionary conduct and that of the *ali'i*. The Sandwich Island Anti-Slavery Society was formed.[127]

Lafon also resented the acceptance by the ABCFM of financial contributions from southern slave-owners. He condemned the Hawaii mission for accepting money from "the blood and sweat of slaves." Lafon made his views know in Boston. He was reprimanded. Lafon resigned. He returned to America. He was followed by three or four others. "The consciences of the rest of the missionaries failed to be awakened upon the subject enough to make them abandon their work." That included the Doles, Smiths, and Thurstons.[128]

The ABCFM in Boston was divided. Its leader, Rufus Anderson, was adamant. The ABCFM had one "grand object:" World evangelization. It could not be diluted by "exporting all the trappings of western civilization [i.e. abolition]." The ABCFM also had to continue to raise money. In 1845, the forces in support of the "grand object" and abolition clashed in Boston. A *Report on Slavery* emphasized "evangelization over civilization." The report declared that "'civil and religious liberty...are still secondary to the primary object of securing holiness.'"[129]

The advocates of the "grand object" embraced the theological notion of "Organic Sin." Slavery, it was postulated, is "organic" to the system of society. It is "the body politic [that] creates false and sinful permanent relations between the individuals," not individual slave owners. Slavery — the buying and selling of "human beings, as merchandise for gain" — was acceptable as long as the "Master" ensured his servant "had satisfactory evidence of being born of God, or having the spirit of Christ." The ABCFM was convinced that "God's method of [dealing with]...slavery...and other kindred wrongs," required that "in dealing with individuals implicated in these wrongs...the utmost kindness and forbearance are to be exercised." Once the report was adopted, "the assembly united in prayer and then sang the Seventy-second Psalm." There now were two classes of wrongs. Idolatry, murder, theft, and polygamy were sins. Slavery and "other kindred wrongs" were not.[130]

In 1848, the ABCFM approved a report titled, "The Control to Be Exercised over Missionaries and Mission Church." It affirmed that each mission and missionary should decide who was pious to God. The abolitionist leader, Charles Whipple, evaluated the report this way: "[T]he one great object of this document was [that slavery's]...continued allowance in the mission churches was both right and unavoidable...." In order to provide comfort to contributors and to lessen the criticism of the ABCFM, Harriet Beecher Stowe, whose brother and husband provided the theological rational for "organic sin," wrote *Uncle Tom's Cabin*. It was the story of the good slave owner compelled by the "shadow of the law," who sold men, women, and children "often without any fault of his own."[131]

In 1850, the Hawaii legislature sanctioned through law conduct that was "kindred" to slavery. "Any person who has attained the age of twenty years," the legislature decided, "may bind himself or herself by written contract to serve another....If any [such] person ... shall absent himself from such service without leave of his master," any judge, upon receiving a complaint, "may issue a warrant to order such offender to be restored to his master." Refusal to continue service, required the judge to "commit such person to prison to remain at hard labor until he will consent to serve according to law."

Contract workers were bought and sold privately. They were flogged and "chained together in the fields." They were allowed only minutes for meals and forced to live in horrendous conditions. Punishment included financial penalties: Ten minutes late in arriving to work meant the loss of more than a day's pay. "Insubordination" cost a dollar. At the outset, men laborers received four dollars a month (roughly $0.15 a day); women laborers three dollars a month. Twelve hour days. Through 1893, Asians workers were excluded from voting. Under the 1887 constitution, so were many native Hawaiians. They were politically powerless: "Control is made easier in Hawaii, as it was in the old South." [132]

The "illegality" of any of this conduct was irrelevant to what was tolerated, encouraged, and commonplace. "The law did not reflect reality; it did not actually protect workers on the plantations." Hawaii and plantation police enforced the planter's rules. In March 1869, the *New York Tribune* found that contract labor in Hawaii "has, for some time past, taken on a development which leaves little difference between it and the slave trade." Native Hawaiians at first embraced plantation work and then quickly sought work elsewhere. They petitioned the government to stop the practice and require the planters to pay reasonable wages. They were ignored. Blacks were encouraged to migrate to Hawaii in 1881. They would not go. Nonetheless, in a later study of contract labor in Hawaii, William O. Smith, Lorrin Thurston, and William D. Alexander, also the son of missionary parents, assured the study's author that contract labor was, actually, "an altogether praise-worthy undertaking."[133]

Caucasians dominated the Hawaii Supreme Court. "The [contract labor] statute was enacted," the supreme court wrote, "in reference to the business of the country." Private sugar ventures and contract labor were indecipherable from the nation's purpose. In a remarkable exercise of raw economic power, the court analogized a plantation laborer to a seaman who signed up for the merchant marine. "It is in degree," the court continued, "as essential to the sugar planters that his employees should remain with him to perform his service as agreed upon...as it is for the seaman to remain on the ship during the voyage." Moreover, the court concluded, the contract was not a "restraint on one's liberty [because, among other analogous reasons,] [e]very man in public office is under an obligation to attend to its duties...but no one thinks that it impairs his liberty." Because the Hawaiian legislature had outlawed slavery and involuntary servitude *after* it approved contract labor, the practices that imbued contract labor did not violate either prohibition.[134]

In 1853, a contract laborer was killed by sever whipping after he tried to escape. The owner's conduct was so offensive the state was obligated to bring him to trial. The owner's defense was that the laborer had escaped and was "voluntarily exposed for several nights, without food or raiment, to the rain, cold and hunger in the forest." Exposure, the defense asserted, was the cause of death. Caucasian Chief Justice William Lee, after instructing the jury about the law governing murder, added gratuitously "That he had known the accused for several years, and always esteemed him as a man not only of cultivation and refinement but of principle and heart." The jury, "after an absence of half an hour," returned a unanimous verdict of not guilty.[135]

Hawaii's judiciary, with the spiritual sanction of the ABCFM and the economic imperative of the sugar plantations, had exercised the power necessary to affirm the legitimacy of "a kindred wrong."

*

Hawaii remained facially neutral during the Civil War. In fact, however, its foreign minister Robert Wyllie believed the south would win. Hawaii's plantation owners were substantial beneficiaries. Louisiana had been the major supplier of sugar to the United States. That supply was now ended. Although Confederate gun boats caused "havoc against northern commercial shipping [in the Pacific,]" there was no indication the sugar trade from Hawaii to ports in the United States was disrupted. The Confederacy had no moral dispute with the practice of forced labor. There also was no practical constraint in the Union over the same conduct.[136]

It also appears that "several hundred [native] Hawaiians volunteered for service in the Union." Two sons of missionary parents, Samuel Armstrong and Nathaniel Emerson who were attending Williams College at the time, joined the Union forces. There seems to have been no organized effort among the mission, who were American citizens and from the north, to actually risk death or injury for moral or patriotic reasons. The call of the Sandwich Islands Anti-Slavery Society seemed, as a practical matter, to have fallen on deaf ears. According to one person who studied the life of Sanford Dole, "Many young men were eager to enlist under the Stars and Stripes and some Hawaiian citizens already in the United States did do so, but those in the Island had already been mustered under the Hawaiian flag." During this time Dole was described as riding "about on horseback" directing natives in drill for a purpose not described. Why mustering under "the

Hawaiian flag" was an alternative to "the Stars and Stripes" at the moment of Civil War was not explained. [137]

In 1861, Dole was almost eighteen years old. Many men who volunteered throughout the duration of the war were younger. New Englanders, like Dole's contemporary Oliver Wendell Holmes of Boston, volunteered almost immediately after war was declared. Holmes was twenty years old and not yet graduated from college. Within a year he was in the Peninsula Campaign proximate to the time James Blount of Georgia was there. Holmes was injured. The lesson in life that Holmes learned from his war experience was not about fairness or equality. He was no supporter of the weak, or southern blacks, or immigrants. The lesson was that "certitude leads to war." What tempered certitude from "overheating and leading to violence is democracy," and the exercise of elementary forms of civil liberty.[138]

In the living room of Washington Place, Mary Dominis received and shared letters from Boston relatives with her new daughter-in-law, Liliu, about the war's justification and its costs to those she loved. Her relatives wrote poignantly of the "great misery and suffering" they lived with and the "streets...full of wounded soldiers," returning from the battlefront.[139]

In 1863, when Dole was twenty years old, he suggested that "somehow [he] must soon get to the United States to volunteer with the North in the Civil War. On this point his father replied quietly that Hawaii would need him still more... and his mother voiced her feeling that while romance was calling him to the colors, he would find little romance in freezing to death. On the other hand, were he actually needed by the Union, neither father nor mother would say nay." Dole did get to Massachusetts right after the war ended. He stayed for a year at Williams College and then read the law with a relative of a former missionary in Boston. In terms of experiences in life that mattered, once Dole was outside the parochial confines of the missionary milieu and values and its declared view on slavery " and other kindred wrongs," he must have been a fish out of water. He returned to Hawaii.[140]

*

When James Blount and his wife Eugenia docked in the Honolulu harbor, they were greeted by Minister Stevens and the members of the Annexation Club. Blount declined their invitation of a house, servants, and a carriage. He also witnessed the presence of hundreds of native Hawaiians led by Joseph Nawahi. They were there to ensure he knew immediately of Hawaiian opposition to the provisional government.

To Blount, whose manner reflected a "sturdy integrity and a logical turn of mind," the central question that tempered his boarder view of the Civil War's meaning was how he thought about the "New South's" economic relationship with the north. His views on race were expressed with subtlety compared with his southern colleagues, although his opposition to civil rights legislation remained as consistent as theirs. He believed, however, that the "New South's... industrialism and nationalism would not follow the northeastern pattern of modernization, which usually included foreign expansion. His economically diversified South would follow what he considered the more traditional American approach to progress: change hinged on minimal connections with the world beyond." Blount opposed the Nicaragua Canal proposal advocated by Senator Morgan. "[T]he internal markets of the nation were more than ample for the envisioned productivity of the New South.... In short, he considered the new plans for greater American influence in the world, through both territorial growth and commercial aggressiveness, contrary to American tenets of self-determination and constitutionalism and also as unnecessary for the progress of his nation and his region."[141]

Blount also supported reform within the diplomatic service. He chastised American diplomats in South America for becoming entangled inappropriately in local affairs. "It is...the right and duty of the Government," he said in 1883, "to see to it that Government...shall do no act that shall affect the honor of the American name.... [T]he United States has a position to maintain among the nations of the earth; her dignity and her honor [are] to be upheld."[142]

The Blounts settled into the Hawaiian Hotel. He rented a cottage near the Hawaiian to conduct his work with some privacy. He heard testimony — transcribed and verified — and received the submission of comments, letters, and petitions. Blount restricted his social interaction to avoid the appearance of bias. His wife Eugenia, however, gathered both intelligence and perspective. She "was busy...meeting and talking with natives and members of the provisional government. Her informal and friendly contacts with these individuals and factions... assisted [her husband] in his investigation."[143]

Blount recognized early that a plebiscite would yield the continuation of the constitutional monarchy. No one, including the *coup* leaders and plantation owners he interviewed, disagreed. It was a factor to be explored further. He also saw the devotion of native Hawaiians to Liliuokalani. It gave him pause. He wrote to Gresham that " I had wondered whether or not this race of people... had fully caste off the old system and conceived the modern ideas in the United States of the control of the government by equal participation by every citizen in the selection of its rulers." This subject, too, warranted further inquiry. [144]

Blount also recognized that the native Hawaiian community was uneasy. In order to ensure the appearance of fairness, he had the American flag removed and ordered the Marines back to the USS *Boston*. The Marines remained a threat, however subtle. That threat — a "perverted influence," as Blount called it — made him believe, albeit tentatively, that "the existing Government owes its being and its maintenance" to the Marines. His suspicions were confirmed. In a series of visits with Dole in his government office and through sources he did not solicit, Blount learned the provisional government had proposed the Queen accept a monetary payment for her support. In a visit to Washington Place, Liliuokalani confirmed the solicitation had come through her counsel, Paul Neumann. She had declined its consideration. She said she awaited Blount's report. Blount remained neutral. In short order, however, he refused Stevens' and Dole's request to have the Marines return to protect against an imminent Japanese takeover. Blount later refused a frantic request by Attorney General Smith to have the Marines impede a rumored rebellion by Caucasians who supported the Queen. Both alleged threats were found wholly bogus. Blount suspected the Marines were sought only to coerce Liliuokalani to acquiesce in the payment offer, once again using the United States as a "perverted influence."[145]

Through April, May, and June Blount questioned supporters and opponents of annexation, including those people present at various locations and events when the *coup* occurred. He interviewed men who had been at Smith's and Thurston's office when the *coup* was discussed and unfolded. He examined the documentation, correspondence, and meeting notes between, among, and involving Minister Stevens, Dole, other *coup* leaders, navy officials, and the Queen and her representatives. He spoke regularly to Stevens. He interviewed planters and native Hawaiian leaders from other islands. In a meeting with Dole and his cabinet he requested their testimony. Smith, at first agreed. Instead, Blount received from Smith a transcribed colloquy among Smith and two other *coup* supporters that, through their own questions and answers, sought to describe various events. In the colloquy, Smith was asked: "You have no knowledge [of the Queen's intention to propose a new constitution] except from the general sources [of speeches and newspapers]?" "No," Smith replied. In fact, he did know through a spy in the Queen's confidence. The colloquy was not submitted under oath.[146]

Dole chose not to submit written comments. Blount's meetings with Dole were reported to Secretary Gresham. Liliuokalani submitted a statement on the sequence of events that preceded the *coup d'état* and what she believed the motivation of its leaders. Blount also received testimony and a thoughtfully crafted narrative and analysis from the Men's Patriotic League. The narrative affirmed the evolving growth, sagacity, and stability of native Hawaiian political involvement and the central importance of the right to vote. It was signed by, among other men, Joseph Nawahi. Implicit in the written narrative was the challenge that, in later testimony, Robert Wilcox echoed: Denial of the franchise was an element in native Hawaiian opposition to annexation and provisional government rule. When Blount received the petitions from the Men's League with seven thousand five hundred signatures, and from the Women's Patriotic League with eight thousand additional ones, he focused especially on the number of registered

voters. The submissions tempered Blount's view of the native Hawaiian commitment to democratic principles.

Blount also documented land and business ownership, demographics, voting
patterns, cultural characteristics, and citizenship records. In the compilation of
this information and through his questioning, Blount received exposure to the
dispute over the ownership and purpose of the Crown lands. He was told that
more than forty percent of the "government land" set aside in 1848 (approximately 1.4 million acres) had been sold to Caucasians in large tracts primarily
for sugar plantations, grazing, and recreation. A valuable resource was now gone.
The 915,000 acres of Crown lands had become more valuable and coveted. Significant portions of those lands already were under long term leases to sugar plantations that preceded Liliuokalani's reign. Blount also was told that sugar planters
had used the government land as a politically coercive weapon. In addition to
monetary bribes to sway votes, the sugar planters "held mortgages on the property of some legislators; some of them [also] were dependent on [the planters] for
pasturage [for cattle.]" The Crown lands could serve the same purpose.[147]

Attorney General William O. Smith authorized William D. Alexander, then
serving as the provisional government's surveyor-general, to submit to Blount a
statement on "the title of the Crown lands of this country," prepared previously
for Smith. Alexander, like Sanford Dole, had supported the sale of the Crown
lands for private use long before the *coup d'état*. Alexander's statement and Smith's
intention was to justify the unilateral incorporation of the lands into the provisional government's authority. They were making an argument.[148]

Alexander began with a conclusion: The original monarch, Kamehameha,
owned the land of Hawaii "in his corporate right," an Anglo-Saxon legal term
comfortable to Smith but not to the Hawaiian culture. Alexander supported
his conclusion by quoting from a portion of Hawaii's first constitution in 1840:
The "kingdom was not the private property of Kamehameha I. 'It belonged to the
chiefs and the people in common, of whom Kamehameha I was the head and had
the management of the landed property.'"

In fact, the constitution embodied a more complex proposition that Alexander excluded. The constitution actually provided that Kamehameha "was the
founder of the kingdom, and to him belonged all the land from one end of the
Islands to the other, though it was not his own private property...." The fact of
common ownership in the land was recognized in the constitution — which Alexander neither understood nor emphasized — and had been recognized earlier
in the Hawaii 1839 Declaration of Rights, which Alexander also did not mention.

Alexander referenced the fact that in 1848, when Hawaii's lands were divided,
the king retained control of a million acres as his own private domain (Crown
lands) to be brought, sold, and inherited, subject still to the rights possessed by
the common people. Alexander focused exclusively on the king's private inter-

est in the land and the proceeds from its use and argued Liliuokalani no longer possessed an interest in the land or the proceeds. In Alexander's argument the common people had no legal interest worthy of mention.[149]

The remainder of Alexander's statement flowed from his assumptions. Three events of consequence — an 1864 Hawaii Supreme Court decision, and the 1865 and 1882 Acts of the Hawaii legislature — were presented in a simplified manner intended to eliminate precisely the subtle political and legal ambivalence reflected in all three actions.

In the 1864 decision, *In the Matter of the Estate of His Majesty, Kamehameha IV, Late Deceased*, Queen Emma, the wife of the deceased king, claimed her inheritance to a part of the Crown lands. Her husband died without a will. Her claim was not related to her being a sovereign but that she had been married to the king. Her claim had legitimacy only if the Crown lands were private property even as that term is understood in Anglo-Saxon law. The Hawaii Supreme Court concluded that she was entitled to a portion of the Crown lands. The court also concluded — in a manner that would ensure continued uncertainty — that, henceforth, the Crown lands could be inherited only by the "successors to the throne" (not their spouse) but, nonetheless, still "be dispose[d]...according to the [king's] will and pleasure as private property."[150]

Shortly after the 1864 decision, the Hawaii legislature recognized Queen Emma's right to the land. In order to keep the Crown lands in tact but still implement the Supreme Court decision, the legislature gave Emma a yearly monetary grant for the remainder of her life to replace the land award she received from the Supreme Court. In 1865, the legislature also sought to clarify the uncertainty left by the 1864 Supreme Court decision. The legislature appeared to prohibit the further sale of Crown lands although still recognizing the king held those lands as private property. In 1882, however, the legislature again recognized and sanctioned the existence of a claim to the Crown lands by a supposed descendant of the Kamehameha line, Princess Ruth. Claus Spreckels — the California businessman with vast sugar and real estate holdings in Hawaii — bought from Princess Ruth her "right" to a small portion of the Crown lands only in Maui as if they were private property that she had or could inherit and sell. Spreckels' acquired legal opinions from former and future attorney generals and Hawaii Supreme Court justices to support the princess' claim to the land. The government agreed. The legislature granted a portion of the Crown lands to Spreckels in exchange for the "rights" he purchased from Princess Ruth. The attorney general then arranged a land swap with Spreckels, acceptable to the king, in order to keep the Crown lands intact. The government, too, recognized Spreckels private right to purchase and own such land as part of the transaction.[151]

The unsettled public and private legal nature of the Crown lands remained. For William Alexander, however, the conclusion from this history was plain. The

Crown lands "have remained, as was settled in 1865, national lands, to be administered for the benefit of the occupant of the throne, who is entitled to receive the revenues of said lands only by virtue of his or her *official* position as chief magistrate." Alexander concluded that, "In view of the above facts, it would seem that, upon the abolition of the office [of the monarch]... the [Crown] lands would [transfer] to the [Provisional] Government." Blount accepted Alexander's report without comment.[152]

The *coup* leaders also sought to game Blount on race. "Dole, Thurston, and the others... had spread the word among annexationalists that Blount's southernism would make him susceptible to racial reasons for annexation." They consulted with the Secretary of Interior, Michael Hoke Smith. Smith was from Georgia. He was a white supremacist who also owned the *Atlanta Journal*. "[T]he provisional government had decided that annexation might [be] advance[d] with the notion that incorporation would help the southerners 'get rid of a portion of the colored population.'" It was a disquieting but predictable strategy.[153]

Blount brought to the investigation, however, "his own deep concerns — indeed, his prejudice — about invasion, occupation, subjugation, and greed, things he felt he knew something about from his experiences as a southerner....." He also understood the correlation between race and economics. On this subject, Blount also knew how to invoke candor. He got it from the Reverend Sereno Bishop. Bishop's testimony reflected the Dole–Thurston strategy.[154]

Bishop was an advocate and early publicist for the annexation cause and the denigration of the Queen. He was the son of missionary parents. He continued to be paid by the ABCFM into the 1870s. It was Bishop's parents who believed that Dr. Thomas Lafon's concern about missionary's treating Hawaiians as servants without pay "to be unreasonable, as our servants were envied by all the common people for their advantages and coveted positions." Bishop approached Blount "as if he knew the special commissioner to be racially biased in favor of annexation."[155]

Blount began by asking whether the intent of diminishing the native vote in the 1887 constitution and allowing Caucasian men who were citizens of other countries to vote was "intended to strengthen the white vote?" "Yes," Bishop replied. What followed revealed both Bishop's prejudice and Blount's skill at encouraging the fullness of it to emerge. Blount: "This constitution was extorted from Kalakaua by a mass meeting?" "Yes," Bishop answered. "That demonstration ...of the white citizens so terrified him that he was ready to do what he was wanted to do." Blount moved cautiously through a few questions, and then asked, "Now, it is inferred from transactions like that [demonstration] that the intelligent people here are of the opinion that the native population as a mass are qualified for government?" Bishop: "I should say to the contrary." Blount: "What is your view about that? I do not know these people at all.... [C]ould you trust to universal suffrage?" "Without limitation we could not," Bishop concluded.

Blount then asked Bishop about Kalakaua's appointment of native Hawaiians to the cabinet. We "did not feel that the natives were fit for office. They were notoriously incompetent," Bishop answered. Blount pushed him. "How about the [supreme] court," he asked. Bishop: "It has always been customary to have three white judges." Blount queried further: "Because they were learned in the law?" Bishop: "Yes; the natives were incapable of being learned in the law." Blount explored some elementary history about Kalakaua and then asked, "How about foreign minister?" Bishop: "They were always white men."[156]

Other witnesses were more subtle. They also further demonstrated the principled difference between the democratic intentions of the native Hawaiians and the unalterable seventeenth-century mentality of the *coup* leaders. Hawaii Supreme Court Chief Justice Albert Judd told Blount that even if voting qualifications were "on the basis of reading and writing English," he "doubt[ed] very much" that a permanent form of government could be maintained. Judd: "[A] republic on our own would not be at all successful." Blount: "Why?" Judd: "Because our natives are so likely to be influenced by demagogues." According to another witness who was dismissed by Attorney General Smith because of his political views, when he asked Smith, "'Do you want a republic here?' He said: 'No....We want to be annexed.' I said: 'To give the natives' franchise?' He said: 'Oh no; we cannot do that.'"[157]

Blount's task was coming to a close. He and Eugenia Blount were ready to return to their family home in Georgia. He formulated his report to the president. He also told Secretary Gresham that Minister Stevens needed to be replaced. The provisional government-controlled newspaper advocated the arrest for treason of anyone who spoke against annexation and the arrest, trial, and deportation of the Queen. The goal was intimidation. Stevens would call on the navy to support it.

Blount completed his report on July 17. He forwarded it to Secretary Gresham. He knew there were expectations and unease on both sides of the dispute. In a quiet moment in the cottage where he had listened and questioned and studied intensely for more than three months, he wrote a letter to Gresham. He posed a question reflective of what he had witnessed and learned: "Can a Christian civilization doom such a people to annihilation by any policy of legislation?"[158]

CHAPTER 5. THE LONG ECHO OF THE CIVIL WAR: JOHN MORGAN

Grover Cleveland was in his second term. He won both times with a plurality vote. His victory in 1892 would not have happened had the southern states not been solidly for him. His cabinet included Secretary of Interior Hoke Smith of Georgia, Secretary of the Treasury John Carlisle of Kentucky, and Secretary of the Navy Hilary Herbert of Alabama. Cleveland approached race and southern proclivities with caution.

Cleveland had not committed publicly or, it appears, privately to the unconditional restoration of Liliuokalani. The imperative he felt to withdraw the proposed treaty was conditioned on continued recognition of the provisional government and uncertainty about the use of force to ensure the Queen's restoration. With James Blount's return the meaningful threat of force proximate to those who would feel it had passed. When Blount met with Secretary of State Gresham upon his return, he believed Gresham favored restoration. Blount had not expressed that opinion. As a former member of Congress, he understood the constitutional limits of the president's ability to effectively and notoriously conduct warfare. Blount was committed to his family and his private life in Georgia. He was not invited to visit Cleveland at the White House. Blount boarded the train south.

Although Cleveland was occupied with problematic national economic matters and the languid evenings of the nation's capital in August, he was informed of the content of Blount's report. He decided not to act. He left the matter to Gresham and the cabinet. Cleveland knew that for Liliuokalani and the provisional government the effect of delay was not the same.

Hawaii was in a form of ordered turmoil. The Queen traveled cautiously between her residences and to church on Sundays. She also retained a close relationship with her supporters. She had power that she shared with them but no authority or control of the means of governance, especially the formation of the police and an army. There also was a palpable cultural and political resistance to the provisional government; an apparatus that at the mid and lower levels was largely native Hawaiian. The new leadership was a disappointment. Engaged in a "feeble and vacillating course," one steadfast supporter characterized Dole's administration. Commerce and tax collection were plagued with uncertainty. Dole borrowed money. He enhanced the arms and skill of what was no longer a wholly vigilant army but one sanctioned with the imprimatur of government. He ordered a new insignia and uniforms and reinforced the palace grounds where executive government had relocated. His office was in the throne room.[159]

Gresham took two steps. The attorney general advised him that he could not use force to restore Liliuokalani without a declaration of war. The attorney general also encouraged use of the threat of force. He proposed that the next minister to Hawaii require the Queen to pardon the provisional government's leaders from any wrongdoing. The minister also could "hint at, or implicitly threaten, the use of force" that could be used "without the necessity for the intervention of Congress." [160]

It was a delicate task. Gresham sought to appoint General Edward S. Bragg as Stevens' replacement. Bragg was from Wisconsin. He was a lawyer. He entered the Union Army in 1861 and rose to the rank of Brigadier General. He was wounded at the battle of Chancellorsville, recovered and participated in General Grant's Wilderness campaign against General Robert E. Lee. Bragg was a Democrat. He had been a five term member of Congress and a supporter of Cleveland's first election. Cleveland had appointed him minister to Mexico. He had "the most fertile imagination," one commentator wrote. "[H]e can find or manufacture expedients to meet any emergency that an opponent can present." He also had "few equals in the power of acrimonious retort and invective." Gresham admired Bragg's "'decision of character.'" He could maneuver the navy, the provisional government, and the Queen to attain Gresham's goal. But Bragg had enemies in Wisconsin and on Senator Morgan's Foreign Relations Committee. Bragg's skill was legendary. Morgan would have known it. The appointment was blocked. The nomination's withdrawal, a sometimes quiet event in Washington, had consequence in Hawaii.[161]

The White House recommended the appointment of Albert Sydney Willis, a former five term congressman from Kentucky with no diplomatic experience. He had not participated in the Civil War. He had no distinguishing accomplishment and no personal relationship with Gresham. He was among the southern Democrats who ran for office before Reconstruction was negotiated away. Willis was fifty years old. He was acceptable to Morgan. Also appointed was Allis Mills as consul general. Mills had served as Blount's secretary in Hawaii. It is unclear he shared Blount's perspective of the *coup d'état*. When the appointments were an-nounced, Blount returned to Washington to meet with both men and Gresham. Blount announced after the meeting that "his official connection with the Gov-ernment had ceased. The Hawaiian matter was entirely out of his hands." Willis did not arrive in Hawaii until November 4. He was directed to act expeditiously. It had been almost four months since Blount had left. [162]

*

Gresham did what he could to keep Blount's report quiet until Cleveland was ready to act. Gresham knew, too, that in the nation's capital preserving secrecy is an improbable task in a controversy with global implications and intensely an-tagonistic interests. By mid-November excerpts and informed speculation about Blount's report seeped into Congress, the press, to the provisional government's minister, Lorrin Thurston, and back to Hawaii. In late November the report was released. Liliuokalani was heartened. Blount was attacked immediately.

The adversaries of constitutional monarchy were able to simplify the public debate in the United States: Monarchy and the presumptions of autocracy and ar-bitrariness that went with it versus Anglo-Saxon dominance and all the presump-tions concerning Christian virtue, intelligence, morality, capitalism, and cultural familiarity that went with it. The consequence was that even those newspapers, including in Blount's Georgia, that disapproved of annexation or America's con-duct were uneasy with the prospect of supporting a monarch. Some northern papers were direct: The monarchy represented "idolatry and depravity."[163]

Blount's report traced the manner in which previous constitutions had been promulgated in Hawaii. Blount concluded they were similar to the way Liliuoka-lani had proposed to do it. He also focused on how the free importation of sugar into the United States, beginning in 1876, had dramatically increased the demand and use of contract labor and the financial, racial, and cultural disparity between the Caucasian and native communities. He documented the effects: Government and Crown lands were brought or leased by Caucasians, the price of property in-creased, and "the price of labor was depressed by the enormous importation and the efficiency accruing from compulsory performance [of labor] by the Govern-ment." Furthermore, Blount wrote, "the distribution of lands under the influence of white residents between the Crown, the chiefs and the people," left the people "with an insignificant interest in the lands." Blount correctly spared no one for their motivation and the consequence: "[T]his division is discreditable to King, chiefs, and white residents." This was not the conclusion Smith and Alexander wanted.[164]

Blount discerned that although the missionary children "sought to succeed to the political control exercised by their fathers," they were thwarted when King Kalakaua appointed cabinet officials who were native Hawaiian or other men who were not disposed to preserve Caucasian wealth. Relying on the testimony of Chief Justice Judd, Blount identified Kalakaua's personal and political failings and the legislative actions relied upon to justify the imposed 1887 constitution. Blount stated, however, that "[n]one of the legislation complained of would have been considered a cause for revolution in any one of the United States... [and the] alleged corrupt action of the king could have been avoided by more careful legislation and would have been a complete remedy for the future."[165]

When Asians were excluded from voting under the 1887 constitution, Portuguese contract laborers were allowed to vote if they took an oath to support the 1887 constitution. "These ignorant laborers were taken... in large numbers by the overseer," Blount noted, "[and] then carried to the polls and voted according to the will of the plantation manager. Why was this done? In the language of Chief Justice Judd, 'to balance the native vote.'" American, German, English, and other foreigners who were not naturalized Hawaiian citizens also voted by taking the same oath.[166]

With respect to the dependence of the *coup d'état's* leaders' on the United States, Blount cited to the documents and testimony concerning Smith's and Thurston's meetings with Stevens. The request for Stevens' intervention was made not on behalf of "American citizens" but the "Committee of Safety," which included British and German nationals with a known purpose to support a *coup d'état*. With regard to the timing of recognition, Blount cited President Sanford Dole's letter to Stevens stating that he was in receipt of Stevens' "valued communication of this day" recognizing the provisional government before the police barracks and military apparatus had been taken. Blount also sighted to the *USS Boston's* Admiral J.S. Skerret's testimony that "the American troops were well located if designed to promote the movement for the Provisional Government and very improperly located if only to protect American citizens in person and property." The Queen, Blount concluded, succumbed to the forces of the United States.[167]

The full report, including the related transcripts and documents, was not yet officially made public. Enough of its content, however, was known to Senator Morgan.

*

John Tyler Morgan was born in Athens, Tennessee, in June 1824. His parents moved to Alabama when Morgan was nine and established squatter's rights on land once occupied by Creek Indians. He was educated by his mother and the Alabama public schools. He did not attend college. He read the law and was admitted to the Alabama bar in 1845. He married Cornelia Willis, who was from a prominent local family.

In 1855, Morgan moved to Cahaba. He joined a small but highly regarded law firm. Morgan was a Democrat from the outset. In 1860, when the Democratic Party split along sectional lines, Morgan was an elector to the convention that supported John C. Breckinridge. The northern wing selected Stephen Douglas. Abraham Lincoln easily won the presidency. Southern succession began almost immediately. Morgan volunteered to comb the state in urging succession and the preparation for war. His support foreshadowed his views not only about race but about the popular vote. He opposed successfully subjecting the decision of succession to a state-wide referendum. He was denounced as acting "derogatory to the rights of a free people." Central to his conduct was certainty about "black inferiority and the need to safeguard southern honor and autonomy." Like many Southerners, including James Blount of Georgia, Morgan believed "'we shall never be conquered."[168]

Morgan volunteered within a month of succession. He was thirty-seven years old. One former colleague described this experience as the first of four epochs in Morgan's life "in which his patriotism, developed by the winds of oppression, sprang into heroic action."[169]

His "heroic action" was direct, ugly, and penetrated deeply into his character. His first combat against Union soldiers was in the early winter of 1862 near La Vergne, southeast of Nashville, Tennessee; shortly after that in the vicinity of Murfreesboro attacking Union supply lines, and then again at Stones River. General Lee promoted him to Brigadier General and wanted him in Virginia. Morgan declined the promotion in order to lead the Alabama regiment with whom he first volunteered. He led them in the "savage battle at Chickamauga Creek...in heavy woods and dense undergrowth." When it ended, "Morgan surveyed the aftermath of one of North America's most brutal struggles. More than sixteen thousand Yankees had been wounded or killed....For this triumph the South paid dearly; in excess of eighteen thousand or nearly 30 percent of the Confederates engaged had fallen. The horror of the mangled bodies and the screams of the wounded, many of whom were being burned to death by battlefield fires, were frightening. The scene at the main Federal field hospital was equally horrifying. Confederate cavalrymen found numerous badly injured adversaries enclosed in wire pens to protect them from animals; they also found large piles of amputated arms and legs, some of which were already being dragged away by wild hogs. Neither Morgan nor any of the other participants in this savage battle would ever be quite the same again."[170]

The war moved deeper into the south. Morgan joined with the main body of the Army of the Tennessee in north Georgia to follow the destruction being laid by General George Tecumseh Sherman. Morgan's troops were engaged and defeated by Union forces south of Atlanta. Morgan was, ironically, designated to recruit black troops in Alabama and Mississippi. He was in Meridian, Mississippi when Lee surrendered at Appomattox.[171]

John Morgan resented and opposed Reconstruction. Only Union soldiers were being honored with burial by the government in Washington. The recovery and burial of the young men he had served with was left largely to local, private efforts led by wives and mothers, including Morgan's wife, Cornelia. He was able to reestablish a law practice. He had neither land nor money.[172]

Morgan's reputation as an orator and advocate for the south's Caucasian identity was recognized by the state's political leaders. "Under this [Reconstruction] regime," Morgan's eulogist described some years later, "[a] debt of millions of dollars had been created ... by means of the newly enfranchised and ignorant blacks.... [T]his flock of harpies had to be swept off the face of the earth.... This was the second trial and triumph of [John T. Morgan's] patriotism." In 1876, the Alabama legislature elected Morgan to the United States Senate. Unlike Blount, Morgan was never subjected to the vote of the people. He considered himself an "ambassador" to Washington, DC. He joined the Senate Foreign Relations Committee and rose to become its chairman. He and James Blount had differed on critical matters. Morgan would have reviewed Blount's report with special care.[173]

*

Minister Albert Willis' arrival in Honolulu was noted with apprehension. None of the fanfare that had accompanied Blount's arrival was evident. Willis moved into the United States legation's residence. He was distant from the Iolani Palace — now the government building — and from the Queen's residence at Washington Place. He did not have Blount's detached purpose, worldliness or learned disciple in dealing with Hawaii's politics. He had met supporters of the provisional government on the steamer from San Francisco. He moved ceremoniously among an established social order that was Caucasian.

Lorrin Thurston, knowing about Blount's report and Willis' purpose, confronted Secretary Gresham in the executive office building. The two men disliked each other. Gresham, despite his determination to deceive, was unable to convince Thurston the United States was prepared to use force to effectuate restoration of the constitutional monarchy. The efficacy of the threat imagined by the attorney general did not work. Cleveland's delay in acting on Blount's report undermined Willis' prospect for accomplishing his assignment in Hawaii before he arrived. Willis' lack of experience would ensure it.

Willis waited until November 13 to request the Queen to visit him at his office. She came alone. It is likely her travel was monitored. Willis said the discussion was informal. Willis claimed to be alone. She recorded in her diary that someone else was behind a Japanese screen. Willis informed the Queen of the president's regret at what had occurred and his intention to correct it. She nodded politely. She had discerned Cleveland's temperament correctly enough to get to this juncture. Implicit in the president's expressed intention was a form of recognition that the constitutional monarchy she headed was the legitimate government of Hawaii.[174]

Willis had only one critical question: Would she agree to pardon those who led the provisional government? She answered that she was bound by the 1887 constitution that Willis and the president insisted must be upheld. It required that treason be dealt with by death or banishment. Her view of the death penalty had not changed since she was confronted with it while serving as a regent during her brother's first trip as king. She abhorred it. Morally and practically neither she nor anyone else desirous of the continuity of government would want Thurston, Dole or Smith to remain in the country. Willis sought the requisite clarity. She wanted to consult with her advisors. He insisted on an answer. She may or may not have said they should be "beheaded." At the time, hanging was the penalty for a capital offense. Willis wrote that she did say it. In her diary entry of the same day she described verbatim a response that did not include that reference. It made no difference. Within days, her intention to behead virtually every Caucasian in Hawaii was in the government-influenced press and then the press in the United States. The "leak" to someone in the government came from Willis, his consul general Allis Mills, whoever was behind the screen or whomever Willis had entrusted to code messages for Secretary Gresham. "That night was one of terror for Liliuokalani." She feared for her life. J.O. Carter came to Washington Place. He reported there were skilled sharpshooters in position atop the Kawaiahao Church. They were within range of her home. Aided by Carter, Edward Macfarlane, and the bishop of the Episcopal Church nearby, Liliuokalani sought refuge. She dressed in the habit of a nun. Accompanied by two nuns, they walked to the church. The black-clad queen entered a carriage occupied by Macfarlane. She "was taken in the dark of night to a downtown hotel" where she was guarded carefully. The provisional government did what was necessary to discredit the Queen and pervert Gresham's effort.[175]

The diplomacy that emerged after this episode was farcical. Willis telegrammed a cryptically-crafted message to Gresham about the meeting. Gresham was appalled that Willis could not explain himself. On November 26 and December 4, Gresham sent Willis instructions. Willis did not receive them until December 14. He had a second meeting with the Queen on December 16. In the interim, she called J.O. Carter and Edward Macfarlane to Washington Place for counsel. She brought Carter with her to the meeting to ensure authenticity in the reporting. She gave Willis a letter two days after their meeting that did precisely what the president requested. It was a futile exercise. Unbeknownst to Willis and the Queen, long before that day the president's staff — probably in consultation with other Democrats in Congress and in the various departments — was drafting his message to Congress declaring failure in his Hawaii policy. It is highly likely the proposed content of the president's message was known in informed quarters throughout the city. The message was submitted to Congress on December 18.[176]

Armed with the Queen's agreement, Willis' boarded a carriage to Iolani Palace. He met with Dole on December 19 on the second floor of the palace in the office of the foreign minister. Members of Dole's cabinet were present, including Attorney General Smith. After listening to an ultimatum from the president to return the government to the Queen, Dole said he would reply after he and his cabinet gave the matter proper consideration. It was a brief meeting. In all likelihood, Dole was informed fully of Cleveland's intention if not the proposed content of his message to Congress. Willis' ultimatum was comparable to a dead letter. [177]

*

On December 18, President Cleveland had submitted to Congress his message on Hawaii. He acknowledged his failure immediately: "I am convinced that the difficulties lately created both here and in Hawaii and now standing in the way of a solution through Executive action of the problem presented, render it proper, and expedient, that the matter should be referred to the broader authority and discretion of Congress." He referenced and then demeaned the reportage about the Queen's intention to behead the Caucasians of Hawaii. The reference showed only that his commitment to the constitutional monarchy had been fragile or that, in the moment, less important than other matters that needed his attention and sway. [178]

The Senate, he wrote, had been "misled" as to the facts. He reiterated the evidence and findings in Blount's report, which he attached along with the entirety of Blount's correspondence, his interviews, and the comments and documentary evidence he received. There also was an uneasy passion in Cleveland's message: "This military demonstration upon the soil of Honolulu was of itself an act of war," against Hawaii's established government and in a city that "was in its customary orderly and peaceful condition." Where it not for the intervention by the navy at the insistence of Minister Stevens, "the Committee of Safety ... would never have exposed themselves to the plans and penalties of treason by undertaking the subversion of the Queen's government," which otherwise "would never have yielded." Cleveland contrasted this conduct in Hawaii with the actions of President Andrew Jackson who declined to support statehood for Texas until it was prudent and becoming to do so. He cited to other precedents in foreign lands where claims of a revolution were met with skepticism until the State Department determined the revolution reflected the popular will. In contrast, the provisional government "has given no evidence of an intention to" secure popular support. "Indeed, the representatives of that government assert that the people of Hawaii are unfit for popular government and frankly avow that they can best be ruled by ...despotic power." [179]

Cleveland laid out the conditions for a solution. He shifted the fullness of the responsibility for failure to the Queen. "In short, they require that the past should be buried, and that the restored Government should reassume its authority as if its continuity had not been interrupted. These conditions have not proved acceptable to the Queen...." [180]

Cleveland had accomplished one goal: He denied annexation to the provisional government. The prospect that annexation would reemerge during his tenure in office — through March of 1897 — was remote. The fight for Hawaii's identity and culture shifted, for now, back to Hawaii and to Congress. Cleveland's message to Congress also was a reflection of weakness. Morgan understood that immediately. So did Lorrin Thurston. They now had a forum previously unavailable in its fullness: The Senate Foreign Relations Committee.

*

December 20, two days after Cleveland's message, the Senate enacted a resolution directing that " the Committee on Foreign Relations shall inquire and report whether any, and, if so, what irregularities have occurred in the diplomatic or other intercourse between the United States and Hawaii in relation to the recent political revolution in Hawaii." [181] Senator Morgan had moved to the center of Hawaii's fate.

John Morgan's view of the south was different than Blount's. He wanted independence from the north's financial and industrial strength and the political power that followed. The south's economic stability would be attained by looking outward for trade. He supported the canal through Nicaragua because it would allow direct southern access to the Far East without having to go through northern manufacturers and shipping interests. "The canal provided 'the best, if not the only hope' of lifting the South from the ashes of the great civil war...." To Morgan, the fate of the canal was "'an Alabama question,' which would greatly increase sea traffic through the Gulf of Mexico, thereby creating a 'great southern Mediterranean,' stimulating the sale of Alabama coal and iron to construct and power new steam-driven ships, and transforming Mobile into a flourishing port." To Morgan, annexation of Hawaii would ensure the canal's construction and the south's redemption. [182]

Morgan recognized that the new fifteenth amendment to the constitution giving black citizens the right to vote had increased the number of representatives to Congress awarded the south. When, in 1890, northern Republicans, including Henry Cabot Lodge, sought to have federal troops enforce the right of blacks to vote in federal elections, Morgan endorsed a bill to require a literacy test for all voters. Literacy tests existed in northern states, including Massachusetts — also at Lodge's insistence — to exclude newly arrived immigrants from voting. The Republican motivation, Morgan contended, was to increase their party's vote in the south. He vowed to defeat the enforcement bill. He succeeded. In southern states, however, the literacy test became law. In Mississippi, the test's immediate effect was to eliminate almost ninety percent of the black voters. Mississippi's skill at manipulating the test ensured the superiority Morgan wanted. Representatives to Congress would be only Caucasians.[183]

For Morgan, the better solution was to deport blacks. He supported bills that would finance their relocation to the Congo and new American territories. During the war in the Philippines in 1898, Morgan encouraged the American military to include an all black company of soldiers in the fighting and encourage them to remain and settle when the fighting ended. His view on race melded with his view of the south's need for territorial expansion abroad. Morgan, unlike his southern colleagues, supported adding states of colored racial majorities to the nation, including Cuba, the Philippines and Nicaragua. Restricting the right to vote in those new nations or potential states would ensure an Anglo-Saxon control that might be sympathetic to the south.

When Lorrin Thurston met John Morgan their purposes could not have been more sympathetic to each other. Morgan was available to Thurston, "All times of the day or night...either at his senatorial office or at his residence." Thurston had returned from Honolulu in order to ensure Morgan knew about Dole's response to Willis. Unlike Dole's and Thurston's effort to game Blount on race during the investigation in Hawaii, Morgan welcomed and defined precisely how to game his investigation into the *coup d'état*. His goal was to have Hawaii not only as a state but to ensure it had a restrictive form of suffrage and its leaders sympathetic to the south. Hawaii had moved into the vortex of the failure of Reconstruction.[184]

*

Dole responded to Minister Willis on December 23. The response was meant for native Hawaiians, posterity, and Senator Morgan. In a thoughtfully-crafted, lengthy letter Dole sought to discredit the Blount report. Blount, Dole contended, had not allowed leaders of the *coup d'état* or the provisional government to testify. He described the report as "undocumented, one-sided." Blount, in fact, had invited Dole and each member of his cabinet personally to testify. Other men who supported the provisional government and annexation had spoken to Blount or submitted comments. Every document in Stevens' files and those that Dole would relinquish were included. Dole knew it.[185]

More revealing, however, was that Dole and his colleagues remained discomforted by one irrefutable fact: They had no popular mandate and would lose badly if the fate of the provisional government or annexation was put to a broadly enfranchised electorate. The notion of subjecting their effort to such a test was antithetical to what they believed. Dole certainly knew he could not be elected president of Hawaii; it was a prospect he avoided for the remainder of his public life. At the conclusion of his letter to Willis, Dole responded to this discomfort with a predictable clarity. "I am instructed to inform you, Mr. Minister, that the provisional Government...respectfully and unhesitatingly declines to entertain the proposition of the President of the United States that it should surrender its authority to the ex-Queen." The "will" of "the brave men...who have faithfully stood by us in the hour of trial is the only earthly authority we recognize. We cannot betray the sacred trust they have placed in our hands which represents the cause of Christian civilization in the interests of the whole people of these islands."[186]

Liliuokalani was saddened by Dole's letter. Her primary task, however, was to regain the nation. She and others who shared her view had acquired, they believed, a vindication of principle. However clumsy the president's conduct he agreed with the facts set out in Blount's report and recognized the injustice the United States had sanctioned in Hawaii. Holding tight to that form of vindication would require her, once again, to take the long view. She wrote in her diary that "1893 over-look to 1894. Thankful to Creator and pray that land might be restored to people and our just rights — my prayer." In the Cleveland-Willis' debacle and in the closing comments of Dole's letter, however, Senator Morgan could not have expected an introduction to his hearings more properly aligned with his intention. [187]

*

Morgan chaired the hearing. The subcommittee also had four members of each party. The hearings occurred between December 27 and February 7, 1894. Overcoats and boots would have been the outer dress of the day. Although sixty-five degrees was recorded on Christmas afternoon, the caustic chill of the earlier part of the month had returned. February was expected to be harsher. The members took their chairs. The furnaces in the Senate's basement dutifully roiled with heat. Whatever modest civility existed dissipated when the gavel struck and Senator Morgan announced the first witness, the Reverend Oliver P. Emerson. Electricity ensured the hearing could be conducted with ease into the evenings. In all likelihood, Lorrin Thurston sat attentively in the audience, close enough to orchestrate his part of the arrangement. [188]

In the parlance of Washington, DC, the hearing had no "stars." No one from the Cleveland administration; no high ranking member of the provisional government; no one who supported the constitutional monarchy or opposed annexation was scheduled to testify. The hearing was not exclusively Morgan's show. None of the Democrats wanted annexation under the circumstances that existed in Hawaii. They were prepared for the inquiry.

The Reverend Oliver P. Emerson was the son of missionary parents. The Queen, he said, was "not an avowed Christian" and the native classes have "some pretty bad characters among them [and] stand a good deal on par with the negro." The disreputable character of the Queen and those native Hawaiians who wanted to vote had been vouchsafed by a minister of God. [189]

Four witnesses were American tourists who happened to be in the vicinity of the palace on the day of the *coup d'état*. They all agreed there was no evidence of violence or any disturbance by native Hawaiians. One of the tourists, Mr. M. Stalker of Ames, Iowa, stunned Morgan. Stalker had expressed the opinion that promulgating a new constitution without compliance with the proper procedure would be a "revolutionary act." Morgan was prepared to rest his case. Senator George Gray of Delaware, a Democrat, interceded. He asked Stalker a more ac-curate question: Did it make a difference that the Queen had withdrawn her pro-posal and would abide by the 1887 constitution. That, Stalker replied, "Would not be revolutionary" or warrant a *coup d'état*. Morgan interceded and tried to break down Gray's question or rephrase it. It made no difference. Stalker stood firm. Gray also solicited that Stalker was a Republican. They remained silent.[190]

The Navy officers were present in their dress blues; some of them tinged prop-erly with gold braid and the insignia of rank and accomplishment. They were likely accompanied by others of lesser rank. The Senate Foreign Relations Com-mittee was central to their institutional well-being. Theatrical performance is a sign of respectful solicitation. Lieutenant Dewitt Coffman, a commander of the Marines that landed in Honolulu, was questioned cautiously by Morgan. Sena-tor Gray examined Coffman with more exactitude about the choice of locations for the troops. Coffman testified that a far more preferable location existed -no-where near the palace grounds — that was known to the Navy. The space was available but not chosen. "Was it nearer to what you considered the property of American citizens?" Gray asked. "Yes," Coffman replied. The palace location was chosen so that troops could protect the provisional government. [191]

Republican Senator William Frye of Maine asked Lieutenant Commander W.T. Swinburne, who also was there, whether the Queen's military could dis-lodge the vigilante forces of the provisional government without also attacking the United States. Swinburne answered: "I thought I would be between the two fires, at least I was not in a good position in the event of an outbreak." It was not the answer Frye wanted. Stevens' recognition of the provisional govern-ment, Swinburne also confirmed, occurred before the provisional government was physically in control of the Queen's military and police forces. Both naval officers also testified that calm prevailed and there was no evidence of any resis-tance or violence. Their conclusions supported Blount's report and Cleveland's message.[192]

On January 8, 1894, while the Morgan hearings were in progress, Senator David Turpie, Democrat of Indiana and a member of the subcommittee, submit-ted a resolution on Hawaii. Turpie was a political giant killer. He defeated Ben-jamin Harrison for the seat. He supported the platform of the Knights of Labor, which included opposition to contract labor. The Turpie resolution provided that the United States would not "consider further at this time either the treaty or project of annexation of the Hawaiian Territory to this country" and that the provisional government "having been duly recognized...shall pursue its own line of polity." The Democratic Party would not leave the field to Morgan. Republicans opposed the resolution immediately. They wanted annexation. The tension in the hearing room must have been palpable.[193]

Blount testified. Beyond questions about the process he used and the limits of his resources and purpose, no member of the committee asked him a question about the substantive content of his conclusions. No new documents were produced which contradicted those documents included in Blount's report.

William D. Alexander testified. Unlike in his submission to Blount, he made no reference to the Crown lands. His purpose was to discredit Blount's report. He laid out peripheral criticism then later withdrew or modified it. He also was the provisional government's conduit for precisely the sensationalism Morgan needed. Alexander stated that Liliuokalani's continuation in office would have reflected "a barbaric despotism," and that Honolulu was "paralyzed" and "mobs in favor of the Crown might arise." His support for the latter assertion was that "a white lady has told me that a half-white lady came to her and told her that natives were putting kerosene in bottles." Senator Gray examined him. Gray asked whether the "apprehension of danger" in Honolulu came from Dole and Thurston and the vigilante army. Morgan interceded. The real problem, Morgan declared without the pretense of a question, was that the Queen's government had a "paralysis of authority...which encouraged the licentious classes, the criminal classes," and justified Stevens' intervention. Alexander agreed.[194]

Stevens testified. He was in his late 70s and now retired. He could not reconcile the timing of his recognition of the provisional government with the reality of the documents in Blount's report. Stevens denied meeting with *coup* leaders even though they acknowledged in the same hearing that he had met with them. Stevens also was asked whether Liliuokalani spoke English. He acknowledged her fluency in two languages. Others witnesses testified, under questioning, that the Queen also was accepted for her fine moral character by the Caucasian ladies of Honolulu.[195]

Testimony also was presented by two reporters, including Charles Macarthur, the editor of the Troy, New York *Northern Budget*. He described his effort to create a story by encouraging the Queen's Counsel, Paul Neumann, and Sanford Dole to settle their differences. Dole was to offer the Queen a yearly annuity of twenty or twenty-five thousand dollars in return for her abdication. When word of Neumann's discussion of this proposition was conveyed to the Queen, she revoked Neumann's power of attorney. Two critical facts did emerge. The reporter assured Dole that the Queen had a serious heart defect and would live only a few years. The cost to the government would be minimal. The reason for the payment — which Dole apparently acquiesced in — was the loss of the Queen's "personal interest" in the Crown lands. "Her rights had been shattered," Macarthur told Dole, "but I thought they ought to pay for them.... [H]e said he would be happy to meet Mr. Neumann and see what they wanted — see if they could come to any terms about this thing by which the Queen would abdicate and surrender her rights."[196]

Although not formally part of his mandate, Morgan also solicited considerable testimony about the strategic value of Hawaii. A Navy Commodore testified. Hawaii was strategically located and Pearl Harbor was unmatched as a location for navy vessels, he said. The need for fleet concentration in the Pacific and the critical need for a canal through Panama or Nicaragua also were essential. Morgan submitted a recent article written by Captain Alfred Thayer Mahan titled, "Hawaii and Our Future Sea Power."[197]

Morgan's report was completed and submitted to the Senate on February 26, less than three weeks after the hearings ended. The report began with a startling if not discourteous assertion about the relations between nations. "Hawaii," Morgan stated, "is an American state." Her leaders were "endeavoring to accomplish what every other American state has achieved — the release of her people from the odious antirepublican regime which denies to the people the right to govern themselves, and subordinates them to the supposed divine right of a monarch, whose title to such divinity originated in the most slavish conditions of pagan barbarity." The fundamental premise of the report was set. The sons' of missionaries — Emerson and Alexander — had created the images and tone. It was the rhetoric of Cotton Mather. Morgan had embraced seventeenth-century New England Calvinism. The temporal power of the United States in the manner he could exercise it and the divine will of God's elect had meshed.[198]

The report made few references to the narrow range of testimony Morgan had allowed. In fact, the report's assertions of fact were detached largely from the factual testimony presented. Morgan justified the *coup d'état* and Stevens' actions by claiming that the January 14, 1893, disagreement between the Queen and her cabinet over the promulgation of the new constitution — which lasted a few hours and was formally resolved with her withdrawal of the constitution within another day — meant that an "interregnum" of lawlessness and the inability to deter criminal behavior, widespread burning and looting of property, and the killing and exile from the nation of Caucasian citizens was plainly evident. "[T]he authority of the Queen," Morgan asserted, "was not respected by the people." His hard evidence was that she had allowed the *coup* leaders to meet and hold a rally without arresting them. Morgan concluded that Stevens' actions were "lawful and authoritative."[199]

The report contained no recommendations for action. The four Democrats dissented. They believed Stevens' actions were "officious and unbecoming participation" that should be censured. There "were no valid reasons...which justify interference by the United States." Although the dissenters were "not inclined to censure Capt. Wiltse," they implicated the Navy and Marines in the wrongdoing. "The force of the United States marines...with their arms stationed at the American legation, and at the consulate...would have effectively represented the authority and power of the United States Government...; and at the same time would have avoided the appearance of coercion or duress either upon the people of Honolulu or the Queen.... [A] less formidable array ... afforded all necessary protection to the lives and property of our citizens..., if they were in jeopardy." The conduct of the United States, the four dissenters concluded, brought "about the conditions of affairs which resulted in the overthrow of the Queen."[200]

The four Republicans endorsed the "essential" conclusions of the report but did not specify which ones. One conclusion Morgan reached was, however, irrefutable. The provisional government had been recognized by two successive presidents. Additionally, two of the four Democrats expressed support for annexation if the domestic conditions in Hawaii were stable, supported by the Hawaiian people, and, by implication, morally acceptable to the people of the United States.

The report was not adopted by the Senate.

*

In the public discourse that followed the Morgan led hearings and report, the fate of Hawaii had taken on a disquieting, insidious tone. Liliuokalani's character and race were declared a personal stigmata, a seventeenth-century puritanical sign of immorality that the Reverend Sereno Bishop in testimony before Blount and William Alexander and the Reverend Oliver P. Emerson in testimony before Morgan bestowed on her and native Hawaiians. It was Bishop, however, who took on the task of imbedding the message into Washington, DC. He became a correspondent of the *Washington Evening Star*. He did not do it under his own name. He used the deceptive *nom de plume* "Kamehameha." He wrote for the *Star* the next five years. He also wrote for other newspapers and magazines.[201]

Liliuokalani, Bishop wrote, was a "debauched Queen of a heathenish monarchy where ... all the white corruptionists, and those who wish to make Honolulu a center for the manufacture and distribution of opium lie together with the lewd and drunken majority of the native race." He also wrote that both she and her brother "had no 'real hereditary royalty but were instead the illegitimate children of a mulatto shoemaker.'" He called her a prostitute. Her hair, he said, had the texture of a black person's. The cartoonists adapted the Queen to the black stereotype: the "picaninny," the frizzy hair, with untamed sexual proclivity, and the facial expression of stupidity or deceptive cunning or savagery. *Judge* magazine combined them all, depicting Liliuokalani with high heels and a short feathered skirt on the front cover of its magazine in February. Bishop later wrote she had engaged in the "lascivious hula" and was a "sorceress."[202]

Minister John Stevens had done the same during his tenure. He circulated a story in government circles in Washington that Liliuokalani had an ongoing affair with the head of Hawaii's security forces. Charles Wilson. Blount, to his consternation, was forced to explore this rumor during his own investigation, only to discover not a single fact that would affirm it, including from Chief Justice Judd. What did emerge was that Wilson had exercised his authority in a way that Judd and his colleagues did not like.[203]

Lorrin Thurston praised Sereno Bishop's writing. "The high standing of the *Star*," Thurston wrote, Bishop's "clear and fearless statements of fact and sledge-hammer logic of the conclusions reached, were invaluable as an educative influence on the American public ....and were a powerful factor in the achievement of the result." An awkwardly parsed and often indecipherable sentence structure in Bishop's memoir, *Reminisces of Old Hawaii*, suggested, however, that Thurston may have been "Kamehameha." [204]

The echo of the missionary voice was not unchallenged. William Saunders Scarborough, the son of freed black slaves from Georgia and professor of Greek and Latin at Wilberforce University in Ohio, announced his opposition to annexation. In the "Ethics of the Hawaiian Question," Scarborough wrote that "the annexation movement was the consummation of one of the most gigantic schemes to steal from a poor helpless people....It is a question of ethics [and] of color and nationality." He pointed to the "caricatures of the deposed ruler" and the "especial pains" by journalists "to enlarge the racial phases of the question." To Scarborough, "If the United States fails to right the wrong it committed by its agents, it will deserve the condemnation of all Christendom."[205]

William M. Springer, a former congressman from Illinois and a sitting federal judge, wrote in the *North American Review*, that "[T]o send our naval forces to the ports of other governments, to land them upon their soil, and allow them to be used for the purpose of overthrowing, in connection with foreign-born subjects or aliens, the established government, would make our Christianity a fraud and our boasted republicanism a mockery." In the same *Review*, however, Minister John Stevens affirmed with certainty the view that Thurston, Dole, Smith, and Morgan shared. Hawaii, he wrote, "must be controlled by other than the native race." Annexation was essential. There were two reasons. Both went to the heart of the deep impulse that moved the leaders of the *coup d'état* from the outset. First, in her proposed constitution Liliuokalani sought the authority to appoint judges to the Hawaii Supreme Court and limit their tenure. Stevens' found this proposal anathema to sound government. It was the court that ensured continuity with missionary values and the preservation of property rights, including in the human chattel of contract labor. But the "paramount reason why annexation should not be long postponed," Stevens' posited, was "that, if it soon takes place, the crown lands and the Government lands will be cut up and sold to Americans and Christian people, thus preventing the islands from being submerged and overrun by Asiatics."[206]

Liliuokalani's claim that the Crown lands were not the property of the provisional government and the persistence of the values reflected in her actions rankled deeply and caused discomfort. What remained unsettled was the fate of Hawaii. President Cleveland's failure of resolve and imagination had left a politically volatile vacuum.

CHAPTER 6. THE LONG ECHO OF SEVENTEENTH-CENTURY MASSACHUSETTS: THE TRIAL OF LILIUOKALANI

By 1894, Honolulu had become a cosmopolitan city. Privately-generated electricity illuminated houses and business establishments in the urban core. Telephones were in usage. Both were introduced by King Kalakaua after he met with Thomas Edison at Menlo Park, New Jersey. Streets were designed wide enough to allow for the anticipated and safe operation of trams. A train moved between the city and the countryside. Structures that housed law offices and commercial interests increased in height and took on the ornate art nouveau style melded with the vernacular of Hawaii's colors and symbols of the land. Throughout the city were Asian, Hawaiian, Portuguese, and some European-owned retail outlets, fish markets, fruit stands, indigenous medical providers, and laundry stores with living space above or behind for family and boarders. The streets were marked with sailors and itinerant vendors and tourists walking, shopping, recovering from rough nights or long sea duty or thinking about staying permanently.[207]

Waikiki was touched carefully with bath houses, most with grand porches — lanais — and a few with guest quarters. They served visitors from downtown hotels. Dances were held on Saturday night. The San Souci hotel, "truly bohemian, with no pretense at modern luxury," was farther down the beach. Robert Louis Stevenson had stayed there only the year before. Men walked along the Pacific's shores in suits and straw hats. Women strolled in white cotton dresses, some with full brimmed hats and parasols. Privately owned cottages, still sparse in number but elegantly crafted, were in between. Within a few years their residents owned homes that were the most "grandiose...stunning" homes in Hawaii. They were designed by renowned architects in the colonial style with expansive lanais, Ionic columns, multiple stories, and finely etched lawns and gardens. They stood not merely with distinction but with a disquieting dominance and stark contrast that comes with the unfettered wealth that, for decades, sugar had provided to its Caucasian owners and lawyers and financiers. The houses could have been in Queen Victoria's India or on a hilltop in colonial Hong Kong.[208]

Iolani Palace was guarded heavily. Gatlin guns were poised on its veranda. Uniformed troops were stationed on its grounds, rifles in tow or stacked for ready access. The vigilante army — now designated the citizens' guard — stood ready for action. Intelligence agents combed the city's bars, restaurants, and fish stands, listening and reporting. Quiet discussion, random at first, became more methodical over time. Restoration of the constitutional monarchy could only occur by those who believed in it. The subtle nuances or even the bold messages from the president and Congress five thousand miles away could not control their nation's fate. The participants included Caucasians; the children of missionaries who had spoken against contract labor and part-Hawaiian men or those men married to native women. Discussions also occurred on the grounds of Washington Place, where Captain Sam Nowlein controlled the guards that protected the Queen. In the early months of 1894, the disappointment of Cleveland's failure seeped deeply into the supporters of the constitution's restoration. At no time did Cleveland or Congress consider their actions would unleash enough anger to provoke the thought of arms.[209]

Hawaii had been formed through revolutionary violence. Kamehameha conquered the islands and quelled any vestige of continued revolt. He was a warrior with tactical and strategic skill. He gave unity and an organized government to eight islands, widely spaced over two thousand miles, with the Pacific's rough vastness serving as an outer border. He and those monarchs that followed sought to ensure limitations on the exercise of monarchial sovereignty. In 1839 and 1840, a declaration of elementary rights was issued by Kamehameha's successor that was similar in content to the ten amendments to the constitution of the United States approved in 1791.

With consolidation of the nation, the culture changed and the need for violence largely dissipated. The generations of Hawaiians that followed, plagued deeply by western and eastern disease and the forced change in property ownership, sought the tranquility of family life, the productivity of the land, the oral traditions that tempered and defined the culture, and the unifying value of a remarkable expanse in literacy. Native Hawaiians, by nature and experience, were law abiding. The idea of war making in the absence of a methodical call to arms and proper training was not in their cultural temperament.

There were two skeptics about the merit for a successful armed counter-*coup*. Liliuokalani recognized the frustration among her people and was aware of the planning. Sam Nowlein was regularly in her presence and lived on the Washington Place grounds. His loyalty to her would have made him careful to insulate her from the details. She had agreed to prepare commissions designating those men who would be in her cabinet should the constitution be restored. She discouraged armed action to anyone who asked. Perhaps she feared that in the long view armed action would yield neither restoration nor a benefit more enduring than had the full exercise of the resistance — in the Hawaiian language papers, the patriotic societies, the boycotted elections — that was displayed solidly. Robert Wilcox also was uneasy about armed action. He thought it might be a "bloody revolution"; more importantly that the provocateurs, however well meaning, were "talking of plans of the dark ages." Wilcox, perhaps more than anyone, understood the reality of armed conflict and preparation. He had witnessed and learned as Kalakaua sought to build an indigenous corps of loyal military and the semblance of a navy. The missionary children had discouraged, ridiculed, and defeated Kalakaua's effort. They wanted to preserve a Caucasian vigilante force loyal to them and their view. They had transformed that force into a uniformed army and some semblance of a marine capability. Wilcox also knew that this moment was not 1889, when he had led troops onto the Iolani Palace grounds with the tacit support of the palace's protective forces and the king. He also knew the geography of Oahu. He wondered why, in the discussions to which he had become privy, the effort centered on the conventional palace *coup d'état* with little regard for the other islands. He knew, too, that the men and culture that owned the cottages and danced at Waikiki would not succumb easily. Wilcox kept his distance.[210]

*

In the early spring, the provisional government moved to fill the vacuum left by Cleveland's commitment against annexation. The government needed the semblance of stability, a familiar construct, and a name change. Without regard to form, Thurston and others decided it should be called a "Republic." In crafting the new constitution, Dole relied precisely on the structure that reflected a council of elders. Dole would not be subjected to election. He would be surrounded by a cabinet of his choosing, an executive council and an advisory board that, when necessary, would act like a legislature. Structurally the "legislature" was in the distance, small in number, and enfeebled. With respect to ensuring that suffrage excluded as many native Hawaiians and Asians as possible, Dole looked to the voting restrictions in Mississippi. Morgan could not have embraced a more compatible ally.[211]

The new constitution also provided that the "Crown Land is hereby declared to have been heretofore, and now to be, the property of the Hawaiian Government, and to be now free and clear from any trust of or concerning the same, and from all claims of any nature whatsoever, upon the rents, issues and profits thereof. It shall be subject to alienation [i.e. sale] and other uses as may be provided by law." Within this unilateral declaration of ownership was an insidious, shrouded complexity.

Dole and William Alexander had accomplished what they had sought to do decades earlier. The Crown lands now were opened securely to sugar and commercial interests — Smith's and Thurston's agenda — and the accomplishment of political purposes. The Crown lands would be a source of needed income for the government. The Queen's interest and any trust relationship retained by native Hawaiians were declared extinguished. The uncertainty in meaning that existed in the 1864 Hawaii Supreme Court decision about the public or private nature of the Crown lands and the subsequent, sometimes contradictory acts of the legislature were resolved in the new constitution with a presumed certainty. The land was declared to "have been...and now to be" the property of the government. The land also could be sold. The 1865 Act of the legislature that prohibited the sale of Crown lands was repealed implicitly. Dole and Thurston had made it an historic artifact, arguably — to any lawyer you sought to attribute meaning to it — of marginal if any weight in a subsequent legal dispute. Under the new constitution, however, a legal basis now existed for precluding the Queen from making a claim of "any nature whatsoever" for the Crown lands in a Hawaii court. She was denied an elementary form of justice. No Hawaii judge would have to assess the meaning of the law.[212]

Dole announced that a constitutional convention would be held. The convention would be composed of thirty-seven delegates; nineteen of whom would be the members of the provisional government and its advisory committee. The remainder would be elected only by those people who declared allegiance to the new Republic. The convention was scheduled for March. Approximately four thousand people registered to vote. Most of the voters were Caucasian and foreign. More than five thousand native Hawaiians, Asians, and Caucasians held a rally in Honolulu. Joseph Nawahi, J. O. Carter, and Herman Widemann spoke against the new constitution and the sham Republic. The men and women's Patriotic Leagues decried that a fair vote of the people was not allowed. They complained about the loss of the Crown lands. The constitution also declared that any public utterance of opposition to the Republic would be considered libel. The insecurity of the president and the Republic's leaders had heightened further and was translated into law.[213]

Dole's insecurity took another form. In May, Liliuokalani was approached again with a proposal for an annuity in return for her abdication and support for the end of any resistance to the government. She declined. She wrote in her diary, "Not a cent will I accept and sacrifice the rights of my people."[214]

In July, President Dole declared the new constitution promulgated. The convention was a gesture. The notion of a referendum to ratify the constitution was not discussed. The Republic was recognized immediately by United States

Minister Willis. A formal protest submitted to him by Liliuokalani was registered dutifully. The frustration and anger intensified. So, too, did planning for a counter-coup.[215]

The effort by supporters to peacefully resist the change in governance in Hawaii had little resonance within the United States Senate or with President Cleveland. In Honolulu, the debate by members of Congress on the merits of the Turpie Resolution was followed with some care. Cleveland encouraged the Democrats to change the resolution's wording. Drop reference to the provisional government's recognition. Substitute the right of the people of Hawaii to decide their own fate. It was a subtlety of little consequence except to Cleveland. In Massachusetts, Republican Senator Hoar condemned Liliuokalani's threat to behead Caucasians and put his party on record as supporting annexation. Senator Lodge joined him. They were prepared to vote against the resolution. Thurston had returned to Washington, DC. He believed the resolution conveyed a useful message: The United States no longer supported the restoration of the constitutional monarchy. He encouraged the resolution's adoption. The resolution passed the senate in its amended form on May 31. The resolution read: "That of right it belongs wholly to the people of the Hawaiian Islands to establish and maintain their own form of government and domestic polity," and that "the United States ought in nowise interfere."[216]

As a matter of law the resolution's content was not binding on the executive or Congress. Republican Senator Richard Pettigrew was not satisfied with Cleveland's moral stand or the resolution's limitations. The fate of Hawaii, he knew, was only postponed. His party coveted its acquisition. Hawaii's fate was within the framework of principles he intended to preserve. He also did not believe native Hawaiians wanted to become American citizens. Given the alien nature of Hawaii's Asiatic population and experience relative to America's demographic and religious character, unsettling effects would be felt in the United States. He also could see the distain with which the native people had been treated and the principles of government the United States' professed had been denigrated. The land and labor would be exploited further if annexation occurred.

On July 2, Pettigrew took to the Senate floor. His style was plain spoken, tinged with irony and a comfort with assessing motivations as well as consequences. Pettigrew ridiculed the leaders of the new Republic in a manner few others had done before. "And now it is seriously proposed," he said, "to annex this impoverished and degraded people.... The missionaries have not only looked out for their morals, but for their property. They long ago succeeded in gaining title to nearly all the land, and now they have captured the Government and set up a Government of their own which has no resemblance whatever to what we call a republic. Under Queen Liliuokalani they had a Limited Monarchy; under Dole they have a Limited Republic — limited to about four men." Any prospect

Pettigrew would be invited to a sedate dinner or a fashionable gala at the home of Republicans John Hay or Henry Adams was gone. Gone as well was any prospect the United States would support restoration even through diplomacy.[217]

*

In June, Lorrin Thurston returned to Hawaii. He and his colleagues in the fledgling Republic were acutely attuned to the political machinations in the nation's capital. They worked at it. They controlled Hawaii's treasury and Foreign Service. They projected their images and maneuvered the press without challenge from their adversaries in Hawaii. They had friends and members of Congress and officials in the executive they cultivated directly. Thurston also kept Dole and Smith informed. Together they were coming to master the communications and diplomacy of the late nineteenth century. Their knowledge informed their policy choices in Hawaii. Thurston, Dole, and Smith also had accumulated wealth in a setting where that mattered. Thurston especially had projected an authoritativeness that few others could. After more than a year of trying, however, they had not succeeded in attaining their goal.

On Friday evening, June 15, Thurston addressed the American League, another institutional iteration that reflected continued Caucasian support for annexation. The League had its own hall in Honolulu. Present in the hall was "a large and representative Hawaiian-American audience." The masculine aura of smoke, fine white-linen suits, panama hats, and the flow of liquor tempered the setting. Thurston took to the podium. The audience settled to attentiveness. Thurston's confidence in annexation was certain. Cleveland's failure to restore the Queen, the issuance of the Morgan report, and the approval by Congress of a neutral position on the fate of Hawaii's governance sustained his position. The Republican Party, he added, "has become united and we have today almost the United Republican Party at our back...The monarchy" — as Thurston reached a crescendo — has been "put to sleep forever in this country." The partisan crowd was moved to stand and applaud.[218]

Thurston expected continued unrest. Cleveland's deference to Congress and the Turpie resolution resolved little in Hawaii. "[T]he question has become," Thurston told the crowd, "one of whether we can maintain peace except by bayonets in the basement of the Executive Building and elsewhere. The conclusion is that this country cannot maintain independent government except with the use of arms....That is why we turn toward annexation." The United States, he expected, would enforce tranquility.[219]

Delay in attaining annexation had consequences, Thurston acknowledged. The fledgling Republic would not include "majority rule [that would] follow the Anglo-Saxon theory of government." Such a principle could only be possible "in a country that has a homogeneous population [of] Anglo-Saxons and Teutons." Two examples were illustrative. Even the United States, he said, believed all men have certain inalienable rights "except Chinamen.... [And] no sooner did the question [of majority rule] arise in the South than the white men were compelled to change this proposition. No matter how much we censure the shotgun and forced balloting policies, the principle of the preservation of right and purity" must prevail. Senator John Morgan had provided a patina of comfort for Thurston and others. What might have been said with some graceful discretion could now be expressed without it. The Republic made its position clear: Native Hawaiians were not worthy of participation in governance in their own land. [220]

*

Disappointment among native Hawaiians was widespread. In July, the Queen was advised that she should send a commission to the United States "to see what could be done for our people... so that a government of the majority might get a hearing in the councils of the great nation to which alone I yielded my authority." She wanted clarity directly from President Cleveland. Among the commissioners who traveled at her expense was Hermann Widemann. His agenda was complex.

Widemann was born in Germany. He had a successful career in Hawaii as a lawyer and judge. His wife was native Hawaiian. He had spoken forcefully at the rally against the formation of the Republic. He was among the men whose counsel she sought in January 1893. He and his colleagues also would be the first formal representatives of hers since Paul Neumann, Edward Macfarlane, and Prince David served that purpose in the wake of the *coup d'état*.[221]

Widemann and his colleagues arrived in Washington on August 1. They stayed at the fashionable, recently built Arlington Hotel. They were a few blocks from the White House and Secretary Gresham's office. They sought a meeting with the president. He was unavailable. They tried again. On August 15 Cleveland declined the request. He sent a note. "Quite lately," Cleveland began, "a Government has been established in Hawaii which is ... maintaining its authority and discharging all ordinary governmental functions...and is clearly entitled to our recognition without regard to any of the incidents which accompanied or preceded its inauguration. This recognition and the attitude of the Congress ... leads to an absolute denial... or encouragement on my part to restore" the constitutional monarchy. Widemann received the clarity the Queen wanted.[222]

Widemann walked next door. He met with Secretary of State Gresham. He expressed the possibility of armed resistance to the newly formed Republic. "You will encounter no opposition from this government," Gresham assured him. "We claim no right to meddle in the domestic affairs of your country." Gresham had encouraged, with the skill of a diplomat and a disappointed maker of Hawaiian foreign policy, precisely what he hoped would have occurred when he had the power and perhaps the authority to support it. Widemann got the signal he sought.[223]

During his visit to Washington, DC, Widemann also explored the matter of the Crown lands. He met with Crammond Kennedy at Kennedy's office in the Kellogg Building, two blocks from the White House. Kennedy was a distinguished and widely recognized international lawyer and author. Gresham or perhaps Paul Neumann may have suggested his name. Kennedy also was renowned enough, even at fifty-one years old, to have attracted Widemann's attention easily. He just had published a book titled, *Some Phases of the Hawaiian Question*, a compilation of his letters to the editor and related articles against annexation. Widemann also was quite precise about the Queen's position: The wrongdoing and claim she had concerning the Crown lands stemmed from the conduct of the United States, specifically Minister Stevens and Captain Wiltse. Widemann's precision also suggested he came to Washington with the intention of seeking counsel for the Queen. The time may have come for her to assess a strategy for the timing and content of keeping alive the battle for Hawaii's identity and sovereignty if Cleveland was no longer supportive.[224]

Crammond Kennedy was born in Scotland. He immigrated to New York when he was fourteen. His oratorical eloquence on religious subjects impressed large audiences in New York and throughout the northeast. He became known as the "Boy Preacher." In 1863, he was ordained as chaplain of the 79th New York regiment. He served in east Tennessee and in the Wilderness Campaign in Virginia. He experienced some of the horror that James Blount, Oliver Wendell Holmes, and John Morgan did. He also had to minister to young men preparing for battle, wounded and dying, in need of a prayer above the field of killing or the place of their burial. He was responsible for understanding their fears and their need to be recognized as Christian far from the comfort of home and in the likelihood of never returning.[225]

Kennedy served on the Freedman's Bureau in the late 1870s. He sought to give meaning to the lives of former slaves after Reconstruction had come to an end. His experience may have moved him to study law, which he did at Columbia. He began his practice in New York. His skill in international matters took him to Washington.

Kennedy was a savvy and formidable advocate. He was engaged by the Queen's claim and offered to examine it. At the time he met with Widemann he was representing Antonio Maxima Mora, an American citizen, whose estate in Cuba had been confiscated by Spain in the 1870s. Kennedy was seeking compensation from Spain through the State Department. He committed to get back to Widemann as soon as he could. [226]

On his return to Honolulu, Widemann shared Cleveland's disappointing letter with Liliuokalani. He also probably described his meeting with Crammond Kennedy. It is unclear whether he described the fullness of his conversation with Secretary Gresham.[227]

*

In December, Attorney General Smith ordered the arrest of Joseph Nawahi. Nawahi had continued to organize, speak, and write against the Republic. So did his wife, Emma. He was visible, thoughtful, respected, and a reflection of Hawaiian nationalism that Smith and others could not tolerate. A shipman of guns had made its way into Honolulu. Government spies learned of the shipment after its arrival. Other men had been arrested first, during the day, at their homes or place of business. Their homes had been searched. The police were looking for rifles in a community that sanctioned private vigilante soldiers and was saturated with weapons. Possessing a rifle was not considered a criminal offense. At most there was a monetary penalty. It made no difference. Nawahi heard of the arrests. They included John Bush, the editor of two newspapers critical of the government. Nawahi often wrote for the same papers. He went to the police station to determine Bush's fate. He was arrested summarily and jailed. Bail was denied. His lawyer, Clarence Ashford, the former Attorney General under Kalakaua, sought it again. It was a futile exercise. Police entered and searched Nawahi's home. No guns were found. The two newspapers were shut down. Elementary notions of free speech and common civil liberties were vitiated. More newspapers were shut down. Nawahi was jailed in solitary confinement in Oahu prison in a dank, mosquito-infested cell. The point had been made. The broader threat reverberated in the native community and another threat to the *status quo* was removed. [228]

On January 4, 1895, the counter *coup d'état* to restore the constitution began. Robert Wilcox was asked by Sam Nowlein to support it. He did. At first, the fighting was largely confined to an intense but brief encounter near Diamond Head. Intelligence had pinpointed the gathering of Nowlein's and Wilcox's forces who were largely native Hawaiian. Their lack of training and arms were readily evident. Wilcox and Nowlein were unable to execute the plan. Wilcox escaped the initial encounter with a contingent of men. They moved deeper into the hillside. He was the last rebel to be arrested. The conflict lasted less than two days. Neither Iolani Palace nor the Republic was ever at risk. No violence occurred on the other islands. Few people there knew the counter *coup d'état* had occurred.[229]

Any semblance of civil order among the Republic's military and citizen guard was gone. Many in the military sought summary executions of the men arrested. "Wholesale slaughter" of Hawaiians and those Caucasians who provided support seemed imminent. Attorney General Smith ordered arrests. No warrants. Caucasian men were the primary focus. They had turned on their own kind. Men walking to work, some sleeping, others miles from the encounter were taken into custody without explanation or cause other than the bald assertion of "conspiracy." Personal grudges were settled. "All that was needed to cause a person's arrest was to assert he was a Royalist." More than three hundred and fifty men were arrested and jailed. Many were not indicted, arraigned, or tried. Native Hawaiians were intimated to give testimony against others or left in prison under threat of indefinite confinement or death. The truth and the coerced assertion of facts were melded. "All of these persons were informed that they were liable to arrest at any time upon the charge of having been identified with the movement against the Republic." Many native Hawaiians refused to lie. Other men, when later on the stand as witnesses, readily acknowledged they had been threatened to testify falsely. At least in appearance, their testimony was negated. The attorney general's scheme did not proceed with the perfection he wanted. Nawahi's attorney, Clarence Ashford was arrested. So was his brother Volney Ashford, the former head of the vigilante force that coerced Kalakaua into accepting the 1887 constitution. He now supported the constitutionalists. Herman Widemann's son Carl was arrested. Two other former attorney generals were arrested. Frederick Wundenberg, who had served as postmaster general under Kalakaua but had once committed to Thurston, Dole, and Smith during the *coup d'état*, also was arrested. Few lawyers who could represent the men arrested were left to do so.[230]

Three men, one American and two British subjects, were arrested, imprisoned, not charged with a crime, then forcibly removed to a steamer for summary deportation. Attorney General Smith was at the dock directing the deportation of them and others. The American requested to see the United States minister, Albert Willis. Smith refused. The British minister was there. He called Willis. Willis came to the dock with his consul general, Allis Mills. Both were helpless. Smith refused Willis' request to keep the man in Hawaii. The American was boarded forcibly. Willis protested to Dole that there was the absence of due process or anything that resembled it. Fruitless. In a moment of recollection, one of the exiles later told the *New York Times*: "We were [in] a very critical position. The Government was in the hands of a mob." Willis made clear to Dole that any American under arrest should not be subject to the death penalty. Dole equivocated. The United States ordered the USS *Philadelphia* into port. It was too late. The men were shipped to Victoria and Vancouver, British Columbia.[231]

After the rebellion ended, more arrests were made. Price Kuhio, Liliuokalani's nephew and an heir to the throne, was among them. So, too, were more newspaper editors. Few opposition papers were left. The story presented to the Hawaiian people would be controlled and one-sided. Some men were imprisoned because they "had been guilty of using intemperate language." Other men taken to prison to languish were later given a choice. Remain indefinitely or accept expulsion from the country. They chose exile. They were put on a steamer to San Francisco. The silence from the Calvinist pulpits was a deafening form of acquiescence.[232]

The Republic, led by its attorney general, had engaged in indiscriminate arrests, threats, the denial of civil liberties, false charges, and the humiliation to families and communities. Hawaiian men were torn from their wives. Old scores were settled. Homes were invaded, children frightened; their fathers taken to an unknown place and an uncertain future. Summary deportations occurred. It was an antecedent in its methods and purpose — a "veritable reign of terror" — to what the United States would not see until Attorney General A. Mitchell Palmer's arrest of southern and Eastern European men, women, and children in Massachusetts in January 1920. Palmer's jail was Deer Island in Boston, with its dank, filthy, and unheated cells. Prophetically, Liliuokalani had visited those cells during her first trip to the United States. The intolerance would be supported and encouraged by Senator Henry Cabot Lodge. His views and those who shared them about anyone who was not of his culture or skin pigment already had tempered and would haunt America for decades to come. One judge in Massachusetts called Palmer's conduct and the arrests "the terroristic methods" of a "mob." Upton Sinclair called it the "White Terror." At these critical moments in 1895, no semblance of independence of judgment or a heightened sensitivity to due process existed in Hawaii's judicial system. Certainly not by the Supreme Court's chief justice, Albert Judd. The elders would not allow it.[233]

Martial law was declared by President Dole on January 7. It extended only to Oahu. Dole suspended the right of *habeas corpus*, the individual right to seek judicial intervention to challenge an arrest. The hostilities already had ended. The civil courts were in session. Neither the judiciary nor the executive branch had been displaced or disbanded. As lawyers educated in the United States, Dole, Thurston, and Smith understood fully they had no American precedent in the Civil or Indian Wars to support them and, as emerged at the trials, no English precedent either. On January 16, Dole created a military tribunal to conduct the trial of those prosecuted for engaging in the counter-*coup*. Dole became the Commander in Chief.[234]

To Smith and Dole, more was at stake than capturing and confining hundreds of men. The ship carrying arms may have come from San Francisco. The United States may have acquiesced in the failed counter-*coup*. Smith apparently believed that capital punishment would serve as an example. Other leaders in the Republic agreed. The Queen had done damage. As long as Cleveland was president, she could do it again. She was good at evoking loyalty and providing the *raison d'être* for the actions of others. The signal had to be sent in Hawaii and abroad to deter any further efforts. The Queen was arrested on January 16.[235]

Smith believed he could charge her with treason. Conviction included punishment by hanging. When the police entered her home, she remained composed. She asked for a moment to prepare. Her attendant arranged an overnight bag. The Queen emerged in a neatly layered black dress. The police carriage moved out of Washington Place. A small crowd of men and women had gathered, some in a painful awe while embracing their children, others in a discreetly expressed delight. The Queen looked at the faces of those mourning, uneasy, frightened for her fate and their own. "She raised a black-gloved hand...and bowed her head in recognition of their loyalty. They moved back, but the heart-rending wailing of Old Hawaii filled the air."[236]

Chief Justice Judd entered her house to conduct a search. The pretense of a separation of powers between the executive and judicial branch was one again pierced. Any prospect that the legality of the military tribunal could be challenged in a court of law was discouraged if not precluded by his conduct. Washington Place was "thoroughly ransacked" in his search for "treasonable evidence." Other than the commissions for a new cabinet referenced in her diary Judd found nothing that would form the basis for the charge. Judd had played the policeman. Smith may have had few people he could trust or control. Judd was his appendage.[237]

The Adjutant General who led the prosecution was William Kinney. He was designated a captain and given a uniform. Kinney was from Salt Lake City, Utah. He was never in the armed forces. He had practiced law with Lorrin Thurston. Neither man had worn a military uniform except for theater. Thurston donned a uniform when he addressed a rally of Caucasians the day before the *coup d'état*. Kinney's uniform was donned to legitimize Dole's decision to bypass the judicial system. The uniform was abandoned after the trials' conclusion.

The trials would be held in the throne room at Iolani Palace stripped of its adornment and Dole's office furniture. The tribunal had few rules of evidence and no solid basis for its jurisdiction; that is, whether it had a legal reason to exist at all and subject anyone to a trial. The tribunal certainly had raw power.

*

Hawaii's form of governance from its outset in 1840 was not a replica of the American constitutional system. What had been promoted or disguised as the introduction of the "separation of powers" into Hawaii governance in 1840 was, for decades to come, analogous to a revolving elect of Caucasian elders who ensured that the appropriate values and men tempered its cabinet positions and especially the judiciary. A privy council or personal advisers to the king was recognized in the first constitution. The missionary leaders, including Chief Justice Judd's father, Gerrit P. Judd, understood that effective influence in the two "branches" of government that mattered — the executive and the judicial — required only that they, too, "aid the King" to ensure that the complexities of the new order in Hawaii could be handled only by men of a certain disposition. The independence of the judiciary was neither promoted nor desired.[238]

The judicial model drawn from an otherwise discredited seventeenth-century New England mentality was set. It was a model known for its intolerance of dissent. It would take some years to materialize in structural as well as practical terms. It evolved gradually as the missionary influence increased. Only modest variations on its form were acceptable but one such variation could not be tolerated: Any consequential deviation from the elect's control of the rules and means of enforcement and adjudication of rights through the judiciary. That intolerance was precisely what erupted in 1887 in the coerced imposition of a constitution upon King Kalakaua and the opposition to Liliuokalani's proposed 1893 constitution. On critical legal questions the judiciary often seemed indistinguishable from the elders. Matters related to property, the Crown lands, and sustaining contract labor as analogous to sea duty — what Lorrin Thurston acknowledged privately was "very generally conceded by members of the bar based on expediency rather than logic" — were but a few examples.[239]

The only institutional arrangements such a form of governance resembled were two arrangements rejected by the Founding Fathers in the United States as antithetical to the separation of powers and representative government. A "Council of State" and a "Privy Council" were rejected during the Constitutional Convention, and the Supreme Court later rejected a request by President George Washington for an advisory opinion because the court declined to be an appendage, in any form, to the executive.[240]

By 1895, in Hawaii, Caucasian men moved from the bench to private practice to government and back to the bench. Dole, Smith and Thurston fit the mold in their generation. So did Albert Judd. In a separate challenge to the military court's jurisdiction Judd had no problem sitting on the case and deciding for the government. In a legal community small in number and almost exclusively Caucasian in race or foreign in birth, the law was manipulated at will. There was no pretense of objectivity in a legal tradition tempered by conflicts of interest, judges and government officials engaged in private ventures, and private attorneys assuming judgeships for a particular case and then stepping aside. A member of the bar — not another judge — would take the place of a sitting judge who could not be available, hear and decide the case, and then move back to his private practice. No oath was taken. The choice of men was made by the judge or judges still sitting. It was a closed and insidious system. Rules, if they could be called that, were informal, inherently prejudicial to the parties in the case, and antithetical to fairness or due process. The process also was a way of ensuring who was important or of the proper temperament and worthy of being retained by private clients to represent their interests. These same men and this same mentality pervaded the attitudes of Dole, Smith, and Thurston and tempered the formation and operation of the military tribunal.[241]

*

During her imprisonment Liliuokalani found solace in playing the autoharp and guitar and, cautiously, writing musical compositions. Some music and poetry got out through the careful efforts of the nuns and school children from the church near Washington Place. The special solace for the Queen came from the music's political communicative purpose. Unknown to her captors, Liliuokalani was able to engage in a colloquy through the use of metaphors and historical and geographic meanings with her people intended to ensure that the truth of her intentions and actions was not distorted by the English language papers influenced by the Republic. Much of what she wrote was published, seemingly innocuously, in the Hawaiian language papers. They were political and personal signals, the confirmation of a commitment to her nation and a view of her duty. "Inexplicably strange are the actions of Willy Kinney," she wrote in Hawaiian when first arrested and the prospect of death for treason was real, "The hot-tempered haole [Caucasian] of Wai'ale. His act was to lie to the people, 'Tell all so that you will live,' Do not be deceived by his cajolery, Say that there is life through Her Majesty, Who sacrifices her life for the lahui [nation], So that you patriots may live." Liliuokalani had not succumbed to Dole or Smith or Thurston or their view of Hawaii's history or future.[242]

The military trial of Liliuokalani was scheduled for February 5. Her trial was followed by every nation represented in Hawaii and she knew it. So did Smith. Her lawyer was Paul Neumann. Neumann had declared his commitment to the Republic only a few weeks earlier. His declaration ensured he could not be accused of disloyalty in his defense of Liliuokalani.[243]

On January 18, the trials began of other defendants, including Robert Wilcox. He pleaded guilty to treason and refused to implicate anyone else. The head of the Queen's guard at Washington Place, Sam Nowlein, also pleaded guilty. He had agreed quietly, however, to offer testimony against the others, including the Queen. Their trial ended on January 21. The trial of four more men began immediately and ended on January 24. "As each group of cases concluded, the commission met privately to pass sentence on the guilty." The six men were sentenced to death by hanging on January 21 and January 24.[244]

On January 19, Liliuokalani's lawyer, Paul Neumann, discussed with her whether it would be in her interest and those men who had risked their lives for the restoration of the constitution for her to abdicate in favor of the Republic. They — and she — were subject to the death penalty by hanging. Although the tribunal sought to preserve the secrecy of each sentence, knowledge of its decisions was known to the Republic's favorite newspapers. It is highly likely that Neumann, who understood the politics and culture of the law in Hawaii, knew the death penalty already had been imposed on other defendants, some of whom he represented. He also would have known that Nowlein had turned against the other defendants, a fact he would have been free to share with her, although at this juncture even Nowlein was subject to the sentence of death. Without disclosing confidences, it would be his duty to advise her to do what was necessary to preserve the lives of others and her own. They both knew that Chief Justice Judd would present the primary evidence against her.

On January 22, the Queen was presented with a document written by Judge Alfred S. Hartwell that declared her abdication. Hartwell had been an "avowed enemy" of the Queen during her reign. He had met with Lorrin Thurston to plan the *coup d'état*. He was the "Republic's man." In addition, no one got to see the Queen or give her a document of such enormous consequence without the attorney general's authorization. She found Hartwell's proposal to be "insulting." She was told, she said, that by abdicating she would ensure that the lives of the other defendants would be spared. She believed herself subject to abject duress; seeking, as she believed she must, to secure fair treatment and to stay "the flow of blood." for those who acted out of "love and loyalty to me." She delayed. Hartwell had given her only a rough draft of his proposal. She was not allowed to consult with anyone except Neumann. She understood accurately that "six prominent citizens [would] immediately [be] put to death." Although she "would have chosen death rather than sign it," she agreed to her abdication on January 24. It was the fact of her abdication that, in her "own handwriting, on such paper as [she] could get" that was "sent outside of her prison walls and into the hands of [the Hawaiian language press] and ... those to whom I wished to state the circumstances under which that fraudulent act...was procured."[245]

In Hartwell's declaration she declared her loyalty to the Republic and recognized she would be subjected to prosecution. She implored Dole to grant executive clemency to all the men found guilty. She also renounced "all rights, claims, [and] demands," and all claims to the throne. Although the Crown lands were not mentioned specifically, they would be among the claims she already had asserted. Immediately the abdication was made public.

Attorney General Smith replied to the abdication. He confirmed that the purpose of Hartwell's work was a set-up to return to 1893 and to affirm for history and the United States the reason for the *coup d'état*. Smith wrote that Liliuokalani would be tried and punished accordingly. She already had explicitly agreed to be subjected to trial in her abdication. For reasons that seem inexplicable except to ensure consistency with their professed rational for the *coup d'état* two years earlier, Smith wrote that "It cannot be conceded that such rights and claims as you now voluntarily relinquish have had any legal existence since January 14, 1893 — [the day of the dispute with her cabinet over the promulgation of her proposed constitution]- when by your public announcement that you no longer considered yourself bound by the fundamental law of the land under which you took office." By selecting January 14, 1893, Smith sought to render irrelevant her protest of January 17, 1893, that she relinquished her authority to the United States. Dole had accepted that protest without objection. Morgan relied on the "interregnum" allegedly caused by the same cabinet dispute to justified Minister Stevens' action. Thurston's theory was that she relinquished the Crown lands through her protest on January 17. At play was Smith's need — more as the revisionist historian than the canny lawyer — to ensure that neither the United States nor Dole's sloppy legal failure could distract from the cause and the success of the *coup d'état*. In his own words and in an effort to humiliate the Queen, Smith rendered her abdication of January 24, 1895, a nullity under his view of the law, and further discredited Thurston's implausible theory. Few Hawaiians believed the abdication had been anything other than coerced.[246]

Liliuokalani was freed legally by Smith of Hartwell's prepared abdication. When she learned from either Neumann or a Honolulu newspaper publication that the death penalty had been imposed on native Hawaiians and others, the Queen no longer believed she was constrained morally by the imposed abdication. She entered the throne room wearing "black — a becoming dress of rich material — and a small flower-trimmed bonnet. Violets and maidenhair fern trimmed her lauhala fan. She was wholly composed, completely dignified, alert, and calm."[247]

She testified in Hawaiian and only briefly. Her audience was her people. She denied the truthfulness of any of the evidence against her. She readily admitted that she had prepared commissions. Judd testified against her. Kinney sought to ridicule her. She remained poised. A statement she had prepared was read into the record by her attorney, Paul Neumann. She, too, went back to 1893. She denounced the Republic. Her position remained consistent with her position from the outset of the *coup d'état* and in her statements to Harrison, Cleveland, and Blount. "A minority of the foreign population made my action the pretext for overthrowing the monarchy," she wrote, "and aided by the United States Naval forces and representative, established a new government. I owe no allegiance to the Provisional Government so established nor to any power or to anyone save my people and the welfare of my country. The wishes of my people were not consulted as to this change of government, and only those who were in practical rebellion against the Constitutional Government were allowed to vote upon the question whether the Monarchy should exist or not."[248]

The discomfort among the tribunal and Smith and Kinney must have been palpable as the translator received and conveyed her words. In the audience, which probably included a recently arrived twenty-five year old lawyer from Providence, Sidney Miller Ballou, all eyes must have been focused on Neumann and the subtle composure of the Queen. Their response, silent for now, was easily discernable: "Never again would the government consent to receive...a document embodying this version of the overthrow." Smith could not control her. His deal, arranged through Hartwell, and his attempt to revisit if not revise history was shattered. Paul Neumann must easily have sensed Smith's discomfort. No doubt he continued reading in his most eloquent oratorical form. "The United States," she wrote, "having first interfered in the interest of those founding the government of 1893 upon the basis of revolution, concluded to leave to the Hawaiian people the selection of their own form of government. This selection was anticipated and pre-vented by the provisional government who, being possessed of the military and police power...so cramped the electoral privileges that no free expression of their will was permitted to the people who were opposed to them."[249]

The tribunal adjourned abruptly. She sat resolutely and with a patience that looked to the long view. Her testimony and statement had ruffled and discom-forted the Republic. The illegal and immoral conduct by the United States and the *coup's* leaders also was the basis for her claim that the Crown lands had been taken from her illegally. Absent death, she still was working toward a future. The constitutional monarchy may not be restored. The Republic may control the police and the military and the citizens' guard. But Hawaii was still not annexed to the United States.

The tribunal ruled that the portions of her statement that dealt with the 1893 *coup d'état*, the United States, and the provisional government be stricken. Neu-mann objected. He was overruled. It made no difference. The statement was re-produced in the Hawaiian language newspapers and distributed by the Patriotic League. The statement also moved quickly throughout the globe.[250]

*

Liliuokalani was found guilty of abetting treason, sentenced to a fine and im-prisonment. She was confined to quarters in Iolani Palace. Her communication with her people continued through smuggled music and poetry. She reiterated to them the need for persistence. The Patriotic Leagues thrived. The diminished health of Joseph Nawahi and the continued arrest or intimidation of other men did not deter Emma Nawahi or Abigail Campbell. The knowledge and sophisti-cated prominence of the new *ali'i* and the educated commoner came to bear fully.

On May 8, while Liliuokalani was still being held in Iolani Palace, Crammond Kennedy wrote to Herman Widemann in response to their meeting in Washing-ton. Kennedy certainly knew about her trial and conviction. Kennedy expressed his willingness to represent the Queen with respect to the Crown lands claim. "I have no doubt that her claim is well founded and ought to be recognized," he wrote. He was skeptical about filing it in the United States Court of Claims. "I do not think it is justifiable under our laws; that is, that it could be enforced by suit in our court," unless Congress authorized it. Given Kennedy's writing about Hawaii and his knowledge of Washington, he also may have known about the court's clerk, Archibald Hopkins, and his relationship to Lorrin Thurston.

Because Liliuokalani was not an American citizen, the State Department, in its common practice, would require the Hawaii Republic to support her claim. "On the contrary," Kennedy recognized, the Republic would state "that the revo-lution did not owe its success to the action of the agents of the United States." If an annexation treaty was pending, perhaps a claim could be made through the legislative process. His idea was to present the Queen's "claim to the Department of State and to justify such a direct appeal upon the exceptional circumstances of the case." He would go to President Cleveland directly and seek his support in declaring the exceptional circumstances. If they had to go to the court of claims, he would argue that the disposition of the Queen and the loss of the Crown lands were "due directly to the conduct of the United States Minister and Captain Wiltse."[251]

Kennedy made plain he "should be glad to serve the Queen...with the understanding that I should have general charge of her interests here including the contingency of annexation." Kennedy wanted a retainer of $5000, against a fee of one fifth of the total of the recovery. His strategy, albeit still tentatively articulated, was based on the assumption that Hawaii, as Liliuokalani knew it, was lost. This was not an assumption she was prepared to accept. Widemann, under the circumstance, would have been unable to give the Queen the letter. Her mail was being read methodically by government officials. Widemann also was preoccupied by the military tribunal's sentence of thirty years in prison for his son Carl's role in the counter *coup d'état*. The Kennedy letter was filed among her papers. What he had done was to provide the Queen with a thoughtful glimpse into a legal analysis and strategy that also affirmed her basic position. His letter also told her about what it might cost her. Kennedy's offer, it appears, passed unanswered.

*

While Liliuokalani was imprisoned, President Dole introduced in the legislature the Lands Act of 1895. Dole characterized it as a "great advance on all previous land legislation." It had two purposes. Meld the Crown lands into the Government lands. They would become one entity under government control. The effect, among others, was to demonstrate further the Republic's distain for recognizing any vestige of Liliuokalani's claim. The second purpose was to allow the lands to be sold or leased primarily for small homesteads. The Act was apparently Dole's view of the Crown lands finally coming to fruition. It was a charade. The 1895 Act was an iteration of the 1848 land division that ensured missionary families and other Caucasians could acquire substantial portions of Hawaii's land at the exclusion of native Hawaiians or anyone else who did not have resources readily available and good political connections. Ninety percent of the lands were under long term lease. Small homesteads were never likely to find a place. Sugar and commercial interest lined up. Within a short period of time, Dole acknowledged that "The results have been somewhat disappointing." More than half of the land was controlled by persons of American or European ancestry. The 1895 Act had another effect. It accomplished explicitly what the Republic's constitution implied. The Act formally repealed the 1865 Act that had prohibited the sale of the Crown lands. [252]

The Queen was released from confinement on September 6. The United States, through Secretary of State Walter Gresham, conveyed to Lorrin Thurston that it looked unfavorably upon the mistreatment of the prisoners, especially if the process of the trials were unfair. The sentences imposed on most of the men imprisoned were diminished or rescinded. Some men were pardoned and released. Clarence Ashford, his brother Volney, and Frederick Wundenberg reestablished their lives and professions in San Francisco. When she arrived at Washington Place, Liliuokalani wrote, the "orchids, the violets, the chrysanthemums, the geraniums, were still in bloom, and seemed to greet me with joy, expressive as silent....But my welcome was not altogether from the silent, waving leaves. Those of my people who had been released from imprisonment were here to greet me also with their fond Aloha."[253]

Joseph Nawahi had been tried and convicted of misprision of treason. His trial, like many of the others, was a theatrical performance directed by the attorney general. Nawahi was released with the others in February. During his incarceration he contracted tuberculosis. During a hopeful convalescence in San Francisco, he died with his wife Emma holding his hand. He lamented at the end that he wanted to be in his home, with her, in Hilo. In a funeral procession that began in Honolulu, when the steamer carrying his body landed and moved gently across the waters to the bay at Hilo where he swam and canoed as a child, thousands of mourners followed the casket. Men and women, many dressed formally in black, from the Patriotic Leagues and other Hawaiian fraternal and women's' organizations, wept openly, respectfully, and with the profound sadness of an enduring loss. In Hilo bay the body was transferred to a specially equipped double-hulled canoe, garlanded, accompanied by others moving gently along side. The eloquence of the eulogies captured barely the depth of Nawahi's contribution to his nation.[254]

On February 7, 1896, President Dole informed Liliuokalani that "the restriction placed upon your freedom at the time of your release from confinement" was modified. She could not "leave the island of Oahu without the consent of the president or a member of the cabinet." She remained under constant surveillance. In November, Republican William McKinley was elected President of the United States. The prospect of another move for annexation was likely. With care and the continued use of the metaphor and the most discreet forms of discussion, Liliuokalani met with Emma Nawahi. She and the Queen discussed the idea of having the Women's Patriotic League "draft a document protesting annexation to be presented to President McKinley along with a similar document from the men's" League. When the time was ripe, Nawahi agreed to tell Abigail Campbell about the plan and the Queen's wishes.[255]

On December 5, bags packed and arrangements made, Liliuokalani presented her request to President Dole to travel abroad. She planned to visit friends in

San Francisco and perhaps her husband's relatives in Boston, she said. Neither Dole nor Smith objected. With the exception of Emma Nawahi, she entrusted her plans and intentions to few others except the attendants who would accompany her. On the same day, Liliuokalani boarded the steamer *Independent*. She was going to the United States of America. [256]

Part II. In the Distance, The Second Battle for Sovereignty

CHAPTER 7. THE PRINCIPLED IMPERATIVE OF THE CLAIM: SAN FRANCISCO

In the winter of 1896, San Francisco was a city of wealth and tumult. The completion of the transcontinental railroad in 1869 allowed commerce to move inland from its port with greater ease. The port attracted immigrants from southern Europe, labor organizers, and pockets of rough and seedy quarters. The wealth from gold and the legitimacy that came with representation in Washington, DC, also made San Francisco "the coastal center of capitalism." The Wells Fargo bank was founded and the Bank of America would soon follow. They financed shipping, land acquisition, and commerce along the coastline and into the Pacific. The influence of Mexico and the Catholic Church remained visibly vibrant. Hawaii stood between San Francisco and Manila and Tokyo. Men and resources moved through Honolulu in both directions. The Army had a fort on Alcatraz. The United States Navy maintained a base and coaling station nearby. The fate of the Navy's base at Pearl Harbor now seemed secure. So, too, did California.[257]

The Pacific Telephone and Telegraph Company had eleven thousand subscribers in the city. Electric streetcars moved people up and down Taylor Street. The park along the bay had been built, and San Francisco's mayor was intent on creating an "ideal city" comparable to Paris and Vienna with grand boulevards that would connect the park to downtown and the neighborhoods. Grand hotels like the California thrived, sometimes with full-time residents. Victorian homes were built. Leland Stanford, Levi Strauss, and Domingo Ghirardelli lived within the city limits. The Emporium and Golden Rule Department store opened on Market and Powell Streets to considerable expectation that would take a few years to meet. Women's organizations "resolved in a mass meeting that certain of their number must be employed in the police department."[258]

Caucasians from the east coast and from Europe, like Paul Neumann, and immigrants from China who had come earlier to work in the mining camps and the railroads, stayed. The densely packed Chinatown was a source of inexpensive labor, commerce, and unease. Its location on valuable land near the city's core and the perceived danger that disease from its alleyways and poor sanitation could spread with epidemic speed occupied city officials. The overt prejudice based on race and political expediency and business acumen made Chinatown's fate precarious. A "dog tag law," as the Chinese called it, required that Chinese immigrants carry an identification card that showed they were in the country legally. They often disobeyed it. The Supreme Court and the courts in California were not sympathetic to their plight. The hypocrisy was laid bare. To Southerners, immigration into the west had conveyed a lesson: Race mattered.[259]

Liliuokalani was familiar with San Francisco. Her first visit in 1878, made at the suggestion of her Oakland-based doctor, included entertainment and social visits throughout the city and surrounding forests and waterways. She also moved beyond the bustle and culture of San Francisco. She visited with the banker Charles Crocker and his wife in Sacramento and stayed in the Golden Eagle Hotel. She was accompanied by her husband, John. He had lived and worked in San Francisco during the Gold Rush era. He had experiences and friends to share. Among them was Antonio Pacheco, Jr., the former Governor. She had friends in the Hawaiian émigré community. Her brother, Kalakaua, had died in San Francisco in 1891.[260]

Liliuokalani also knew men who had been exiled to San Francisco following the *coup d'état*. They included Clarence Ashford and Frederick Wundenberg, each of whom had become supporters of the constitutional monarchy. Wundenberg was importing and exporting grain through offices at 222 Sansome Street in the city's core. Clarence Ashford was practicing law in the Mills Building near the Merchants Club. Also living in San Francisco was George Macfarlane. He had served in England under King Kalakaua and, later, as his personal chamberlain. He now was engaged as a financier, including projects with Claus Spreckels. Spreckels operated his integrated sugar empire — growing, refining, importing, and distribution — from San Francisco.

The Queen remained only briefly but productively in San Francisco. The Macfarlanes and Spreckels came to visit and look after her. They knew the Ashford brothers and Wundenberg. Annexation, her intentions in Washington, and, it appears, her thoughts about the Crown lands and the possibility of retaining counsel if necessary were part of the discussion.

She took the Sunset Limited via New Orleans at Macfarlane's suggestion. She was able to see the area around Los Angeles and Denver and then across the nation into the Deep South. She was taken by the "boundless panorama" and places for sugar and rice farms, and new colonies, and she thought, "And yet this great and powerful nation must go across two thousand miles of sea, and take from the poor Hawaiians their little spots in the broad Pacific... And for what? In order that another race-problem shall be injected into the social and political perplexities with which the United Sates in the great experiment of popular government is already struggling?" She changed trains in Washington, DC, for Boston. Snow was evident as she moved up the coastline.[261]

*

Liliuokalani was, from the outset of her visit, of "unique notoriety." She knew it. She was in the United States to change the perception of who she was and what and whom she represented. She had an agenda to be executed with deliberateness and, for now, with a modicum of indirection. Substantively, she held tightly to the moral imperative of the Blount report, largely ignored Morgan's report and her own coerced if not nullified statement of abdication. In a term of art lawyers use frequently: The issue had been joined. The field was no longer left exclusively to those men who sought the annexation of Hawaii.[262]

In Boston, Liliuokalani found hospitality and practical help. Julius Palmer offered his assistance without cost. He had traveled earlier in his life to Hawaii and met her through a mutual acquaintance. He was sympathetic to her temperament and cause and he knew the politics of the nation. He was a skilled publicist. He also knew her adversaries and the slice of Boston's culture they reflected. She knew, as Palmer did, that she had become the personification of the constitutional monarchy in a manner that was both personally denigrating and politically harmful to her purpose. He understood what she wanted done.

Correspondence with J.O. Carter and Emma Nawahi began immediately. Carter had assumed responsibility for her personal matters and finances. Each of their letters began with directives and reports about Washington Place, her other properties, and her indebtedness. The Queen also needed intelligence; what was occurring politically and culturally, what guidance might they offer, and how to coordinate her efforts in the United States with their efforts in Hawaii. She received it from both of them. From Nawahi, the intelligence came in letters, tightly spaced, sometimes three or four pages in length, written in Hawaiian. Her first one was dated December 16. They wrote to each other two or three times a month. They often wrote in metaphors, a code, a method for the two women to talk without detection. Nawahi described the efforts to organize petitions, discussions with the men's Patriotic League and with Abigail Campbell. She suggested ideas for actions in Hawaii and the United States, commented upon the Queen's adversaries in both locations, and reported on the political machinations in the Hawaiian community on Oahu, Maui, and Hawaii. Nawahi had her own source of intelligence inside the Dole Administration; someone who could detect the movement and decisions of Dole and Smith. The two women exchanged newspaper articles. Nawahi also used her letters to keep other people aware of the Queen's activities, health, and disappointments. She also expressed concern about the integrity of their letters. Liliuokalani's receipt of a poem from a seventy-two-year-old "Jewish mother of Greenbush, Mass.," was referenced in a newspaper article before Nawahi received the letter. The use of a code was critical. In a March letter, she wrote to the Queen: "God help us in our womanly works."[263]

Liliuokalani became visible in the manner she wanted. Her movements were covered by the press. Her plan unfolded not merely in Washington but elsewhere. The *New York Times* reported from Boston, "Liliuokalani in a Sleigh, She Enjoys the First Ride of Her Life." She took services at the Episcopal Church, and attended a doll auction for charity. The auction included a talk that praised the intelligence of native Hawaiians, mentioned that the Queen was a devout Christian, and said that she was right to propose a new constitution for the nation. The Queen was introduced. She sponsored a Hawaiian doll for the auction. The event was reported in the *Boston Globe*. Her visibility no doubt also was witnessed by Senators Lodge and Hoar. During the summer she visited Hawaiian émigré friends in Cape May, New Jersey; later she traveled to Niagara Falls; and later still to see the premiere of "Captain Cook" at the Madison Square Garden amphitheater. The box seats were "fittingly draped with the Hawaiian flag." At Cape May "all but four states" were represented at the local hotels, where dances, galas, luncheons, and musicals were held. Two congressmen and members of the administration were there as well. She agreed to write an autobiography with Palmer's guidance. These were not merely events to make her better known — prudent, tasteful, and Christian, the antithesis to what Sereno Bishop and other men had portrayed — but to expose her views and to meet people with influence in a political and social milieu that mattered to Hawaii. In January 1897, the Queen, her two retainers, and Julius Palmer got on a train for the nation's capital.[264]

*

Washington was in a transformation. In early 1895, Henry Cabot Lodge delivered a trilogy of foreign policy speeches on the floor of the United States Senate. He was a freshman. He had served three terms in the House of Representatives. He was not yet a member of the Foreign Relations Committee and "his voice on foreign policy was much less respected than that of the senior senator from his state, the venerable George Frisbie Hoar...."Lodge also "was not an impressive speaker. Though tall and elegant, with a well-trimmed Vandyke beard, he had a high-pitched, grating voice. His personality was chilly and austere, not of the type to make him popular within the Senate's convivial precincts. But he had energy, intelligence, determination, and foresight. His speeches accurately predicted the imminent revolution in foreign policy."[265]

Lodge spoke on January 19 — during the Hawaii trial of the men and the Queen implicated in the counter *coup d'état* — to "assail Cleveland's anti-annexationist policy." Lodge claimed the chief "gainer" in Hawaii and the Pacific would be Great Britain. "[T]he islands," he said, "should become part of the American Republic." Three days later, in a second speech, the threat also included the Japanese despite their protestations or any indication they sought control. "I do not mean we should enter on a widely extended system of colonialization. That is not our line. But I do mean that we should take all the outlying territory necessary for our defense, to the protection of the Isthmian Canal [not yet built,] to the upbuilding of our trade and commerce, and to the maintenance of our military safety everywhere. I would take and hold the outworks, as we now hold the citadel." He ridiculed James Blount in a way that had become notorious for those who shared Lodge's view: "I cannot bear to see the American flag pulled down where it has once been run up, and I dislike to see the American foot go back where it has once been advanced." He was oblivious to the rights or the culture of native people. His view was the echo of the first missionary to leave Boston and now, the view of their children. On March 2, Lodge completed his trilogy. He "revealed his debt to Alfred Thayer Mahan." Hawaii was "in the heart of the Pacific," Lodge said, "the controlling point in the commerce of the great ocean....Upon those islands rests a great part of the future commercial progress of the United States." He spoke about fleet concentration and said that "we must have suitable posts for naval stations." Hawaii must be one of them.[266]

By 1896, Lodge had joined the Foreign Relations Committee when the Republicans took control of Congress and the White House. John Morgan became the senior Democrat. In early 1896, Henry Adams, who was "a zealous advocate of Cuban independence," arranged a clandestine meeting between Lodge and representatives of the Cuban insurrection movement. Lodge disliked the Spanish temperament and hospitality during his visit to Spain. The prospect of further expansion into more "outworks" was critical to Lodge's agenda.[267]

Throughout his life, Lodge made no effort to hide his moral primacy. He despised the new European immigrants and the newly wealthy, "parvenus" as they were labeled in his circle. "He rarely met the poor." People like Senator John Morgan had come to understand Lodge's fundamental character and what it meant for Morgan's agenda. "[W]orsening race relations in the north [emerged visibly with] the immigration of millions of southern and eastern Europeans, which began in the 1880s and accelerated around 1900. Northerners concerned about the dilution of 'Anglo-Saxon racial stock' by Italian Catholics and Russian Jews were attracted to southern racial policies. Henry Cabot Lodge, in 1890 a staunch supporter of the suffrage rights of southern blacks, in 1896 was an enthusiastic defender in the Senate of preserving American racial superiority by adopting literacy tests to restrict European immigration." Lodge's discomfort and implicit reliability as an ally to Morgan increased further as blacks began to move north in larger numbers. "Fear of southern black exodus [to the north] had existed during the Civil War, but these fears diminished as black migration tapered off immediately after the war. But black migrants to the North...increased ... [and]... led to discrimination in public accommodations, occasional efforts to separate public schools, [and] increased lynching... [E]ven former bastions of abolitionism, such as Boston and Cleveland, experienced growing racial prejudice and discrimination."[268]

Although "an average of 101 blacks were lynched a year mostly in the south between 1895 and 1900," in 1897 President William McKinley "declared that 'the north and the south no longer divide on the old [sectional lines],'" as he and the Republican Party "turned an increasingly blind eye to violations of civil and political rights of southern blacks." Between 1890 and 1915, forty-seven Italian immigrants were lynched, some for merely treating blacks equally. Following the 1891 lynching of eleven Italian immigrants in New Orleans supported by "The Committee of Fifty," Theodore Roosevelt said: "[T]he lynching 'was rather a good thing.'" A grand jury investigation yielded no indictments. In 1896, the United States Supreme Court decided *Plessy v. Ferguson.* The court held that the constitution permitted "separate but equal" accommodations for African-Americans on publicly available railroads. Justice John Marshall Harlan, however, created a choice for those who wanted to follow it: "In respect of civil rights common to all citizens," he wrote, "the Constitution of the United States does not, I think, permit any public authority to know the race of those entitled to be protected in the enjoyment of such rights."[269]

"The opening 'nineties [also] saw the old regime, Anglo-Saxon, conservative, making its last stand at the White House." Women "who could give all their time to social perfections undistracted by suffrage [or] divorce" were on the wane. During Cleveland's time and especially with McKinley's move into Washington, social and cultural axioms were changing. A Midwestern Americana emerged; new money; industrial, retail, and banking fortunes snuggled tightly against the presumption of taste and manners held exclusively by inherited wealth or the old families with their connections to the pilgrims and puritans. Chicago had held a world's fair that influenced national architecture and political strength. Cleveland, Cincinnati, and the small towns of Illinois, and western Pennsylvania had an identity that mattered.[270]

Mark Twain embodied a perspective that challenged immersion in the literary influences of France, England, New York, or Massachusetts. The accumulated experience in Indiana of Booth Tarkington would soon aid in defining literary tastes and what was normal and acceptable within the American culture. There also was Theodore Dreiser of Terre Haute, Indiana. He chose to write about the underbelly of America, its cities, and the hard choices and roughly hewed values of people that were direct, harsh, confrontational, and uneasy to swallow. Frank Norris was from Chicago. He wrote the same way. He moved to San Francisco. Their presence was not felt in Washington social circles.

Washington society was largely the dinner party, the gala at someone's home, the elegant luncheon at the White House. Men had their Cosmos Club and Metropolitan Club located on 17th and H Streets; and it was still most fashionable to be invited to the dinner gatherings at the home of John Hay where a Supreme Court justice or the novelist Henry Adams might be present. Evening gatherings was where women dominated and reputations were made. A rose center piece at a dollar a stem in winter would appear, and proscriptions about dress — the "smart society hastily took to hats and boned collars" — were established. The women were educated, worldly, competitive, and tough; into discussions about suffrage, the Red Cross, and the efforts to appreciate the contributions of Civil War veterans, north and south. Few members of Congress had offices on Capitol Hill. Homes were built and designed to include space for private meetings and quests. Julia Foraker, wife of Senator Foraker of Ohio, "settled down in a big yellow house" she had built to accommodate her husband's political needs. It meant women were a critical part of welcoming, small talk, dining, note-taking, and making judgments about character and policy. Mrs. Foraker commented poignantly that "Everybody knew everybody else."[271]

Liliuokalani had made an impression on Mrs. Foraker in the mores of society that revealed the Queen's challenge as she entered the city. "Toward the very end the Harrison Administration flared with a brief, exotic sparkle," Mrs. Foraker wrote. "This was when Hawaii made us aware of her. To annex or not became the question. In the cold, snow-stormy winter of 1893 it was pleasant to think about owning those dream-like islands, and the President was known to be preparing a favorable treaty to send to the Senate. We heard a great deal, too, about the islands' picturesque queen who, decidedly, had a mind of her own. 'Come, Liliuokalani, Give Uncle Sam, Your little yellow hannie' — People hummed on their way to dinner parties for the Hawaiian Commissioners."[272]

The Queen entered Washington with a studied visibility. She was watched and judged. She expected and embraced it. She stayed at the Shoreham Hotel. She received a cordial visit by the Secretary of the Treasury. She arranged a meeting with President Cleveland just before his departure. She expressed her gratitude for what he had done and her appreciation of the limitations imposed upon him by others. Within short order, a plot was reported "to assassinate her...because she is the greatest obstacle to annexation." The concreteness of the details aside, the plot did not deter her from attending the Episcopal Church on 14th Street, appearing in a box at the theater, visiting Arlington Cemetery, and hosting receptions for charity groups, members of Congress, and the diplomatic corps. It appears she also was able to meet informally with Senator George Hoar, perhaps through Julius Palmer. The meeting tempered Hoar's attitude about her and annexation. He was undergoing his own transformation. The abolitionists — Hoar was a genuine adherent when it mattered to the nation — slowly became the core of the anti-imperialist movement in New England. The movement's purpose, once formed nationally, was "to aid in holding the United States true to the principles of the Declaration of Independence," and opposing "any candidate or party that stands for the forcible subjugation of any people." In time, its members would include Hoar, Senator Richard Pettigrew, and James Blount, Jr. This led Hoar to rethink his position on Hawaii. Race was at the core of the imperialist policy and the northern view of economic expansion abroad.[273]

When Liliuokalani learned the Shoreham would be booked for the impending inauguration, she moved to The Cairo, an exotic thirteen story structure on Q Street, northwest, where she had a "glorious view of the country and down the Potomac." Through the diplomacy of Julius Palmer, she was able to get a seat in the diplomatic gallery for the inauguration of William McKinley. Once she was seen, a "storm...burst from the reporter's gallery."[274]

She had been told by Emma Nawahi that William O. Smith, Alfred Hartwell, who had written her abdication, William Kinney, who had prosecuted her, Francis Hatch, who had been a law partner of Lorrin Thurston and had taken his place as minister to the United States, and Thurston would arrive in Washington in March. They came to negotiate a new treaty. They hired John Foster, the secretary of state under President Harrison, with whom Thurston had negotiated the first, unsuccessful treaty. The treaty had formidable adversaries. The beet sugar industry from Louisiana and California, the labor unions concerned about contract labor and Chinese immigration, and anti-expansionists like Senator Pettigrew were among them. Although the Republican Party was on record as wanting "control" of Hawaii, neither the president nor his new secretary of state, John Sherman, was willing to be very supportive. The Queen had met Sherman in 1887 during her visit to Mount Vernon. It was Sherman who, as a member of the Foreign Relations Committee, had joined the "essential elements" of Senator Morgan's report but not, apparently, his conclusion. McKinley could not resist the pressure from other members of his party. A treaty was negotiated and introduced into the Senate on June 16.[275]

The treaty eschewed reference to the Christian civilization as it *raison d'être*. It embraced, instead, the "natural dependence of the Hawaiian Islands on the United States" and the "preponderant share acquired by the United States and its citizens in the industries and trade." The treaty contained two provisions similar to the first treaty introduced in 1893 but withdrawn by President Cleveland. The "republic of Hawaii hereby also cedes and hereby transfers to the United States the absolute fee and ownership of all public, government, and Crown lands...of every kind and description belonging to the government of the Hawaiian Islands," and "Congress...shall enact special laws for their management and disposition;" provided that all revenues not expended for military or local government purposes "shall be used solely for the benefits of the inhabitants." Land was Hawaii's single most valuable resource to be bartered in the transaction. Contact labor, with some anticipated modifications, remained available for the sugar industry with as much support as the government could provide. The president also would appoint a five member commission, two of whom had to be residents of Hawaii, to aid in formulating an organic act that would establish Hawaii's form of government as a territory. [276]

The Queen submitted her protest the next day to the secretary of state. The treaty, she wrote, "purporting to cede those Islands to ...the United States [is]... an act of wrong toward the native and part native people of Hawaii...[and]...the perpetuation of the fraud whereby the constitutional government was overthrown, and, finally, an act of gross injustice to me." She referred specifically to James Blount's report "commissioned by the president," which concluded that "I yielded my authority...in order to avoid bloodshed." The representatives from Hawaii, she continued, did not include a single Hawaiian, nor had "the government which sent it ...ever received any...authority from the registered voters of Hawaii." The United States was receiving the territory of Hawaii from men "whom its own magistrate [the president and secretary of state] pronounced fraudulently in power." The treaty also ignored "915,000 acres...no way heretofore recognized as other than the private property of the constitutional monarch...Because...said treaty [does] confiscate said property...those legally entitled thereto, either now or in succession, received no consideration whatever...." Her protest was the formulation of a recognizable, classic legal argument: The taking of private property. The argument paralleled the Fifth Amendment to the United States Constitution that no person shall be deprived of property "without due process of law; nor shall private property be taken for public use, without just compensation." [277]

Julius Palmer added clarity to the Queen's legal position on her ownership of the Crown lands in a letter to the *New York Times* in reply to William Kinney's critique of the Queen's protest. Palmer focused, implicitly, on the treaty's language that the United States took only the land "belonging to the government of Hawaii." As the Queen had done previously, Palmer referred to the 1848 action of the king that created and retained the Crown lands in his private ownership, and set forth his view, which she also shared, that the 1864 Hawaii Supreme Court decision involving Queen Emma's claim to a portion of the Crown lands recognized the private nature of the land. Palmer then formulated a subtle but critical interpretation of the 1865 Act of the Hawaii legislature which prohibited any further sale of the land. His view was that the 1865 Act prohibited any further sale, inheritance, or distribution of the land to anyone except the heirs and descendants of the Kamehameha lineage, which included Kalakaua and Liliuokalani. Consequently, no disposition of the land -including by the Republic — could occur without the consent of Liliuokalani. The Republic had neither the ownership nor the right to dispose of it. In the terms of the proposed treaty, the Crown lands did not belong to "the Government of Hawaii." Palmer also chided "the lawyer[s]" from Hawaii (all four representatives were lawyers) "who know the facts" and have conveyed nothing more than a "quit-claim deed;" that is, an unverified, "defective deed" to the United States. The lawyers, he claimed, merely had sifted the burden to the United States. The Queen continued to take the same position. In the public realm the legal issue now was joined.[278]

*

The Salvation Army hall in Hilo, Hawaii was near the center of town. "It's a crude little place, which holds about 300 people.... The rough, uncovered rafters show above, and the bare walls are relieved only by Scripture admonitions in English and Hawaiian." There was no room, seats or standing space, available inside the hall. Many native Hawaiians stood outside with patience and deep interest. It was a women's meeting called by the Patriotic League. The women seated and standing all were dressed in "Mother Hubbards of calico or cloth and wore sailor hats — white or black."[279]

Two women entered. The crowd parted. The women were "tall, dressed in handsome flowing trained gowns of black crepe and braided in black. They wore black gloves and large hats of black straw with black feathers. The taller of the two — a very queen in dignity and repose — wore nodding in red rose in her hat, and about her neck and falling to her waist a long, thick necklace of closely strung, deep red, coral-like flowers, with delicate ferns interspersed." The woman was Abigail Campbell, President of the Women's Patriotic League. Her companion was Emma Nawahi. They carried petitions against annexation.

The minister said a brief prayer. Those assembled ended it with a softly spoken "amen." Mrs. Nawahi took to the floor. Her thoughts "were of her subjects, not of herself." Reflected among the people in the audience was a fierce determination and "an adoring fondness" that ensured attention. "We ...have no power unless we stand together," Nawahi said. "The United States is just — a land of liberty. The people there are the friends — the great friends of the weak. Let us then — let us show them that as they love their country and would suffer much before giving it up, so we love our country, our Hawaii, and pray they do not take it from us. Our hope is to stand — shoulder to shoulder, heart to heart. The voice of the people is the voice of God. Surely that great country across the ocean must hear our cry."

Mrs. Nawahi described the petition's purpose and urged the women to sign it. The men's petition will be separate, she said. The politics of Washington required it. "We have right on our side," she added, as she looked to the audience with an appeal: "Say, Shall we lose our nationality? Shall we be annexed to the United States?" The response was unequivocal and thunderous. "Never," was said over and then over again. The women prepared to sign and committed to gather more signatures.

Mrs. Campbell was introduced. "Her large mouth parted....She spoke only a few words...as though she were taking them all into her confidence, so sincere and soft was her voice as she leaned forward... 'Stand firm, my friends. Love of country means more to you and me than anything else....Sign the petition — those who love Hawaii. How many — how many will sign?' She held up a gloved hand as she spoke, and in a moment the palms of hundred of hands turned toward her."

More than twenty-nine thousand men, women, and young adults signed the petitions. A delegation of four men was selected to bring them to the United States for presentation to the Queen and the United States Senate. Resolutions also were approved by an assembly of elected Hawaiians from the various islands meeting in Honolulu. They were threatened with arrest for treason. In defiance and in challenge their leader said: "Let us take up the honorable field of struggle, brain against brain." One resolution, also to be presented to the Senate, made plain that the Republic held power only "by the force of arms," that the Hawaiian people were "accustomed to participate in the constitutional form of government...in which the principle of government by majorities has been acknowledged and firmly established." They sought only to exercise the right to vote on annexation as "proclaimed in the Declaration of Independence, the United States Constitution," and as provided in the resolution — the Turpie Resolution — approved by the United States Senate. Senator Morgan came to Hawaii during the petition drive and the formulation of the resolutions. His intent, expressed with confidence, was to convince native Hawaiians they would have the same rights to vote that blacks exercised. He was disappointed. He could hardly have an audience more informed and capable of recognizing his cynicism. Once confronted and exposed, he left. When Senator Pettigrew came to Hawaii he learned the obvious: Hawaiians did not support annexation or the Republic or believe Morgan. Pettigrew's commitment was now better informed.[280]

When the delegation of native Hawaiian men arrived in Washington, DC, they met with the Queen. Senator Richard Pettigrew provided them introductions to other members of the Senate to present their views and to put an additional face on the reality of who was harmed by the decision pending before the Senate. Senator Hoar agreed to introduce the petition onto the Senate floor and into the national debate. Liliuokalani welcomed their presence. She asked the women's League if it could raise more money to keep them in the United States longer. In a moment of lament, however, reached with an insight born of personal need and political value and prophetic in terms of where she wanted her nation and its governance to move, Liliuokalani wrote to J.O. Carter that "some Hawaiian Ladies should come over. I thought of that when I was in S. Francisco and would like to have brought ... [them]...over but money was lacking. I have no doubt of Mrs. Campbell and one or two of our Hawaiian ladies could come...and

Mrs. Nawahi is very smart and diplomatic. She could make some kind of favorable impression."[281]

All of the officials in Washington who were adversaries of the constitutional monarchy were men. They were seeking to impose on her and her nation a loss impossible to accept. Women in the nation's capital had posed a different problem, a challenge no less consequential if the Queen did not meet it with propriety, culturally and politically. She recorded meeting women from civic and charitable societies; and the wives of prominent officials often joined them in social settings that could yield an attitude, an atmosphere, a direct comment or a subtle frown that could change a vote or influence a speech. The observations of Julia Foraker made from a distance conveyed the atmosphere within which Liliuokalani moved. She was a woman ahead of her times in a country, especially in Washington, DC, where transformations in women's lives and roles were occurring but not with ease. The depth of consultation and intelligence she shared and garnered from Emma Nawahi and through her and at times directly from Abigail Campbell was without readily discernable precedent in American governance. If there was to be another constitutional monarchy in Hawaii, they would be cabinet officials, ministers of foreign affairs and interior, and the right to vote would come sooner than it did in the United States. But in meetings or visits of state or in the informal, quiet moments where the men of politics and government weighed and balanced each other's strengths and potential weaknesses and where judgments about trust and suspicion were often formed in this moment of resistance, Liliuokalani stood largely alone.

*

In January 1898, the Queen's book, *Hawaii's Story by Hawaii's Queen*, was published. It contained photographs she chose deliberately to establish her stature in appearance and manners and the dignity, in uniform, of her husband, John, who was an American by birth and a Bostonian within his family's history. The book was written with a special care; restrained but direct about her critics with a thoughtful, readable prose reflective of her diary writings and her letters. She took on race and cultural condescension directly and the problems they had caused in Hawaii and in the United States. She also raised the impropriety of taking the Crown lands. She clarified both the history and principle that underlie her claim and the beneficial purpose of the Crown lands: "For four years and more, now, these people have confiscated and collected the revenues reserved from all time in order that the chief highest in rank, that is, the reigning sovereign, might care for his poorer people."[282]

The book also was a reply; first to the ugliness of Sereno Bishop and then as a political tract intended to convey an intention. It reflected the Queen's skill at elevating the dialogue; putting people on notice, framing the issue that in the long view their moral posture was at stake and would be judged in time. The book's closing plea formed her intention: "Oh, honest Americans, as Christians hear me for my down-trodden people! .... With all your goodly possessions, covering a territory so immense that there yet remains parts unexplored...do not covet the vineyard of Naboth's, so far from your shores... The people to whom your fathers told of the living God, and taught to call 'Father,' and whom the sons now seek to despoil and destroy, are crying and He will keep His promise, and will listen to the voices of His Hawaiian children lamenting for their homes.....It is for them that I would give the last drop of my blood; it is for them that I would spend nay, am spending, everything belonging to me. Will it be in vain? It is for the American people and their representatives in Congress to answer these questions. As they deal with me and my people, kindly, generously, and justly, so may the Great Ruler of all nations deal with the grand and glorious nation of the United States." Some book reviewers understood and amplified her goal.[283]

The debate about Hawaii in the Senate and the broader discussion about expansion yielded a perverse form of irony. It "fostered the convergence of northern [, western,] and southern racial attitudes. Beginning with the clamor for annexation [of Hawaii]...imperialists argued partly in racial terms of Manifest Destiny, the 'white man's burden.' Most imperialists," as John Morgan already had confirmed and welcomed, "rejected full citizenship rights for persons thus incorporated into the United States." Henry Cabot Lodge was wholly immune from the prospect native Hawaiians should vote on the fate of annexation. An influx of immigrants and blacks increased further through the Great Lakes. Cincinnati, Ohio, Evansville, Indiana, West Frankfort and Springfield, Illinois were poised to undergo ugly racial and ethnic tumult in the next decades. A "Louisiana Senator wondered how northerners could justify trying to foist on the South 'a government they will not tolerate in the newly acquired territories.'" Senator Foraker of Ohio was for annexation.[284]

Nonetheless, there were not enough votes in the Senate to approve the annexation treaty. The requisite two-thirds majority of the Senate's members had not coalesced. The Republicans, Senator Morgan, and Lorrin Thurston knew it. All their cajoling, appeal to patriotism, denigration of the Queen, and the advocacy of Harry Bingham, the grandson of missionary pioneer Reverend Hiram Bingham, was to no avail. The Queen and others who opposed annexation had caused a stalemate in law and politics. Individual Senators began to withdraw support for the treaty. The fate of Hawaii would be decided in Hawaii; a proposition the Queen welcomed. She did not believe the Republic could survive. She and those who shared her view preferred ordered chaos and the prospect of regaining a Constitutional monarchy through the ballot.[285]

But the Queen was a realist. Her letters to J.O. Carter reflected a recognition that Henry Cabot Lodge, Senator Morgan, and the delegation from Hawaii would persist until they had what they wanted. "The Annexationalists are capable of doing anything," she wrote to Carter, "... no matter how wicked it is. If you were here you would see a great many things which you cannot imagine all under the form of propriety. Perhaps you may censure my opinion but one must be here to know." Two events ensured annexation: War with Spain and the use of the joint resolution.[286]

In April 1898, the Senate debated whether to go to war with Spain over the independence of Cuba. Julia Foraker was in the gallery watching with a packed audience. "In the diplomats' Gallery," she wrote, "was the Hawaiian Queen, Lili-uokalani, somber and yellow and fateful; she looked like a pythoness that day." Liliuokalani sought to listen to a debate she knew was critical to Hawaii's fate not because the United States needed any more than it had in Hawaii to pro-tect its interest in the Far East but because the Navy had found comfort on its shores; its men and money were welcomed by the Republic and treated respect-fully by the people. In addition to fleet concentration, Honolulu had become part of the Navy's Pacific culture. Perhaps, as well, the Navy's continued presence was viewed as the vindication of an institution discomforted by the criticism provoked by the actions of Minister Stevens. With a bigger role in the Pacific that included an essential duty, the Navy had little care for the fate of native Hawai-ians. The resolution passed. The United States was at war.[287]

A new tactic also was undertaken in the Senate and the House: Use of the joint resolution to effectuate annexation. Passage would only require a majority vote in each house of Congress. The approach was as much a product of the House's in-terest in having a say about appropriating money, administering newly acquired land, and preserving its prerogatives over Indians affairs as it was an effort to gain Hawaii as a territory by a simpler means. The resolution was introduced by Congressman Francis G. Newlands of Nevada in the House of Representatives. Newlands and Senator John Morgan had this in common: "[T]hey agreed on the inferiority of non-whites and applauded the white, American control of Hawaii's government...." Newlands' projected "an even-whiter Hawaii" through American immigration. Morgan hoped, instead, for "the colonization of American blacks and their restriction [along with native Hawaiians] to an inferior grade of citi-zenship." The content of Newlands' resolution contained the same language as the original treaty. Although it ceded and transferred all property and the rights in the Crown lands "absolutely and without reserve" to the United States, it did so with respect to the property "which belonged to the Government" of Hawaii. On its face, the fate of the Crown lands — ownership and who would benefit from their proceeds — appeared settled in law and in the power of enforcement by the United States. The legality of annexation through a joint resolution was questioned almost immediately. During the debate in the Senate, a resolution was proposed by an opponent of annexation to require a plebiscite open to all adult males. It failed badly. The Newlands' resolution was approved in the Senate on June 6 and signed by President McKinley the same evening. Sanford Dole was still president of Hawaii. Thurston, Smith, Kinney, and Hartwell were celebrating a victory of historic consequence.[288]

*

Two days after the president signed the resolution, Liliuokalani sat quietly in the Ebbitt House, much closer to the White House and less expensive than the Shoreham or The Cairo, to write a letter to J.O. Carter. She could imagine and feel easily what later she saw firsthand. Native Hawaiians were "desperately gloomy" and "never...in worse condition" after this loss. When she arrived in Honolulu, she knew they would look to her to define the spirit of the moment. In her letter to J.O. Carter, she also looked to the future. She had written her brother-in-law, Charles Bishop, to request a ten thousand dollar loan, and he consented to it. The loan would help pay needed expenses for travel and repairs on Washington Place that she already had authorized Carter to make. She also sought a loan from Claus Spreckels, which he agreed to provide. "When I get home," she wrote, "I will have to set my wits about me" to pay off the debts that were outstanding and to mold the remainder of her life. She also had to preserve her integrity and be mindful of the integrity of those with whom she shared a culture and a love of the land that they called home. She was fifty-nine years old, capable of a regal politeness even to her adversaries despite the loss. She certainly had no intention of encouraging native Hawaiians to violate the laws of the United States or to risk the loss of their employment or land. She also had no history of acquiescing easily into other people's agenda. She had known the duty of a queen. An illegal and immoral act had occurred against her nation and her. It required her to be conscious of not only how to preserve her financial well-being or that of others but also to think about generations still to come, to legacy, heritage, and memory, and to take the long view. She planned to cross the United States, she informed Carter, and to be in San Francisco for a few days before boarding the steamer *Gaelic* to go home.[289]

Precisely what occurred in San Francisco is unclear in its details. She apparently met with George Macfarlane. A tentative understanding was reached, including preliminary negotiations over a power of attorney and a strategy for continuing the fight. Clarence Ashford would be involved in the legal work. Frederick Wundenberg would provide some assistance. On July 23, *The New York Times* — three thousand miles away — reported that "among the intimate friends of Liliuokalani" it was understood that "[w]hen she reaches Honolulu...and informs her people of the result of her mission, she will publicly protest against the transfer of the islands, and will present her claim for the crown lands, confiscated by the republic, which consists of nearly 1,000,000 acres of land...It is said she will also present her claim for between $300,000 and $400,000 collected as rentals by the republic. Prominent American lawyers, it is said, have been engaged to handle the case against the United States Government."[290]

Chapter 8. The Lawyer and the Argument: Washington, DC

In the late fall of 1898, Liliuokalani returned to San Francisco. Her stay at home had been poignantly hard. She was greeted at dockside in Honolulu with an embedded, enduring sadness. Tears flowed. She did what came to her heart to ensure they understood her empathy. " 'Aloha,'" she said "with her musical voice rich with emotion." It is a word of deep meaning, generational in that moment, a shared disappointment that, together, they would all live with in their own way. Her friends and supporters and those men and women who were there just to see her face and the comfort of its expression escorted her to Washington Place. Its veranda was tinged with greenery in a gentle festiveness. Torch bearers in black tie with tails stood with a dignified comfort. Emma Nawahi stood quietly amid the many others talking, holding hands, and seeking solace. Nawahi knew better than anyone what her queen had endured. They both knew there was more to be done. Children waited in quiet awe, bowing gently in respect, and then playing, eating the simple refreshments, unaware of a future for which the Queen and others were still responsible.[291]

When matters settled, and with her wits in place, the Queen had turned to repairs of her properties and a clearer understanding of her financial resources and debts. Her health had deteriorated. The stress, disappointment, and the constancy of travel had taken a toll physically. Her doctors cautioned her about more travel. There was speculation she had cancer of the throat and would "live but a short time." On August 12, the flag of the United States was raised at Iolani Palace. Native Hawaiians were not in attendance.[292]

In San Francisco, the Queen moved into the California Hotel on Bush Street, near Kearny. The city had been enthralled by the feat of Admiral George Dewey. His success in Manila was received in San Francisco with particular warmth.

Troops had left the city's port to fight on behalf of California. With their success, San Francisco was not only secure but also had the prospect of increased commerce. A movement began to raise public funds for a Dewey monument. "[O]ur generation," the monument's advocates would write, "has fought the war that has broken down the last vestige of Spanish dominance in this hemisphere." Making a "liberal contribution for the Dewey monument" was "one of the best ways to give your patriotism expression." In the quietude of her room, Liliuokalani began her correspondence with Emma Nawahi and J.O. Carter [293]

She met with George Macfarlane. They entered into two agreements they both understood to be preliminary and revocable. She signed a power of attorney so Macfarlane could act with authority in retaining counsel and determining compensation. She also entered into an indenture — a contract to pay — that Macfarlane needed in order to form a syndicate of investors or lawyers to help finance travel, research, and document preparation. The value of her claim was the estimated value of the Crown lands, perhaps as high as ten million dollars plus the value of the rents and fees collected since the *coup d'état*. The lawyer would be Clarence Ashford. His duty was to determine the legal basis for the claim and prepare a brief. It would tell Macfarlane the prospects for success. Macfarlane would be the strategist; Fred Wundenberg his liaison in San Francisco. It also appears that Philip Lilienthal, the head of the Anglo-California Bank, would support Ashford's effort. Strategy, Macfarlane said, would be determined later. Macfarlane left for Honolulu to pursue his business interests and direct the required research. Liliuokalani departed for Washington via Salt Lake City, Utah. [294]

The Queen was uneasy with the arrangement. She knew Macfarlane for many years and trusted him. He was a cosmopolitan figure; Scottish, handsome, squared-jawed, with a finely cut mustache; a successful banker, able to assure comfort in his ventures for investors in London and New York. Her discomfort lingered when she reached Washington, DC. She had rented a home at 1418 15th Street in a sedate, "unhurried" residential neighborhood near the Episcopal Church she liked to attend. She wrote to Carter on November 24 and asked him to meet with Macfarlane in Hawaii to discuss the terms of the agreements and support his research. She had come to the nation's capital to follow the evolution of the commission the president had appointed to propose a form a government for Hawaii and the legislation they had recommended. With the aid of Macfarlane she intended to ensure her claim for the Crown lands would be heard and incorporated into the debate and the law. One element of the commission's effort already had engaged her: Who could vote. [295]

The commission had included Senator John Morgan. He had properly positioned himself to ensure Anglo-Saxon dominance in Hawaii's governance and a sympathetic ear for the South. President Dole was named. So, too, was Republican Congressman Robert Hitt of Connecticut. Hitt had been a supporter of annexation. There were no native Hawaiians. The commissioners had visited Hawaii while the Queen was still there. She traveled the islands, essentially following the commission's path. It was a classic political move with the moral imperative of the long view. She had been requested by the Patriotic Leagues to advocate the inclusion of broad suffrage requirements into an Organic Act the commissioner's would recommend. The Leagues also wanted her to retain the Crown lands or be compensated for their loss. She welcomed the duty.[296]

In the reality of annexation, the principle of broad suffrage that she and native Hawaiians had sought since 1887 could be vindicated. She demonstrated to the commissioners that she had neither withdrawn from her definition of duty nor succumbed to their intention to diminish the native vote. "I understand," she later wrote to Carter, "they will propose to Congress to allow 'franchise to Hawaiians.'" It was one provision of the proposed Organic Act she could embrace. She also was witnessing the slow emergence of forces that were powerful and exacting: The United States was confronted directly and solely with the conflict between its own principles and values and those of the missionary mentality that had dominated the islands. Native Hawaiians were no longer an easily available shield to hide behind; a ploy to be used, or a diversion to be elevated.[297]

Congress reconvened in December to examine the proposed Hawaii legislation. Macfarlane had instructed her to file a "simple protest," which he or Ashford prepared. It was two paragraphs in length. It was filed in the Senate, House of Representatives, and with the secretary of state on December 19. It was filed under her name. The protest recognized the singular legal perpetrator of the wrongdoing against her: The United States of America. Its "assertion of ownership... [was] a taking of property without due process of law and without just compensation," she wrote. The claim had taken on a constitutional character. By virtue of annexation, Liliuokalani was now an American citizen. "The Crown lands," she concluded, "should be "restore[d] to me...by your Government under what must be a misapprehension of my right and title."[298]

*

By early January 1899, Liliuokalani was frustrated with the lack of response from Macfarlane and the absence of his advocacy in Washington, DC. The *Washington Post* had published an article denigrating her claim. She wrote Wundenberg. "I must impress upon you," she told him, "the necessity of appointing or sending here a representative to work for the claim and to contradict all false statements... very soon." The reply came from Macfarlane through Wundenberg. Macfarlane was still in Honolulu. He had received some of the documents he sought to support her claim. He had secured a copy of Kamehameha III's will that, presumably, would demonstrate that he treated the Crown lands as private property. The will needed to be translated and mailed to Wundenberg. He also had a copy of Queen Emma's release of her rights to the Crown lands which she had claimed as King

Kamehameha IV's wife, a document that was implicated in the 1864 Supreme Court decision. He had a copy of Claus Spreckels' conveyance of the interest he acquired from Princess Ruth, implicated in the 1882 Act of the legislature and the memoranda of history and law that allegedly supported Princess Ruth's claim to the Crown lands in Maui. Archibald Cleghorn, the Queen's brother-in-law, also had gathered old legal texts that referenced these transactions. Macfarlane told the Queen he intended to share his research results with J.O. Carter.[299]

Macfarlane advised the Queen "that it would be time wasted for me or any of us to have been at Washington before this time." He wanted to wait until Congress delved deeper into the "Territorial question." He expected to be back in San Francisco in February. On February 15, Wundenberg assured her that he and Clarence Ashford "have completed our work and only await Macfarlane's arrival."[300]

Liliuokalani's concern did not diminish, even though Congress adjourned without resolving the proposed legislation. What her experience had shown was that influence and advocacy were exerted in different ways throughout the year, including in the executive branch and among members who stayed during recess. Her greatest apprehension came from wanting to know the content of the brief — the legal argument Ashford had developed. She asked him for it. He had prepared the document and wanted to be certain he would be compensated for it. "The conditions surrounding the status of the title to the Crown Lands," he wrote her in reply, "taken in connection with their history...are such as to render knowledge thereof peculiarly valuable [and]...so much stock-in-trade." His agreement with Macfarlane was not settled. He was gracious and apologetic in denying her request. Macfarlane was still in Hawaii on business. It was the middle of March. She replied to Ashford on March 21. She understood his position, she said, but expressed her concern that as "the party most interested in the claim," she did not want to say anything publicly or privately that could be harmful.[301]

She also wrote to Macfarlane directly. She wanted to alter the indenture, her contract to pay. In a series of letters that followed among her, Macfarlane, and Carter, two issues emerged with clarity. Macfarlane expected her to pay one-third of the value of her claim, although how that would be calculated was not specified. She expected the payment to be one-fourth or one-fifth and she did not think a syndicate was necessary. He assured her that he understood from Wundenberg "that it is a splendidly prepared brief, and makes out your case much better than the attorneys anticipated." He would not risk mailing it to her, he wrote. He had the brief placed in a vault at the Anglo-California Bank for safe-keeping. The lawyers expected to receive one-third, he reiterated. If that was not acceptable to her, he would help her negotiate with a new lawyer.[302]

In Washington, the Queen was questioned by friends for not being more forthcoming about her claim. Paul Neumann was in Washington. He criticized the inadequacy of the December 19 protest. He was considering, he told her, representing an alleged descendant of royalty who also wanted to make a claim for the Crown lands. Macfarlane cautioned her about Neumann and the "many so-called claim-lawyers" that would not get her the land or money to which she was entitled. She did not want to leave Washington, go to San Francisco to review the brief, and then return. Macfarlane also made clear, however, that his strategy required Congress to complete and approve all the terms of the new government before he would file the claim. She was uneasy with this approach. She suggested in a letter to Carter that Congress was not the place to begin the process. What may have lingered was her letter from Crammond Kennedy in 1895 and the manner in which she and Palmer approached both branches of government and the capital's culture in the fight for independence. The place to start was with the president and the secretary of state.[303]

Through June, July, and August, the disagreement between the Queen and Macfarlane intensified. The tone of the letters was cordial, respectful, and serious. She tried to convince Macfarlane to share the brief with her. He would not. What emerged in this colloquy about timing and strategy among San Francisco, Honolulu, and Washington, DC, was the Queen's decision to cancel the power of attorney and the indenture. Although the correspondence continued, finality was reached when the Queen learned that a formal dispute existed between the Dole Administration and the attorney general of the United States over the attempt by Dole to sell or lease public land, including the Crown lands, in large acreage amounts. In November, the attorney general issued an opinion that not only prohibited any further sale but made clear the United States owned the land without equivocation.

She understood properly and with the sophistication that came with her knowledge of the federal bureaucracy that now the "U.S. Government considered their claims to these Crown lands as permanent and of course making any claim in [the] future difficult since they have issued this protest against the sale." The executive was bound or at least more entrenched in its position. She wrote to Carter: "It actually makes me heart sick and tired — this long waiting." [304]

Macfarlane, she believed, was preoccupied wholly with his business venture in Hawaii and that her interests were not attended to timely or properly. She never received the brief. She was, once again, largely on her own. Julius Palmer and her old friend Herman Widemann had died. Neumann was back in Honolulu and distracted by other possible claimants. In Washington, DC, she was supported by the memory of those members of Congress who had felt the fullness of the Patriotic Leagues' effort and her effort to articulate a legal and moral position on the Crown lands. She had the benefit of her continued presence and social and political connections with members like Senator Hoar whom she had befriended. She knew enough about the claim and its *raison d'être* to argue for it with anyone.

She needed that knowledge and skill. The Dole Administration was prepared to argue for its own version of the Organic Act.[305]

*

The Shoreham Hotel was on the corner of H and 15th Streets, two blocks from the White House. "There was no other hotel in Washington quite like it." Architecturally it merged the Romanesque Revival motif with French inspired dormers reflective of the Second Empire look and an entranceway designed in the Queen Anne style. Its dining room, about to undergo a renovation, was considered among the most elegant in the city. The location carried its own history. During the Civil War, General George B. McClellan lived there and President Andrew Johnson moved in to wait politely for Mrs. Lincoln to vacate the White House after the president's assassination. The property was purchased by Vice President Levi P. Morton, who built the hotel. He named it after his birth place, Shoreham, Vermont.[306]

When William O. Smith moved into his suite in December 1899, the Shoreham had become not only fashionable but the residential apartment for members of Congress, especially those from New England and New York. Smith was no longer the attorney general of Hawaii. He was there, he told Senator Lodge, on behalf of his private client, the chamber of commerce. He did not disclose that his expenses were being paid by the Hawaiian Sugar Planters Association. Although not there representing the government — that was Alfred Hartwell's and Francis Hatch's responsibility — Smith's actions were integrated fully into theirs and reflective of the way they all tended to view public and private interests. It was difficult to tell when Smith was not serving both masters. Hartwell joined him at the Shoreham. [307]

Smith met regularly with members of Congress as they took up portions of the Hawaii legislation. He was confident of the working relationships the delegation had, including with Senator Joseph Foraker of Ohio. Smith also remained active socially. "When a gentleman comes to Washington with official standing," he wrote to his colleagues in Hawaii, "he must call upon the ladies [during special 'calling days']...if one expects to have any recognition from them." Senator Foraker's wife, whose colonial revival home was only a few blocks from the Shoreham, would have been among those ladies who received such visitors. Smith also attended a dinner at the Metropolitan Club hosted by Hartwell for current and former cabinet officials. Congressman Robert Hitt of Connecticut, whom Smith and others already knew from his role as a member of the commission that formulated the proposed Organic Act, was invited. There were ten men at Smith's table, including Lorrin Thurston's former retainer and continued confidant, United States Court of Claims Clerk, Archibald Hopkins. Hopkins had just moved his office to the court's new location at the corner of Pennsylvania Avenue and 17th Street — the former Renwick Art Gallery. Smith also had retained the prominent Washington attorney and successful lobbyist with members of Congress, Clarence Woods DeKnight. Their relationship appears to have preceded Smith's arrival and to have met Smith's need for solid intelligence on Washington power centers. He paid DeKnight the last retainer in their arrangement of $250 a month on January 31, 1900.[308]

Matters did not go precisely as the Hawaii delegation intended. Senator Richard Pettigrew was obstinate in his criticism of the entire legislation especially a recent Hawaii Supreme Court decision that, once again, upheld contract labor. Smith thought that Pettigrew's arguments were "injurious." Smith also noted that Pettigrew was "denounced as a traitor by such men as Senator Lodge...and that he, Pettigrew, [was] largely responsible for the deaths of the soldiers who were being killed in the Philippines." Pettigrew also made clear, either publicly or privately, that his documentation of the recent court decision was received from J.O. Carter. The Queen's fine hand was at play. Robert Wilcox came to testify in support of the Queen's position that she owned the Crown lands. He was most comfortable speaking Hawaiian, and, probably, also knew Italian. He was awkward in English but it did not deter him from expressing his view or conveying in a manner that resonated to members that the Queen was supported fully by the native Hawaiian community back home. [309]

In the contentiousness of this debate, Smith's deeper discomfort emerged over the subject probably most central to his reason for being there: Who could vote. "My own experience," he wrote to a member of Congress, "convinces me... that with an excessively large native vote, without property qualifications, the government of the islands would be in control of the natives, to the great detriment of the 'white' interests." Historically, Smith continued, "the native is only one generation removed from serfdom....He had little education or training in the practice of self-government." They "remain 'children of the tropics,' and have hardly ever parted with the economic ideas which the race has held over a thousand years....Thriftlessness is a characteristic of the people." This "condition of the race is not," Smith concluded, "due to the oppression of the whites."[310]

Perhaps seated quietly near a window looking out upon 15th Street and the movement and clatter of people or the Victorian townhouses easily within her view, the Queen focused on the same provision concerning voting that disconcerted Smith. Pen in hand, in a cursive style still crafted with the clarity she had learned in her youth, she wrote to Carter. The expanded franchise, she posited with a subtle pleasure, "will please a majority of the people [and the] nation." [311]

*

On March 2, the Senate approved the Organic Act that established a form of government for Hawaii. It would have a governor, senate, and House of Representatives. Suffrage, with minor qualifications, was largely universal. The master-servant contract was effectively prohibited. Preserving it was no longer the duty of the state. Smith, however, already was reviewing a report in his hotel room about "a class known as Peons" from Puerto Rico that would be suitable as laborers in Hawaii for "about thirty cents American money" a day. Under the Organic Act, the judiciary would remain essentially the same until Congress could examine it closer. With exceptions, the criminal and civil laws would remain in tack. They had been compiled by attorney Sidney Miller Ballou at the Republic's request and incorporated by reference into the Organic Act. With respect to the Crown lands, the Organic Act provided, in part: "[T]he portion of the public domain heretofore known as the Crown Land is hereby declared to have been, on the twelfth of August, eighteen hundred and ninety four, and prior thereto, the property of the Hawaiian government, and to be free and clear from any trust of or concerning the same, and from all claim of any nature whatsoever, upon the rents, issues, and profits thereof. It shall be subject to alienation and other uses as may be provided by law." Both the United States and the Hawaii delegation had done all they could in the language of the law to deny the Queen's interest and any trust obligation. [312]

The Crown lands were distinctly scrutinized during the debate. For all the efforts that Dole, Thurston, and Smith had made to meld the Crown lands into the public lands, open them for sale, and declare the Queen's interest nullified, Liliuokalani's effort had preserved a continuity of interest in Congress. In the House of Representatives, as Smith described it in his monitoring of the debate for his colleagues in Hawaii, "an amendment was introduced which required that every transaction [on the public lands, such as a sale or lease] should be referred to the Interior Department of the US....The amendment in the Senate, signaling out the Crown lands to be subject to the U.S. laws and leaving the rest under Hawaiian law" was, to Smith, "extremely unsatisfactory." The amendment was not approved. [313]

When the bill came before the Senate for a final debate on March 1, Senator Clarence D. Clark of Wyoming, who shared Senator Hoar's general perspective on public matters, "presented an amendment authorizing the payment of $250,000 [to Liliuokalani] which amount was to be a charge upon revenues of the Crown Lands and paid at the rate of $50,000 a year. In consideration of this [the Queen] was to give a deed to the Government relinquishing all her right and title to those lands." Clark's amendment reflected the principle she advocated: The correlation between her ownership of the Crown land and the wrongdoing that resulted in its taking. The debate was contentious. Senator Pettigrew "said he was opposed to the [entire] bill and to any effort made by Congress to provide a government for the islands. He favored turning the Hawaiian Islands back to the people." Pettigrew's speech would be among his last as a United States Senator. McKinley and his manager Mark Hanna did all they could in South Dakota to prevent Pettigrew's reelection to the Senate. Pettigrew could not overcome their money and influence. The Queen would soon lose a friend and an advocate in the senate. In the debate on the Clark amendment, Senator Orville Platt of Connecticut denied the Queen had any interest in the lands. The amendment was defeated by the Republican majority.[314]

Senator Hoar was not deterred. On March 10, he proposed an amendment to the Diplomatic and Consular Appropriations bill to give to Liliuokalani two hundred and fifty thousand dollars. It was an amount that emerged with regularity. In 1893, Archibald Hopkins had proposed a similar amount to Lorrin Thurston as his own estimate of what he thought Congress might provide the Queen. Hopkins, however, had not connected the amount to the loss of the Crown lands. Senators Clark and Hoar did. Senator Lodge would only agree to a smaller amount and an annuity: Twenty thousand dollars and ten thousand dollars a year during her natural life. He counted on her death. On the Senate floor, Hoar said the Queen had been subjected to "cruel calumnies" about her character and Christianity — including from him — that he had come to realize were inaccurate. Senator Ben Tillman of South Carolina, who was as rabid a segregationist as Senator Morgan but had not agreed with Morgan on the value of Hawaii to the south, insisted that any obligation to the Queen was incurred by the Republic of Hawaii not the United States. In his private correspondence, Smith wrote that he was asked by Morgan how he felt about the ten thousand dollars annuity. Smith had no objection to an annuity paid by the United States. The annuity, if approved, was not connected to any acknowledgement of wrongdoing by the United States or the leaders of the *coup d'état*. Senator Platt of Connecticut contended the Queen had not the slightest claim. The appropriation would be, Senator Lodge said, "an act of grace." The amendment was defeated. [315]

The transformation in the reason to support the Queen's claim from an obligation to an "act of grace" was not based in law as that term might be understood in a court of law but based on the politics of law as that term was understood in Congress and in the public dialogue. The "act of grace" was the euphemism for denying accountability and seeking supplication by the Queen. That Lodge suggested it, at least in that moment, may have suggested the viability of a political rationale that opponents of the Queen's claim might find acceptable. Lodge's rationale went to the heart of the problem Liliuokalani now confronted. If compensation was provided, it could not be because the United States had committed a wrong. Senator Tillman's contention embodied the related problem. If compensation was owed the Queen, the duty and the wrongdoing lay on the Republic. Smith, Dole, and Thurston would ensure such an acknowledgement was never made. She was prepared to understand and work the politics as it was presented. She was not prepared to forgo the claim's *raison d'être*: The illegality and immorality of the *coup d'état* and the role in it of the United States. The long view required that the principled position since 1893 -solidly demonstrated by Neumann and

Palmer, the research of Ashford and Macfarlane, and through the amendments of Senators Clark and Hoar — continue to be pursued. She would not relieve Dole, Smith, Thurston, Stevens, Morgan or Henry Cabot Lodge of the judgment of history. In her commitment to principle and with her knowledge of Washington, DC, she intended to return to carry on the fight.

She prepared to go home. Dole was appointed the new governor. More importantly, Hawaii was under a new form of franchise. An election was scheduled. The people could vote for members of the legislature and Hawaii's first delegate to the United States House of Representatives.

*

Liliuokalani returned to the United States in November 1901. She stopped in San Francisco to recover her health, still fragile. She was sixty-three years old. She borrowed money through mortgages, rented her property to ensure a flow of income to manage the debt, and traveled with more frugality. She relied on J.O. Carter to help her. [316]

The Queen also returned with a new sense of commitment. Annexation and the Organic Act were resolved. Restoration of the constitutional monarchy was no longer at stake. The fate of Hawaiian nationalism — her personification of it — and the Crown lands still were at stake. Paul Neumann had died and other claimants to the Crown lands were ignored as illegitimate. The elections in Hawaii had a predictable and favorable outcome: Native Hawaiians controlled the legislature. Three political parties had been formed. The Caucasians dominated the Republican Party; a group of native Hawaiians and Asians, including the Queen's nephew, Prince David, became Democrats; and Robert Wilcox, with a canny political acumen, formed the Independent or Home Rule Party. Wilcox's party prevailed. It controlled the legislature. Native Hawaiians had voted. Within a short period of time, Wilcox orchestrated the passage of a two-hundred and fifty thousand dollar payment to Liliuokalani for the Crown lands. Dole vetoed it. Wilcox then orchestrated a one-time fifteen thousand dollar payment to her to be paid over a two year period. The money was in the nature of an annuity. She appreciated his commitment and the temporary financial relief it provided. Wilcox also was elected Hawaii's delegate to Washington, DC. He would be entering a hostile environment. He was neither Caucasian nor shared the values of the Republican Party. He was, however, a reflection of Hawaiian unity at home and the responsible exercise of the franchise. Before the new legislative session began in Hawaii, a delegation from the Home Rule party had visited Liliuokalani at Washington Place. She received them in her reception room on the first floor. She spoke to a larger audience. She "urged her people to stand firm. In Robert Wilcox they had [a delegate] who would work for them in the United States. As for her, 'your interests will be my interests, as they always have been, and I shall ever stand by you as a loving mother. Be assured, my people, of my aloha, for it is real and lasting.'" [317]

She also had witnessed demographic change in Hawaii. Annexation was an invitation. European and American immigration was occurring. Asian immigration increased and Puerto Rico became a greater source of contract labor. The United States ensured stability. There was a naval presence. There was no threat of violence. The courageous effort by a small group of native Hawaiians and others in 1895 was nothing comparable to the unexpected insurrection by Emilio Aguinaldo for independence raging in the Philippines. [318]

When she reached Washington, DC, the Queen rented a private residence at 1517 20th Street. It was less expensive than Washington's hotels and would allow her more privacy. She had moved away from the conventional centers of power although physically she remained within a few blocks of the White House. It now had a new occupant: Theodore Roosevelt. He had his hands full in the Philippines. The Queen's friend Senator Hoar was involved in an ugly, contentious battle with both Roosevelt and Hoar's colleague from Massachusetts, Senator Lodge. It was not a quiet insider's fight.

In October 1899, at the Metropolitan Club, the same people who had held a tribute to Commodore George Dewey just before his departure for the Philippines exactly two years earlier reconvened in the same location. At the 1897 event, Dewey's friend, the chief clerk at the United States Court of Claims, Archibald Hopkins, "read a prophetic poem toasting the departure of the Commodore and predicting his return under the Admiral's flag." In the 1899 gathering, Hopkins read a new poem in tribute to Dewey's success in the war. Hopkins may have suggested Dewey should be a candidate for president. Dewey, it was rumored, discouraged the reference loud enough to make the *New York Times*. In order to clarify the inaccuracy of the newspaper account, Hopkins gave the poem to the *Times* for publication. One stanza read:

> An epoch on Times great clock
> The day he won his fight;
> Henceforth our Anglo-Saxon stock
> Keep step for law and right.

The United States had defeated Spain. Hopkins' erudition was legendary and his cultural perspective, expressed with clarity, was welcomed by those in attendance. By late 1901, however, the war had changed dramatically. Dewey's luster was displaced by something darker. Emilio Aquinaldo and his forces, which had cooperated with the United States to defeat Spain, had been informed that the United Sates intended to take control of the islands. Aquinaldo wanted independence. He was not subdued until March 1901. [319]

The news that was raging publicly when Liliuokalani arrived in the city in November was the acknowledged use of torture — water boarding — by American troops. Senator Hoar was at the forefront of those complaining. He had opposed the war. He got the Senate to authorize a broad-based investigation. Lodge eventually took control of it. Water boarding was documented fully and acknowledged by then Commissioner of the Philippines, William Howard Taft. Other people, "while conceding that American soldiers had engaged in 'cruelties,'" contended that the torture reflected the "barbaric sensibilities" inherent in the Filipinos. "I think I know why these things have happened," Senator Lodge offered in a senate speech. They had "grown out of the conditions of warfare, of the war that was waged by the Filipinos themselves, a semi civilized people, with all the tendencies and characteristics of Asiatics, with the Asiatic influence, and the Asiatic indifference to life, with the Asiatic treachery and the Asiatic cruelty, all tinctured and increased by three hundred years of subjection to Spain." Use of the water cure, as it was called, was the fault of the Filipinos. Taft's task, not easily accomplished and highly commended, was to ensure civility, education, and safety for the Philippine people. Through his very public criticism, Hoar, only a few years from serious illness, had lost his political credibility within the majority party. He would no longer be as helpful to the Queen as either of them wanted. She also may have wondered what might have occurred in Hawaii had she resisted America's intervention in the *coup d'état* in 1893.[320]

By 1902, Liliuokalani had been in the nation's capital, particularly its northwest quadrant, with considerable frequency and over long periods of time. Its geography and culture had become familiar to her. She made friends. Her correspondence with women especially had increased. She reflected a unique experience: Widowed and willing to socialize alone, a national leader and a queen, sophisticated in manner and intellect, loved and admired by her people with whom she fought for independence with grace, prudently and classically dressed, and an engaging conversationalist. She added an unexpected dimension to Washington's social life when she chose to engage in it. Politically she was persistent in temperament, unequivocally Hawaiian, and had access to men of power few women could aspire to except through marriage or moments of cordiality. She would need all her wits to continue this fight. In this impending round of politics and law, she also wanted a lawyer.

*

George Washington University was chartered by Congress in 1825. The nation's first president had left a modest endowment to support it. He wanted a national university that would educate civil servants and an academic tradition that would teach and encourage republican government and service to public purposes. President James Monroe and Congress had agreed. The university's law school was established in 1865, near the end of the Civil War. It was the first law school in the nation's capital.

By 1902, the law school had a solid faculty that included Justice John Marshall Harlan, author of the dissenting opinion in *Plessy v. Ferguson*. The law school's graduates were among the most knowledgeable and experienced in understanding how government worked and who within it made decisions. Among the law school's most prominent and successful graduates was Clarence Woods DeKnight. His office was in the Kellogg Building, a few blocks from the White House. Crammond Kennedy's office was in the same location.

DeKnight was born in Virginia. He had a range of noted skills. He conducted litigation in the local courts and was able to engage in formal administrative disputes before agencies of the government. He knew Congress. He had practiced before the court of claims. In all likelihood he knew Archibald Hopkins and the judicial approach of the court's members. He had both personal wealth and success at the bar. He traveled abroad yearly. He was recognized in social and charitable circles in Washington, New York, and Newport. He was a man of solid accomplishment and social charm. In 1902, he was thirty-five years old. When William O. Smith had retained him in 1899 and 1900 to provide intelligence, it was a prudent choice. [321]

It is unclear how DeKnight met Liliuokalani. She had been introduced to Colonel John Boyd, the Washington, DC, representative for Collis P. Huntington. Huntington was a financier and the owner of real estate and railroads throughout the nation. His business interest began in Sacramento, including with Charles Crocker and Leland Stanford. Liliuokalani knew Crocker from her early visit to San Francisco. On June 2, Boyd and Clarence DeKnight visited her at her residence to discuss the Crown lands claim and their offer to "bring my case before Congress." Hawaii's Delegate, Robert Wilcox, was there. She agreed to their offer. DeKnight would have been obligated ethically to inform her he had once been retained by Smith in a legal matter that he knew then or certainly now was antithetical or adverse to the Queen's interest, at least the way Liliuokalani viewed it. DeKnight's work for Smith also might have been viewed as an asset presuming he disclosed it to her. He knew Smith, must have met with him and evaluated his skills. He knew Smith had deep resources financially and, through others, substantial political and cultural relationships in Washington, DC. DeKnight also knew something of the subject matter of interest to the Queen.

The Queen may have recognized in DeKnight's temperament and approach to the law an attitude that engaged her. He was respectful of her knowledge, sought to learn and use it, and expected her to play a practical role in their strategy. He had one other virtue: DeKnight was in Washington, DC. She entered into an agreement with DeKnight and Boyd. It appears to have been a contingency; one-third "of what is won" and expenses provided by the Queen. Wilcox agreed to be helpful. They also seemed to accept that the presumed full market value of the lands — ten million dollars — was the underlying basis for the claim. [322]

The Queen and DeKnight began to plan their strategy. They would not liti-gate in the court of claims. They would approach Congress comprehensively. The vehicle for doing so was imminent and available. Governing Hawaii was going to require additional legislation from Congress to authorize local government, a new judicial system, rules governing the sale and lease of the Crown lands, and an assessment of what was needed at Pearl Harbor for the Navy. Congress also recognized the need to broadly assess the Dole administration. Only recently it had been reported that " the native majority [in the Hawaii legislative] was at variance with Governor Dole, and on the final day a resolution was passed asking the president [of the United States] to remove him from office." A delegation was sent to Washington to make the request directly. Obvious to Congress and the president was that this "small territory...has occupied a disproportionate amount of ...time." The Dole administration was at the "last extremity of financial embar-rassment [and] a political and social organism torn by factions." The problem was not only Dole's ineptitude or the native Hawaiian "deep, unchangeable hatred" of those who ensured the "loss of their nationality" or even the rupture in unity among the Caucasians who expected tranquility and acquiescence in exploiting the land. Part of the discord was a broad resentment "due to attempts to coerce, by men who were accustomed to controlling government officials....There is a 'star chamber' policy in the Dole government with no match on American soil." [323]

As expected by DeKnight, in June 1902 the senate authorized the committee on the Pacific Islands and Porto Rico [sic] to investigate the general conditions of the islands of Hawaii and the administration of its affairs. Through the interces-sion of Senator Hoar and the efforts by Clarence DeKnight and Robert Wilcox to define the inquiry, the members would examine "whether or not the former Queen...now possesses any legal or equitable right, title, or interest in [the Crown lands]" or "any claim against the United States, legal or equitable." The subcom-mittee would be chaired by Republican Senator John H. Mitchell of Oregon. The other members were Republican Senators Joseph Burton of Kansas and Addison Foster of Washington, and Democrat Senator Joseph Blackburn of Kentucky. The hearings were tentatively scheduled for September. Only Senators Mitchell, Burton, and Foster planned to attend. [324]

Liliuokalani needed allies and people to testify. De Knight also had a good deal to learn. He needed to plot a strategy. He expected roughly-hued adversaries who had the power of the Republican Party and more resources than the Queen could bring to bear. He also knew that in Hawaii Dole, Smith, and Thurston had control of the executive branch and its presumed connection to the president of the United States. The hearings would be held in Honolulu at the United States Naval Station. The Queen could go home.

CHAPTER 9. ON HALLOWED GROUND: CONGRESS IN HAWAII

The United States Navy had found comfort and duty in Hawaii. Coaling stations, equipped fully, manned and protected, were established near Diamond
Head and the Honolulu harbor. Sailors and marines no longer remained on ships
awaiting shore duty or leave. Barracks were constructed, small towns were laid
out, and fortifications expanded. Exploratory expeditions were undertaken to
Midway and Guam. Soundings were taken to determine the feasibility of a communications cable to Curzon. The Navy was authorized by Congress to take land
for expansion. Public land and Crown land were among those lands acquired.
Plans were laid for the further dredging of Pearl Harbor. "Naval Station, Hawaii"
was recognized in the Pacific lexicon. In July 1902, Rear Admiral William Henry
Whiting was placed in charge of the station. He had led forces to quell the insurrection for independence in the Philippines. Among Whiting's more imminent
duties was to welcome and accommodate the members of the senate committee
on the Pacific Islands and Porto Rico.[325]

The Queen and DeKnight began their preparations while she was in San Francisco awaiting the steamer for Honolulu. On June 29, he sent her the senate resolution identifying the committee's purpose and its composition. He had talked
"with Senator Burton," he wrote, "and he informed me that he expected to sail
from San Francisco" a few weeks before the hearing. DeKnight would depart on
the same vessel. DeKnight had scheduled a meeting with Senator Mitchell. DeK-
night also cautioned the Queen that there would be others on board or aware
of the committee's purpose and that "it would be well not to let these parties
know anything about the object of our visit." DeKnight followed up on July 3
— while the Queen was aboard the *China* steamer on her way home — to inform
her the committee had met in Washington, DC. DeKnight would "start with

Burton should he go in advance" of the other members. DeKnight also requested the Queen to recommend and secure local counsel of high caliber and skill as an oral advocate capable of examining witnesses in a contentious setting. DeKnight expected to call witnesses in order to substantiate her position on the illegality of the *coup d'état* and the role of the United States. The Queen chose the former judge A.S. Humphreys.[326]

Humphreys had been in Hawaii for only six years. He was from Mississippi. He held no government position under the Republic. He received his appointment as a circuit judge in the new Territory through the intervention of others in Washington. He had no admirers in the Dole Administration. Humphreys had sought to have Dole's attorney general impeached in 1899, and in 1901 Humphreys was attacked by the Hawaii Bar Association when he charged three members of the bar for contempt of court. Humphreys was thirty-three years old. The Queen agreed to pay him a flat fee. He would take the lead locally in preparing a memorandum setting forth the Queen's argument and, with DeKnight, conduct the examination.[327]

By late August, three members of the committee had arrived. DeKnight met with Humphreys to develop strategy. The Queen arranged for DeKnight to see parts of Hawaii. Emma Nawahi was his guide. Perhaps in a moment of deftly executed camaraderie and her own recognition of generational change she told him that her niece's friend, Noa Webster Aluli, had graduated from the University of Michigan law school and was accepted at Yale for a master degree. Aluli was planning to return to Hawaii to practice law. The Queen also received a note from George Macfarlane who was in Honolulu. Macfarlane had met the wife of Senator Burton. Macfarlane had impressed upon her the Queen's position on the "Crown lands case, and [she] will undoubtedly influence" her husband. Macfarlane also proposed she meet the Queen. "Mrs. Burton," he added, "bought your book in San Francisco and read it on the ship here." The Queen informed DeKnight. Senator and Mrs. Burton came to visit her at Washington Place.[328]

*

If there were any detached observers in the hall at the Naval Station, the hearings must have been a remarkable site to behold. Newspaper notices were published inviting "any citizen" to testify, submit written comments, and identify "subjects deemed important...to the betterment of the people and the government of the islands." Forty-three sessions were held over a twenty-five day period, mainly in Oahu but also on Maui, Lanai, Molakai, and Hawaii. One hundred and seventy witnesses testified. Dozens of written comments were received. Lawyers representing different parties, Humphreys and Hawaii's attorney general most notably, were allowed to examine any witness they chose. Decorum was required but not politeness. Senator Mitchell, the chairman, preserved a modicum of order. Criticism was leveled with confidence and certainty.[329]

Humphreys emerged almost at the outset as a force with which to be reckoned. He testified vehemently, with documented support, against the use of contract labor and the importation and mistreatment of Chinese and Puerto Rican immigrants brought to Hawaii on ships financed by the sugar planters. He read from reports of the "inhuman treatment" still not acted upon and the subsidy provided by the Dole Administration through the use of the police to enforce the contracts. The problem was exacerbated rather than lessened after annexation. The Hawaii Supreme Court, Humphreys explained, had decided that various protections of the United States constitution still did not apply in Hawaii, including the thirteenth amendment's prohibition against slavery.[330]

Humphreys also was the first witness to identify the existence and prevalence of the *ad hoc* appointment of lawyers to sit on Hawaii Supreme Court cases without taking an oath or subject to any form of objective scrutiny for ethical conflicts or prejudice. The cases, Humphreys continued, included "issues involving ... life and liberty, and some of the members of the bar who sat were young men right out of law school." Senator Foster asked: "And no appeal can be taken from their decision?" Humphreys: "No." A few moments later, Senator Foster asked: "And they were not really decided by men appointed by the president of the United States?" Humphreys: "No." "I should say [the system] is infamous," a current judge agreed, "and calculated to create dissatisfaction and distrust and cause very little weight or respect for the decisions of the supreme court in many instances."[331]

The judiciary was revealed as a self-perpetuating, closed, insider's game. This was the criticism that the Queen implied in wanting to change the judiciary in her proposed constitution. It was a change her adversaries could not tolerate then or now. The judicial system had been touted in the United States for its principled decision-making and relationship to Anglo-Saxon jurisprudence during the fight for annexation. As with the restrictions placed on the franchise, the United States was confronting the reality of what they had ignored and approved. Perhaps the committee members felt at that moment an indescribable, distinct shudder of discomfort. William O. Smith, there to monitor the proceedings on behalf of public and private clients, also was serving as the president of the bar association. He defended the practice. He, too, had become a judge under the arrangement.[332]

The committee heard testimony on the importance and need for county and local government and the election of local officials, especially from native Hawaiians. When Hawaii's attorney general testified, he acknowledged that "the government of this territory...probably [is] almost as much centralized as it was in France under Louis XIV." However, he continued, the government that "protects life, liberty, and property...is a good government whatever it may be, whether it is a monarchy, oligarchy, republic [or] democracy." Governor Sanford Dole took

a seat at the table. He opposed both local government and the value of electing officials. Senator Burton asked him for an explanation. "I think there are a
great many of [the native people]," Dole responded, "who find difficulty and
would be unequal to the task of electing executive officers." A colloquy ensued
between the two men that reflected Dole's parochialism and fear and the senators stunned response. America, Dole insisted under severe criticism, possessed
precisely the form of governance that existed currently in Hawaii. It should not
be changed.[333]

*

Clarence DeKnight introduce himself for the record. He introduced Judge
Humphreys, who already was well known to the audience and the committee.
Humphreys submitted a petition signed by the Queen. The petition explained
her ownership and interests in the Crown lands and the issue most critical to the
hearing: The role of the United States in the *coup d'état*. The petition estimated the
value of the Crown lands at twenty million dollars. Humphreys and DeKnight
also requested that the committee chairman require the Territory to produce all
relevant data on the size, nature, and value of the Crown lands and the proceeds
derived from their rental since January 1893. Senator Mitchell granted the request.
DeKnight explained that he and Humphreys intended to subpoena twenty-seven
witnesses that he and the committee could question. On September 17, as the
committee convened aboard the steamer *Claudine* on its way to another island,
DeKnight called Prince Kuhio. [334]

Kuhio was a candidate for Congress against Wilcox in the November election. Kuhio, the Queen's cousin who had been convicted and jailed for his participation in the *coup d'état*, had joined the Republican Party. It was the party of Dole,
Thurston, and Smith. Kuhio thus began to create a distinct center of political
power among native Hawaiians as well as a relationship with the forces that had
ensured annexation and thwarted the Queen. He also had a constituency that, in
critical ways, was antithetical to the Queen's interest. When asked previously
about the Crown lands claim, "he hedged nimbly: 'he wasn't sure;' 'he didn't have
the first-hand information;' 'he hadn't been present during certain transactions.'"
Kuhio was going to testify even if not called by Humphreys. Kuhio's party dominated the committee. [335]

The tone and content of Kuhio's testimony was subtle. In a matter of fact manner he contradicted the Queen's position about whether she retained an ownership interest after the *coup d'état* while positing that he was neither well informed
about the Crown lands nor in Honolulu when the *coup d'état* had occurred. His
caution emerged immediately and obviously. Senator Mitchell asked him, "Are
you acquainted with the claim that has been made by the Queen?" Prince Kuhio:
"Well. I have heard of it." When DeKnight asked him, "What is the sentiment
of the people...in regard to the claim for damages done by the United States in

landing troops...and for the Crown lands?" Kuhio answered, "From a Hawaiian point of view...they have always, as far as I know," supported the Queen. Later DeKnight asked him, "[D]o they feel that the United States damaged her?" Kuhio: "Well, I suppose that is the feeling...." Senator Mitchell interceded to attain clarity. "Were [the lands] held by the monarchy or any particular person...the Queen for instance?" Kuhio responded: "Oh, no." Mitchell: "The lands would not go to the heirs of the Queen?" Kuhio: "No; it goes with the Crown." [336]

DeKnight moved Kuhio to safer ground. He asked: "Do Hawaiians love the Queen....?" "Oh, yes," Kuhio replied. "So that they would be pleased to see her receive some recognition?" DeKnight followed up. Kuhio: "Yes; that is my belief." At this juncture Senator Burton moved the testimony toward what, presumably, he believed was a middle ground: The "act of grace." "Do you believe that if the Queen was paid in this way," Burton asked, "it would have a tendency to create a good feeling on the part of the Hawaiians — I mean the native Hawaiians — toward the American people?" Kuhio: "That is my belief." [337]

Other witnesses testified with more directness. The tone and documentation that Humphreys had provided on other subjects he planned to provide on the Crown lands. The testimony returned to the events of 1893, the illegality of the *coup d'état*, the correctness of the Queen's proposed changes to the constitution, and the decisive conduct of the United States. Other witnesses, men who had been there and experienced the events prepared to testify. There was legal and moral support for compensation for the Crown lands. Judge Gilbert Little testified that the Queen "should be indemnified for the loss of the Crown lands." When Senator Burton asked why, Little replied that "the overthrow of the monarchy... was without right and without any pretense of justice, and without warning or motive.....The Queen desired that her citizens should have one vote, without financial qualification, and should have that one vote counted — the same condition that existed in the South at the time of reconstruction." Senator Mitchell probed deeper. "It is generally understood everywhere in these islands that she could not have been overthrown except for the American Government?" Little: "Yes, sir; that is the sentiment." Judge Little felt the need for more explanation. "[A]fter dethroning her of course," he said, "the oligarchy cut off her income and made the Crown lands public lands...[and it is] the persistence of the United States government" that keeps them in power. They "have taken away from the Hawaiians their queen, their country, their flag, and everything that they held near and dear ... the last remaining, lingering sentiment in favor of their sovereign is that she be indemnified for the loss of the lands which belonged to her under the constitution of the country now merged in our own." [338]

Smith, Thurston and others were uncomfortable with the vehement tone and direction of the testimony and colloquy. Both resonated with a challenge to the *coup d'état* and the legitimacy of Dole's reign, the abuses and corruption that tempered the Territorial government, favoritism, and, by extension, Smith and Thurston's power and presumed legacy. The fate of the Crown lands was the thread that melded together the discord over the sovereignty and legitimacy that Smith thought was settled with finality in 1893, 1895, 1898, and 1900. The Queen had provoked the debate, and gave voice to a broader discontent. Damage had been done. The committee called an adjournment to the proceedings.

On the morning of September 23, the committee reconvened. Senator Mitchell announced to a startled crowd, except for those men in the room already privy to the committee's decision, that testimony concerning the "settlement of a sum of money" will be allowed to proceed only within a narrowed parameter. "Since no question can ever arise looking to the restoration of the monarchy," Senator Mitchell announced, "the committee is unanimously of the opinion that it is not necessary or proper to inquire through oral testimony at this time into the causes that led to the dethronement of the Queen and the part that the United States Government had in that matter, if any." The committee had determined that "evidence respecting her dethronement...are now matters of political history and official record, and upon that record of evidence must the question be determined, if its determination is necessary." The testimony that will be allowed, Senator Mitchell explained, related only to "The sentiment of the people...respecting the claim of the Queen and ...the wisdom and advisability...of recognizing her claim by making her some reasonable provision." [339]

DeKnight's strategy had been undermined. He knew that, in the end, Congress would make a political decision however melded into the terminology of law. The "act of grace" rationale as the decision's basis was a fragile argument standing alone. When Senator Mitchell made his announcement no doubt DeKnight and Humphreys already had been informed and, perhaps, even had an opportunity through Senator Burton to argue the need and political value of allowing the testimony as planned. There was no correlation between the testimony and evidence DeKnight planned to introduce and the restoration of the constitutional monarchy. The evidence was intended to support the claim for compensation and to support the argument in Congress that the legal substantiality of her position was too difficult to penetrate to justify the claim's denial. It was prudent for DeKnight to want the members to learn firsthand what had occurred, in the reality of the setting, from men who had witnessed the *coup d'état* or its effects. Senator Foster had not been in Congress in 1893, and the committee members would need the fullness of the experience of others to persuade their colleagues thousands of miles away in a setting filled with competing demands and agendas that the claim was justified fully. The witnesses all would testify under oath and be subject to examination by the Hawaii attorney general as well as the committee members. DeKnight, Humphreys, and Liliuokalani were confident of the record that would be made.

Perhaps unknown to DeKnight, except after the fact, was that in the evening of September 22, William O. Smith and Lorrin Thurston "spent three hours with the Senators showing them the reports of Blount and Morgan," and arguing "that the whole matter had been passed upon and the evidence in great detail was already in possession of the Senate." Smith, as he later wrote to his colleagues "in private correspondence," recognized immediately the risk involved in questioning what, for almost a decade, he and others had sought to settle. They still had not succeeded. He also must have appreciated, as DeKnight did, there was little likelihood members of Congress would take the time to analyze either the Blount or Morgan report or the testimony that both men had solicited. To Smith, the testimony he already had heard criticizing the Dole administration and the United States was "something like emptying rubbish into a waste barrel, or gathering the sewage in the sewer. It was rank time," he wrote," for all the disgruntled, the vicious and the discontent." Whether the senate committee agreed with Smith and Thurston's precise sentiments, it did agree to severely constrain the testimony. What followed was the elevation, now compelled, of approving a sum of money as an "act of grace" disconnected from the events of 1893. Even with such a constraint the testimony took on an unsuspected meaning. [340]

Many of the men who testified under this new rule were confined to assessing the obvious: How did native Hawaiians feel about the Queen getting a sum of money for an unarticulated wrong. In posing this question, however, the senators and DeKnight elevated a new correlation: The fate of Hawaii depended on the fate of the Queen's treatment and the Crown lands. Would native Hawaiians, the question was posed in various iterations, more likely feel good about the United States and the future of Hawaii's governance if a sum of money was provided. Former cabinet officials, Fred Wundenberg, and Prince David testified affirmatively to both propositions under questioning by Humphreys, DeKnight, and the committee members. [341]

Curtis Iaukea testified. He had been in King Kalakaua's cabinet and the personal chamberlain to the royal family. He agreed with both propositions while taking the position the Crown lands were not owned by the Queen but the revenues from the Crown lands were her private property. Delegate Robert Wilcox testified without equivocation that "The general feeling all over the country, all classes of people, is to give the Queen a big compensation for the loss of the Crown lands and her position as Queen." Humphreys asked, "What would be the effect of such a settlement by the United States....?" Wilcox, intent on making his point, responded that "The Territorial Government got out of the Crown lands in the last ten years nearly $1,000,000 and that $1,000,000 would all go to the Queen." Humphreys asked again, "What the effect would be?" Wilcox: "To harmonize the people here in their feeling and make a good feeling toward the United States." [342]

In support of the "act of grace" theory and the benefit to Hawaii's governance, everyone who had supported the *coup d'état* testified in support of the Queen. Lorrin Thurston, William O. Smith, and Governor Sanford Dole were among them. Providing money would be "a very honorable and gracious thing" and "wise policy." For Lorrin Thurston, what happened in 1893 "is passed and gone." Dole was perhaps the most candid. When asked the sentiment of the people toward the Queen, Dole answered: "I am not very intimately acquainted with it." Under questioning by Senator Mitchell and probably coaxed by Smith and Thurston, Dole agreed it "would do a great deal toward smoothing down some of the irritation caused by overthrowing their government." [343]

J.O. Carter testified. Judge Humphreys asked whether the Queen was "a lady of fortune?" "Not at all," Carter replied. She had encumbrances on her property, made payments on loans, and supported older Hawaiians and others in her care. She had about two thousand dollars in available cash and "her income for six years is about $13, 000." The official accounting of the size, nature, and revenue from the Crown lands also was admitted into evidence. DeKnight was able to produce credible testimony that, contrary to the previous low estimates by the government, the value of the Crown lands was between twenty and twenty-five million dollars. Whatever sum the committee might decide upon would have credible economic data to support it. More importantly, the visibility of the land's fate and treatment going forward made it more difficult for Dole and his colleagues to sell it to private interests. [344]

When the hearings on Oahu came to an end, and before the committee prepared to move again to another island, Senator and Mrs. Burton returned to Washington Place "to say goodbye." Clarence DeKnight escorted them. They experienced the beauty and culture reflected in her home and the Queen's graciousness as a host and depth as an intellect. They saw the manner in which she had melded the Hawaiian character of her life into the classic nature of her home's internal décor and external architecture and gardens. Perhaps they also sat with her among the flowers and leafy shade in the high-backed rattan chairs that she was pictured in at various moments since the end of her reign. Senator Burton, the Queen wrote at the end of a momentous day, "assured me of [the] success of [the] claim to [the] C[rown] Lands. It was a sad parting."[345]

*

Clarence DeKnight accompanied the committee members back to San Francisco. After they departed for home — the Burtons to Kansas, Senator Mitchell to Oregon, and Senator Foster to Washington — DeKnight settled in at the Palace Hotel. He wrote to the Queen. His letter reflected a tentative confidence in getting the claim acted upon favorably. He expected Humphreys to prepare a brief of law for his own use and wanted the Queen to encourage its preparation. DeKnight discouraged her and Humphreys from making any public statements. The Queen's additional responsibility was to compile all her expenses, determine the value of the property she was forced to sell while in prison, and list her outstanding debt, including any "Royal" debt incurred while she was in office and was obligated to pay. DeKnight also wanted her to ensure that the Hawaii legislature made no further effort to approve a "lump sum" payment. There should be no basis for the committee to assume the United States had no obligation for its actions. He wanted to be certain that nothing disrupted the difficult task that lay ahead in Washington, DC.[346]

DeKnight wanted the Queen to return to Washington, although the precise political and social path to follow once arriving was uncertain. The full Pacific Islands' committee had to approve any bill submitted to the senate. The committee's chairman was Senator Foraker. The bill also would have to be approved by the senate appropriations committee because money from the United States Treasury would be expended. DeKnight and Colonel Boyd expected to meet with Senators Mitchell and Burton on October 29, after they returned to Washington. Robert Wilcox, who also had stopped at Washington Place to bid goodbye to the Queen, agreed to be supportive when he returned after the election in early November. DeKnight had one last message: Senator and Mrs. Burton "wished to be kindly remembered...and the thanks of Senator Mitchell for the flowers."[347]

By the first week in November, Liliuokalani was on the steamer for San Francisco. She already may have known that Prince Kuhio had defeated Robert Wilcox. Kuhio would be the new delegate to Congress starting in March. Wilcox would remain in office until Kuhio was sworn in. The Queen would soon lose a supporter who was still evolving in his capacity as the nation's representative albeit with some personal difficulty. Kuhio's victory only elevated the correctness of her decision to retain Boyd and DeKnight. She also must have sensed a tentative form of completeness. What had occurred at the hearings had affirmed the persistence with which she embraced the claim for the Crown lands. Her principled argument was now part of the Congressional dialogue and the basis for expectation in Hawaii. She had not wavered on the argument's correctness.[348]

After a brief respite at the California Hotel, she boarded a train to cross the United States. Robert Wilcox, she noted to herself, would ensure the Hawaii legislature did not act. She identified two men who could sign affidavits "showing that Minister Stevens was offering [her] money" to acquiesce in the *coup d'état,* a fact that "should not get to the ears of the opposition" until it was timely to do so. She itemized and calculated her debt at eighty-five thousand dollars. She had sold twenty-seven thousand dollars in bonds and property between 1893 and 1900 to manage her obligations. DeKnight may have wanted to use this information in private discussions with members of the committee.[349]

The *New York Times* noted her arrival in Washington the evening of November 23 at the Ebbitt House Hotel. She had rented a home at 1517 20th Street. For a few days, however, she would recuperate and think. She also could experience some joy and unencumbered moments in the heart of the city. She had ensured that the legitimacy of the *coup d'état* and its leadership were questioned into the twentieth century.[350]

CHAPTER 10. ON DISTANT GROUND: CONGRESS IN WASHINGTON, DC

Into the late nineteenth century the Ebbitt House Hotel, located on the corner of 14th and F Streets, was among Washington's more eclectic and interest-
ing addresses. A bookstore, cafes, and townhouses defined the streetscape. The
indigenous urban sounds of horse and carriage, bicycles, delivery carts, and the
steely screech and rumble of the growing streetcar service nearby mixed in a
rough smoothness with tourists, some irascible, inquisitive, or lost, and people,
directed, worried or anticipatory in mood, walking to the commercial offices next
door. The exterior of the Ebbitt was in the Second French Empire style with an
enlarged mansard roof. In form, the exterior was now American in character with
the stars and stripes unfurled daily. The Ebbitt House resembled the executive
office building adjacent to the White House. There was a presumption of *gravitas*
and the subtle exercise of power among its diners and in its private rooms. William McKinley had stayed there before his inauguration. The Ebbitt also "was a
favorite of journalists, and their offices on the ground and basement floors had
become known as 'Newspaper Row.'" Their presence explained why, on the day
of Liliuokalani's arrival, the *New York Times* reported her presence and purpose.
That same evening the Queen was visited by Clarence DeKnight. His office was
less than a block away.[351]

DeKnight reported that he and Colonel Boyd had met with Senators Mitchell
and Burton. Both senators were "pleased" with the investigation and that "everything promises success." DeKnight returned repeatedly to gather facts and opinions and test the Queen's recollection, including a "long conversation about the
constitution" that she sought to promulgate in 1893. On December 1, the Queen
moved to 1517 20th Street and within a month to 1508 21st Street only a few blocks
away. She was closer to apartment houses and the Georgetown section of the

city than she had been before. DeKnight continued to visit or telephone her with news. The most critical news was that the committee report on its investigation in Hawaii was presented to the senate on December 14 and a bill for the claim was expected to be submitted by Senator Blackburn of Kentucky. He was on the committee but had not made the trip to Hawaii. Blackburn was in Congress at the time of the *coup d'état*.[352]

The report was predictable, problematic, and enlightening. The committee members, without dissent , found that the Dole administration bore little relationship to "a government republican in form." It was "un-American." Dole had aggregated power away from departments of government and the legislature. Neither entity could serve its purpose. The new Territory had, the committee believed, "many of the old elements of monarchy." The time had arrived "when the real interest of the people of Hawaii require that many...of these old, ancient, unrepublican, and undemocratic forms and practices should be eliminated.... [T] here are among very many of the leading men of the islands — as well as those in power — evidentially a strong disposition to adhere with a strange degree of pertinacity to the old forms." The committee report recognized that the "common people of Hawaii are intelligent, educated, and discriminating." The committee also believed it essential to point out that — contrary to William O. Smith's characterization during the debate on the Organic Act — native Hawaiians were "not a product of the tropics but [are], like the white man, a product of the temperate zone." They "have been rightfully led to believe, and do believe, that by annexation there has been opened the right to a more enlarged participation," that Dole and others had denied them. The committee proposed changes to the structure of the Territorial government and the creation of county and local government. They also may have suspected that, with the proper encouragement, it would not be much longer before Dole moved on to something else.[353]

The subtle but corrosive problem for the Queen, Boyd, and DeKnight was that the analogue to the "old elements of the monarchy," however well intentioned as a criticism, was inaccurate. Participation in voting, an active legislative process, and the responsiveness of departments to "the common people" during the reign of Kalakaua and Liliuokalani easily exceeded, even under the 1887 constitution, similar attributes of governance permitted under the provisional government, the Republic or the new Territory. Congress failed to look deeper or recognize the history and culture of the men who administered and influenced Hawaii. Candor — or more studied familiarity with Hawaii's constitutional experience and the history rather than presumptions of the missionary conduct and values — would have taken the committee back to America, actually to a time period before it became the United States, to find the proper analogue. It was unlikely, however, that the Republicans on the committee or in Congress would have been capable at this late date of such an acknowledgement. A modest albeit still inaccurate analogue of what the committee might have been thinking was relied upon by Hawaii's attorney general: The reign of Louis XIV. To some members of the committee and Congress, however, the constitutional character and limitations that defined the Hawaii monarchy never existed. Unless you knew her and Hawaii's history, Liliuokalani had been a mere monarch and her reign void of elections, parties, dissent, rules, civility, or a judiciary. The burden on her to be known continued to be critical. Being in Washington, DC, was essential.

Contrary to the implication of the rule it imposed restricting testimony and evidence during the hearings in Hawaii, the committee reached conclusions concerning the title to the Crown lands and the title that now was vested in the United States. The committee stated baldy that "the legal and equitable title" to the Crown lands was in the United States; that "legal title...never vested *personally* in the former Queen Liliuokalani;" that "the establishment of a provisional government" was recognized not only by the "people of Hawaii" but also the Queen; and, that "all legal claim of the late Queen [was] at once and forever cut off" by the formation of the Republic. Consequently, "whatever allowance is made to the ex-Queen...must rely solely upon considerations of national grace [and] public and private justice."[354]

The committee identified the 1864 Hawaii Supreme Court decision and the 1865 Act prohibiting the sale of the Crown lands. The committee analyzed both actions with the same selective use of facts that had tempered the approach Sanford Dole and William Alexander had taken before and after the *coup d'état*. The Queen, this approach supported, had no personal title to the Crown lands when she ascended to the monarchy. The committee's course of reasoning — if it existed — was unavailable to public scrutiny. Similar conclusions but no meaningful evidence or analysis had been presented by some witnesses during the hearing in Hawaii but precisely opposite conclusions were presented by others including the Queen. Judge Humphreys and Clarence DeKnight had sought a serious fact-finding inquiry and something in the nature of a trial and exchange of legal analysis during the same hearings. Their goal was to educate the committee and provide an evidentiary basis for decision. Their effort was denied. Instead the committee report, now suspect in its substantive content and the process relied upon to reach its conclusions, reflected political law intended perhaps to diminish or eliminate opposition to the appropriation of money the senators wanted for the Queen. One critical consequence of this approach and the conclusions reached was that the committee could avoid the most delicate and contentious issue in Congress and for the president and his party: The legality and morality of the role played by the United States in the *coup d'état*.[355]

Unexpectedly, however, the Queen's persistence — and the committee's acknowledgement that there can be "no question...native Hawaiians" believed the "overthrow of the monarch [was] due mainly to the aid given the then insurgents by the ...United States Government" — meant that providing money to the Queen was essential to the fate of Hawaii as a governable territory. Without recognition of the claim, there would not be "complete harmony among the people... so very necessary to...good government in the new territory." Having elevated the importance of the claim, the committee believed that making "some reasonable provision" for Liliuokalani would be not only an "act of grace" but an act of "wisdom." The committee unanimously supported providing two hundred thousand dollars for the Queen. The consolation for Boyd and DeKnight was that, however fragile the argument, the committee would make it to the Senate on the Queen's behalf.[356]

On January 23, Delegate Robert Wilcox visited the Queen at her private residence. An opportunity had presented itself that she chose to take. It was visiting day at the White House. Apparently together, Liliuokalani and Wilcox visited President Roosevelt and his wife. She wrote later that evening that it was a brief visit. It also was essential to her purpose for being in Washington.

On February 9, Senator Blackburn introduced a bill "for payment to Liliuokalani...in full satisfaction of all claims, or pretended claims, two hundred thousand dollars." The bill was referred to the senate committee on appropriations for review. Both DeKnight and Wilcox were pleased. If the money was approved, Wilcox hoped, "it will suffice for now — later another [effort] will be made." The evening before the bill was introduced the Queen noted in her diary that William O. Smith was "in town to lobby."[357]

The bill took a turn toward uncertainty. Republican Senator John Spooner of Wisconsin raised an objection in the appropriations committee. DeKnight was not sure why. Spooner had a long history of "paternalism" with respect to Native Americans, blacks, and the peoples of the Philippines and Puerto Rico. He, along with other Republicans like Senator Lodge or Senator Orville Platt of Connecticut, had abandoned what little pretense remained for the party's once professed support for civil rights, especially when the decision involved areas outside the nation's borders. Senator Foraker, once a stalwart supporter of the same approach, had modestly altered his views. He was the chairman of the full Pacific Islands and Porto Rico Committee and within limits — reflected in the committee's willingness to do everything necessary to avoid examining the role of the United States — was prepared to support a payment to the Queen. On February 26, when the bill passed out of the appropriations committee with a favorable vote it passed the senate without debate. Spooner's objection did not materialize on the Senate floor. "Rejoice and praise the Almighty," the Queen noted the same day.[358]

DeKnight still had to be uneasy. No appropriation for the Queen was contained in the appropriations bill approved in the House of Representatives. In a process fraught with the exercise of often stealth maneuvering and motives, the two bills were sent to a "conference committee" to be reconciled. In an appropriations bill where members and the president are often at odds regardless of the merit of a particular appropriation, few members are prepared to risk a fight unless it touched deeply into their own interest. The conference committee was composed of three members of the senate and three members of the House. It was their obligation to reconcile the differences in the two bills and then report them back to their respective bodies for a new vote. An objection was raised in the conference committee by Congressman Robert Hitt of Illinois. Hitt had been a member of the committee that included Senator Morgan of Alabama and Sanford Dole that was responsible for recommending a governing structure for Hawaii in 1898. Hitt also had a working if not personal relationship with William O. Smith.[359]

On February 28, late in the afternoon, Wilcox and Boyd visited the Queen. "Boyd asked who the enemies are who would enter objections…Wilcox said — W.O. Smith." Boyd, Wilcox, and DeKnight would try to block Smith's efforts. Senator Hoar told the Queen he supported the appropriation. Senator Blackburn continued his effort, acknowledging on the senate floor, perhaps in a moment of candor and pique and abandoning the committee's report, that "no dethronement would have occurred and the United States would not have appropriated to itself the rentals had it not been for the landing of the United States marines…." By March 3, the claim had failed. The bill never got out of the conference committee. DeKnight came to see the Queen. The claim, he told her, "was blocked by Rep[resentative] Hitt — because of W.O. Smith." There may have been other factors but Smith had found a receptive advocate in Hitt. The Queen felt she had been "maligned." The notion expressed publicly by Smith, Thurston, and Dole during the hearings in Hawaii that an "act of grace" was essential lost its seeming imperative in the quiet confines of the United States Congress.[360]

DeKnight reported that Senators Blackburn, Burton, and Mitchell were prepared to try again when Congress reconvened in the winter. Liliuokalani settled into her disappointment and considered her next move. Prince Kuhio would soon be in Washington as the new delegate from Hawaii. Robert Wilcox's loss also would mean the Hawaii legislature would be less likely to provide any assistance. She was uncertain whether Kuhio would either. She knew Wilcox would not challenge Kuhio in two years. He already had suffered serious health problems that seemed chronic.

On March 8, James Blount died. He had stopped practicing law after he completed his investigation in 1893 and returned to his home in Macon. "He was a wealthy man, and one of the largest landowners in Middle Georgia. He [left] a widow, two sons, and daughters," one obituary read. His land was special to his identity and comfort and his legacy. His work in Hawaii and his belief in its independence remained a valued, principled accomplishment that he continued to share with his children. A decade had passed since his report. Perhaps, in her reflection, the Queen found some moment of warmth and remembrance in learning that James Blount had named his home *Hale Nui*, Hawaiian for "the big house."[361]

*

In November, the Queen returned to the United States. Her spring and summer had been devoted largely to property maintenance especially problems with drainage and resolving an offer to rent some of her land. Her train had stopped in Chicago. The reason for her visit, the *Boston Daily Globe* reported, "is a mystery." The passage of time had not diminished the ease of her attaining notoriety. She sought to manage it. Her assistant whom she brought with her informed the *Globe* that "she is not giving her claim a thought. All that she could do with propriety in that direction has been done." She arrived in Boston on November 16. She was a guest of Mr. and Mrs. William Lee in Brookline. Mr. Lee was a cousin to her husband, John. She had found a form of comfort in Boston not, it appears, because she was attracted to the city but because her husband's family had embraced her. She had learned more about his family's origins in an area outside of Trieste, Italy, in or near the Austrian border and the Dalmatian coastline. She had not visited Boston since the winter of 1896, the *Globe* noted. She was expected to receive "a cordial welcome" from intimate friends. By November 24, she was in Washington. She took a room at the Ebbitt House Hotel before moving to the private residence she had rented. A few days before her arrival, Senator Blackburn had introduced a bill "to pay to Liliuokalani...in full satisfaction and discharge of all claims, legal and equitable, two hundred thousand dollars."[362]

The Queen continued to rely upon DeKnight and Boyd. Prince Kuhio agreed to accompany DeKnight to a meeting with the Queen to discuss strategy. Kuhio was kept informed. The bill introduced by Senator Blackburn was referred to the Pacific Islands and Porto Rico Committee. The bill was reported out favorably on January 15, 1904. In order to diminish the uncertainty an identical bill was introduced in the House of Representatives by Kuhio. Liliuokalani had chosen, once again, to subject herself to the unsettling, disquieting uncertainty of the legislative process in Washington. At stake was a principle she believed in and, despite the committee report's argument she had no legal or equitable claim, Senator Blackburn's bill stated plainly that the money she would receive would be in "full satisfaction and discharge of all claims, legal and equitable." Her interest in governance and politics which emerged in her teenage years and were honed especially during her brother's reign had not diminished. She had a cause that was critical to her position that the 1893 *coup d'état* was illegal, and now a committee report that correlated the fate of her treatment with the fate of Hawaii as a governable territory. She had a particular bill around which to form and direct her skill, and an ability to create impressions and change minds in order to aid her attorney and others in accomplishing her purpose. She had not succeeded in resolving her claim. But she seemed to embrace doing it in the capital of the United

States against the United States. In the long view she was creating a memory and an example for others to follow. She knew it. She also was acutely aware of her age, her financial fragility, and that fine line, a razor's edge perhaps, between pursuing this cause and risking a debilitating ridicule. She was not there yet and, it might safely be presumed, she would know intuitively when that moment was about to arrive.[363]

On February 12, the debate in the senate began. Immediately Senator Platt of Connecticut sought by amendment to eliminate any expressed correlation between the payment to the Queen and the "full satisfaction and discharge" of her claims. "The purpose of the amendment," Senator Platt said to his colleagues, "was to [make] clear the payment was a gift.....I do not think she has any claim, legal or equitable." Blackburn and Platt were lawyers. Blackburn agreed only that she had no legal claim. Senator Hoar, also a lawyer, added that "I think myself the ex-Queen has equitable rights." Hoar turned to Platt. Blackburn interrupted. He wanted Platt to know the Pacific Islands committee had agreed unanimously "she has a well-grounded equitable claim."[364]

Blackburn was moving toward the only argument the committee report had allowed: An "act of grace." Senator Spooner started to expose the limitations imposed by the report. "Does the committee predicate anything upon the theory that she was dethroned by the United States?" Blackburn: "No." The effect of the choice Senators Mitchell and Burton made in Hawaii — either to satisfy Smith and Thurston or because they believed their choice would yield an outcome they could sell to their colleagues — was a flawed strategy. Once relieved of having to confront the culpability of the United States, Spooner and Platt had a simple rejoinder that could appeal to those members who did not sit through the hearings in Honolulu or Hilo or on Molakai and had matters of more personal urgently that warranted their attention and the need !for votes.

The Queen's interest was taken by the provisional government and then the Republic, Spooner and Platt said. The United States acquired the Crown lands almost six years later without conditions or limitations or liens. The United States had done nothing wrong. Blackburn strained to adhere to the committee position. "I have very decided convictions in my own mind," about the responsibility of the United States for the overthrow but, Blackburn continued, "that is beside the question presented by this committee." In the absence of a role by the United States in 1893, there was no equitable argument to fairness or justice. The meaning of the 1864 Hawaii Supreme Court decision or the 1864 Act of the Hawaii legislature were not part of the debate with respect to what would be legal or equitable. Senator Mitchell interceded. He said that "nothing could go so far to harmonize matters in that new part of our country" than to recognize the claim. His argument, once central to the committee's rationale for acting, seemed diminished in the context of the debate's evolution. Perhaps at that moment Senator Blackburn lamented not making the trip to Hawaii or agreeing in committee to the "act of grace" rationale that its Republican members believed essential. Mitchell could only say to Spooner that "our government has become the beneficiary of her misfortune." Spooner, no doubt sensing the burden Mitchell was forced to support, went deeper into exposing its weakness. "Perhaps," Spooner began, "the Republic committed suicide and became merged with the United States....Perhaps," he added, "they who dethroned her...would be glad to have some other purse than theirs open to reparation for their wrong."[365]

A motion was made to recommit the bill to the committee on Pacific Islands for further study. Through a calculated maneuver the motion was defeated by a vote of sixteen to recommit and nineteen to continue the debate. Fifty-five members did not vote. There was, as the senate terms it, the absence of a quorum; that is, not enough members to ensure a proper vote. The bill was still alive. On February 15 the same motion to recommit was subjected to another vote. The motion was defeated again. Twenty-three members voted to recommit; twenty-six members voted to continue the debate. Another amendment was introduced to diminish the amount paid to the Queen to one hundred and fifty thousand dollars. The amendment passed without a roll call vote of individual senators. Finally the vote on Senator Blackburn's original bill with a reduced payment came before the senate. The vote was twenty-six members for it and twenty-six members against it. The bill did not pass. Among those voting against it was Senator Hoar's colleague, Henry Cabot Lodge. Among those voting for it was Mrs. Foraker's husband, Joseph.[366]

On February 16, Senator Hoar wrote a note to the Queen expressing his disappointment and letting her know he intended to request a member who had voted against the bill to ask that the vote be reconsidered. He was disappointed as well that he was not able to speak forcibly in support of the claim. He also had recognized and commended her for the care she provided to dependent children and friends. She found it "gratifying to know the interest you take in my behalf," she said in reply. She wrote him that "having dependents who I feel a moral obligation to aid — especially children of my friends and members of my court whom I desire to educate" was gratifying although it required "a good deal of self-sacrifice on my part." She also added that she hoped "Senator Foraker will also [have] an opportunity to speak." Senator Hoar was able to convince one member who voted against the bill to ask for reconsideration. Hoar could not get additional support. The bill was defeated. Twenty-three members voted for it; twenty-seven members voted against it. The vote would be the last gesture of support Senator Hoar would make on behalf of Liliuokalani. His illness took him back home to Massachusetts more frequently. His voting record and view of civil rights in and outside of the United States separated him further from his party. She would soon lose a friend and advocate.[367]

On March 18, the Queen wrote to J.O. Carter. In a manner typical of the form and cadence of their correspondence she expressed her concern about the state of her properties and anxiety about finances. They would have added only to her disappointment over the loss in Congress and her unease about the future. The same sensitivity was reflected in a previous letter to Carter in early February. Her script had remained concisely drawn and her willingness to express her thoughts still reflected a candor between old friends separated by a vast continent and ocean. At that moment she was in a different world that Carter understood only through their letters and talks when she was home. They shared intimately a cultural bond and a depth of knowledge about each other accumulated over many years of tumult and friendship. In the previous letter, she had expressed gratitude to her creditors "for not insisting on immediate payment in full," and understanding her commitment to ensure she would fulfill her obligations. In a thoughtful insight to the life she had led and the personal and public obligations she still had, she also wrote to Carter that "I am very thankful for all the benefits that I am enjoying and for all the good friends who have helped to make my life endurable. The 'Giver' of all good things has truly been merciful."[368]

*

In early May, Liliuokalani left Washington. She had decided to visit the world's fair in St. Louis, Missouri, organized to celebrate the one hundredth anniversary of the Louisiana Purchase. Planning and construction took much longer than the people of St. Louis anticipated. The fair had been extended well into 1904. It is unclear what the Queen expected. Perhaps she thought it would be a unique experience embraced by America's cosmopolitan cities to display their strength and accomplishment and to offer a place, an opportunity and even some funding for innovative thinkers to display their ideas for the first time. Chicago had done it in a variety of ways, especially in its introduction of a new architectural vision lead by Daniel Burnham and Frederick Law Olmsted. She would have seen and experienced some of their work in Washington in the new railroad station Burnham designed and the remarkable alteration already emerging in Washington's parks and urban design that Olmsted had crafted. She probably already had read about the large Ferris wheel at the fair and the Palace of Electricity or perhaps she was interested in listening to the music of John Philip Souza or trying an "ice cream cone." The remarkable photography of Jesse Tarbox Beals also was being published. Perhaps, too, she wanted to find a productive diversion that would allow her to reflect on the Crown lands claim before she returned to Honolulu.

She took the train to St. Louis. By all reports the Queen had expected to stay a few weeks. Within a short period after arriving, she was reported to have taken ill and restricted her activities. The cause of the illness was left vague. In addition to the grandeur, she may have witnessed in her brief stay a display of cultural and racial denigration that was the subject of protest and severe public criticism. In the compelling need to promote anthropological research and to demonstrate the breadth of America's accomplishments and conquests in the world, expansive villages of Filipinos, Africans, Eskimos, and other native cultures were created. A display of cannibalism was concocted for public excitement. Some Filipinos had been denied warm clothing during their trip across the country. They became ill. Some died. In promotional photographs and art work, the characteristically "savage" dark-skinned people of these foreign cultures were contrasted with the "civilized American" of Anglo-Saxon stock. In "using America's new imperial image, the world's fair's sponsors 'exploit[ed] the wonders of the colonial possessions.'" This world view also may have been a source of the Queen's discomfort and disappointment.

Within a few days Liliuokalani left St. Louis to return to her native Hawaii.[369]

CHAPTER 11. DISQUIETING CHARADE: THERE IS NO LAW FOR YOU

In November 1904, the United States elected Theodore Roosevelt to a full term as president and Senator Charles Warren Fairbanks as vice president. The election was an affirmation of increasing America's naval prowess. Only a few months earlier, Japan had used its naval skill to surprise and stymie the Russian fleet at Port Arthur, Korea. European nations that already possessed sophisticated naval armaments entered into a fervent competition to expand further. Domestic opposition to the exercise of America's military strength abroad diminished noticeably.

The Democratic Party had nominated Alton B. Parker, the chief judge of the New York Court of Appeals, perhaps in the expectation he would challenge Roosevelt in his home state. The Republicans anticipated such a move. At their convention in Chicago, United States Speaker of the House of Representatives Joseph Cannon from Illinois had Roosevelt nominated by the Republican governor of New York whom Roosevelt disliked. Cannon also had orchestrated a solid victory for Roosevelt at the convention, including the vote of one of the Illinois' delegates to the convention, Fenton Whitlock Booth of Marshall, Illinois. Booth's cousin was Booth Tarkington, who already had provided a definition of America as seen through the simpler, small town life in *Gentleman from Indiana* that included — and would, more so, in time — stories about Tarkington's childhood experiences with his cousin Fenton. Booth, a graduate of the University of Michigan Law School, had returned home to practice law in Marshall. Perhaps drawing off a family history — his uncle had been the governor of California and later its United States senator — Booth entered politics. He had been a state legislator and become a close friend of Cannon's by the time of Roosevelt's nomination. Booth was thirty-five years old. Cannon sought to make him a federal judge.

The position went to someone else. Cannon promised that he could convince Roosevelt, once elected in his own right, that Booth should get an appointment to the United States Court of Claims in Washington.[370]

The Anti-Imperialist League had decided to support the Democrat candidate if the party would adopt the League's position that the Philippines should be "free and independent to work out their own destiny." The Democrats agreed. The Republicans affirmed their party's conduct in the Philippines. The party's platform read: "[W]e have suppressed insurrection, established order...[and] civil liberty, and enabled the United States to exercise influence in China" through the navy. The Alton B. Parker strategy and the aid of the League failed. Roosevelt captured fifty-six percent of the vote and carried thirty-two states including his native New York. Roosevelt also carried Illinois. On March 17, 1905 — within two weeks of his inauguration — Roosevelt appointed Fenton Booth to the United States Court of Claims. The first person who likely greeted Booth — after the reigning chief justice and his colleagues — and from whom Booth would have learned the machinations and culture of the court was the chief clerk, Archibald Hopkins.[371]

Roosevelt's victory confirmed an attitude that had emerged with the acquisition of Hawaii. The United States had few constraints in notions of morality or civil rights or elementary principles of international law that should impede the full attainment of the nation's commercial objectives and definition of security. The debates in Congress were about which kind of ships in which ocean should be built that would best serve the nation's future. Hawaii had become a place for tourists, investors, and immigration, and a critical naval station. Sanford Dole — the formal, visible remnant of a disruptive past -was appointed a federal judge. Native Hawaiians were voting regularly and held civil service positions throughout the islands. Within the broad framework of Alfred Thayer Mahan's late nineteenth-century vision, Hawaii was secure, tranquil, and no longer a source of unease in Washington. In November 1904, when Liliuokalani arrived in San Francisco, there was little in the national temperament that ensured the historical distinctiveness of the Crown lands taken through the conduct of the United States would receive appropriate attention. Her physical presence in the nation's capital remained critical to ensure the visibility and imperative of the claim.[372]

Liliuokalani was not without resources. She still retained a formal agreement with John Boyd and Clarence DeKnight. Prince Kuhio, who had accompanied her to Washington, had been reelected as Hawaii's delegate to Congress and available to her. Kuhio had developed some friendships although he was still constrained by seniority, his race, and the ease of access that other men in Hawaii already had with senior members of Congress. The Queen also could move graciously in Washington's rarified social milieu when necessary. Her financial resources had diminished. She and J.O. Carter agreed she would receive six hundred dollars a month during her stay, which he would wire to her. Together they preserved a studied frugality. The amount would deplete her modest cash resources in a few months. There also were realities she understood and witnessed. Native Hawaiians remained disconnected from the land, which was increasingly controlled by sugar plantations and real estate and commercial firms. It was no longer within her authority to resolve those problems and she was too constrained financially to affect their resolution. Her persistence in Washington would ensure or make clear — perhaps in a grating and, for some, discomforting way — that neither she nor the native Hawaiian people were content with conditions in their nation. On January 13, 1905, Senator Blackburn "submitted an amendment providing for the payment of the claim of Liliuokalani." It was referred to the committee on appropriations.[373]

Her conduct and correspondence in Washington made plain she also had come for a respite. In Washington, friendships were less demanding, defined by newer experiences at a different age than in Hawaii. The reality of her condition as a deposed monarch was less visible, easier to manage in her daily social interactions, especially when she moved into residential areas where a walk to the park or a carriage ride to the American Security and Trust Bank did not require an explanation about her recent loss in Congress or the invariable glance of sadness. She also liked the weather and Washington's greenery. In February, she wrote to Carter of possibly returning in late March. In mid-March she decided to stay for two more months. "The weather has been lovely the past week," she wrote, "and with the change I find my health as much better....The buds on the trees are already coming out in some places which promise a pleasant spring." She wanted to experience it. On March 18, she attended the wake of Senator William Brimage Bate, a Democrat of Tennessee. Bate, like Senator John Morgan, had fought at Chickamauga as well as the first battle of Manassas and the battle of Shiloh. The Queen had befriended him. She also knew Bate's wife and visited her home to express her sorrow. "I have not forgotten the kind interest he took in my cause and was very active in trying to make it pass," she wrote Carter. The wake was held at the Ebbitt House. She also noted that the inauguration of President Roosevelt had occurred and "Everything since...seems to have quieted down and Congress has closed." The letter had the tone of familiarity; the events described as a backdrop to a more centered need for a quiet comfort or simple joy or an easy moment of solace. She booked train tickets and the steamer passage to return to Honolulu in early June.[374]

*

In 1905, Turkey retained significant remnants of a massive empire in Eastern Europe, the Middle East, and into the Arabian Peninsula. Turkey controlled vital waterways and the heart of western and eastern religions often with as cruel a hand as the British in the same part of the world. In Washington, Turkey's minister had a presence of consequence. His Excellency, Minister Bey, was a distinguished diplomat attuned to the social and political niceties of America's capital. The United States was no threat to the Ottoman Empire. Turkey was still a decade away from acquiring the opulent but tasteful Everett House residence on Sheridan Circle and sustaining the visible erosion and ultimate collapse of its possessions. Minister Bey had become acquainted socially with Liliuokalani.[375]

On April 28, the Queen received a letter from Dr. Hermann Schoenfeld, a member of the Committee on Higher Education at The George Washington University. The previous evening he had dinner with Minister Bey and Judge W. B. Matthews, "an eminent lawyer" who also represented the university. Bey and Schoenfeld both knew about the claim for the Crown lands. The "question of the very legitimate claims of Your Majesty was accidentally mentioned, and the long delay in...satisfying them...was painfully noticed." Schoenfeld suggested that if Judge Matthews, "with his wide influence in both Houses of Congress, his legal strength and his power, were able to handle the case...a favorable and speedy outcome...would be assured." Minister Bey, Schoenfeld continued, "cordially assented to my suggestion." Either man would be willing to "present Judge Matthews to your kind consideration."[376]

The Queen's response was cordial, affirmative in tone but expressed cautiously. The response came from her assistant. The Queen agreed to "duly consider" the offer but noted that "in the meantime she would be indeed pleased to meet" Matthews and "doubly pleased to have the pleasure of seeing" the minister and Schoenfeld at their earliest opportunity, "as her Majesty intends returning to Hawaii" on June 1. Retaining Matthews or at least rethinking her relationship with her counsel was of interest to the Queen. On May 3, she informed John Boyd and Clarence DeKnight that because Congress had adjourned "without affording me any compensation as to my claims, I feel that it would be utterly useless for you to give any more of your valuable time to my case." She recognized, she wrote, that "I am advancing far in years, and therefore would be at liberty to make arrangements other than those made with you." She requested they return the power of attorney and cancel their agreement with her. "I can only feel intensely sorry that your efforts were not crowned with success," she added. On May 22, Boyd and DeKnight sent her an invoice for three thousand five hundred dollars.[377]

*

Liliuokalani returned to Hawaii. The dismal economy in Hawaii was causing widespread discomfort. The apparent slow-down also may have increased her caution about expending money. Fatigue, emotional as well as physical, needed her attention. The invoice from Boyd and DeKnight loomed large and burdensome. On July 9, Hermann Schoenfeld informed the Queen he had met with DeKnight who agreed to "transmit to me all the material in his hand and an absolute release" of his retainer with the Queen but not until September 1. DeKnight first wanted to be paid. Three thousand five hundred dollars was a considerable sum, now beyond her means except at the cost of other choices. Judge Matthews, according to Schoenfeld, had "arranged all the preliminaries [and had] informed his Congressional combination" of his likely representation of the Queen.[378]

The Queen directed Carter to pay Boyd and DeKnight. Judge Matthews was informed by the Queen's "agent," presumable Carter, that she "desir[ed] to dispense with his services," although there is no record they had entered into an agreement. Schoenfeld wrote her in a tone of dismay and frustration. Schoenfeld and Bey believed Matthews the "*only* man who could obtain" compensation. In a direct and realistic characterization of DeKnight and Prince Kuhio, Schoenfeld wrote," Unfortunately Your Majesty will learn too late that your present advisers, or any one blood related to you, will never obtain a cent for you."[379]

Liliuokalani could no longer afford a skilled advocate in the law. She was sixty-seven years old and still had obligations to protect other people in her care. The loss of the Crown lands to men who neither respected their original purpose nor provided compensation for taking them from her or ensured meaningfully that native Hawaiians had benefited from their use was a reality she could — in 1905 — legitimately accept as final. Going back to Washington was beyond her means. Perhaps, too, the fine line between graceful effort and warranted ridicule had been reached. Finding justice would be almost wholly dependent on her persistence.

*

By November, Liliuokalani decided she was not prepared to accept the illegality of the *coup d'état*. She drafted and edited letters to Joseph Cannon, the speaker of the House of Representatives, Charles Fairbanks, the vice president of the United States, and President Roosevelt. She also had drafted, in Hawaiian, what appears to be one of three variations of a petition that would accompany the letters. The petitions vary in length and content and at least two of them ring loudly as having been drafted by someone sufficiently familiar with the history of the Crown lands to know the previous legal actions taken by the Hawaii judiciary and legislature. The Hawaiian language document was not in her handwriting. Certainly she had the personal knowledge and documents necessary to guide anyone, including Carter, in preparing a suitable petition with her cooperation. But the language in two of the draft petitions reads like the author had a nineteenth-century education in law. They are awkwardly parsed and not easily understood except by lawyers of a similar bent and even then with difficulty. They may simply have been the result of cobbling together previously prepared documents and petitions.[380]

It appears that the petition she did submit to Speaker Cannon — probably written by her and Carter — bore the closest relationship to her writing style and her view of which facts were relevant to the claim. In the petition she placed the moral burden on the speaker and Congress, which have "the right to mete out justice and equality," the standard she wanted relied upon in dealing with the claim's fate. The petition's substantive content was a recitation of facts that began on January 17, 1893, the day of the *coup d'état* and the intervention of the United States. In clear, easily understood prose, she set out the events in chronological order. She attached copies of Minister Stevens' directive to Captain Wiltse to land troops and her letter in protest yielding to the United States. She valued the Crown lands and the proceeds she had been denied at ten million dollars. "It is almost thirteen years," she wrote toward the end of the petition, "since I entered my protest against the revolutionary movement...and still my rights have not been adjudicated by the government of the United States." This claim, she concluded, "is placed before you without the aid or assistance of any attorney or counselor at law. Wherefore, in the name of the Supreme Being, Petitioner humbly asks the honorable Congress to give a just and equitable decision on behalf of this claim."[381]

On or about December 16, the Queen visited the town of Lahaina on Maui. She received a letter while staying there that described the presence in Honolulu of two Paulist fathers "giving a series of lectures " on "'Death,' 'The Reincarnation,' 'The Second Coming,' 'Life,' etc." The two priests had drawn a considerable audience. In reply, the Queen expressed "great curiosity to see these two Catholics ...who are so glib of tongue....Their energy cannot fail to secure them fondness. From the experiences I have had," she wrote with frankness and an acute sense of history, "and of which our people have been deprived of our country — and many other small nations have been gobbled up by larger nations, which have been the work of all missionaries — no matter what nationality....Missionaries come with the Bible in one hand and in the other hand taken our countries, our independence — our nationality."[382]

*

There were three hundred and eighty four members of Congress in 1905. Many representatives had to rent office space, use their homes, or borrow space in the Capitol building. As a delegate, Kuhio likely used his home. When he arrived in Washington, Congress already had approved construction of its first office building. The Beaux Arts architectural style had been approved and the exterior, under construction in 1905, was reminiscent of the Colonnade du Louvre in Paris. The name of the office building already had been selected: The Joseph Cannon Building.

Prince Kuhio had clarity of mind about the distribution of political power and his place in it. He was appointed to committees of considerable importance to Hawaii if he could stay long enough to gain both seniority and displace the presumption he was merely a representative of Hawaii's Caucasian-controlled Republican Party. His relationship with the Queen was strained. The Crown lands claim was only part of the reason. Kuhio actually was a beneficiary of the Hawaiian Renaissance that Kalakaua and Liliuokalani had supported and encouraged and that Robert Wilcox, Emma and Joseph Nawahi, and other men and women helped define. Kuhio had a refinement and education that Wilcox had acquired in a much different environment, when the struggle for Hawaiian nationalism required the risk of death, and knowledge had the virtue of being empirically as well as academically acquired. Kuhio had to forge a different kind of demographic alliance to succeed. He became, in effect, the native Hawaiian entrance into government positions, business, and the Republican Party. The Queen was his cousin, unequivocally revered, and unwilling to treat him deferentially. She believed he had a duty to her and to the preservation of the principle involving the Crown lands and the overthrow of the monarchy she embodied. She also wanted him to promote, in practical and political ways, the prospect of getting her the value of the Crown lands.[383]

On March 7, 1906, the Queen wrote the prince. "The subject of compensation, "she explained, "occupied my mind — that the United States ought to make some redress to me for what she holds that should be mine. The full value of the Crown lands according to the report given to the Commissioners who came out to investigate under Senator Mitchell [in 1902] was $20,000,000 — so I thought I would ask for $10,000,000." With some comparatively-based innuendo, she added that "I noticed that you have asked for $200,000 for me. It is rather small, but it is better than none at all and will have to be satisfied." On March 23, Kuhio acknowledged the reality of his constraint in the House. His handwritten note to the Queen reflected a respectful deference. "I can say that all Hawaii agrees that you should be compensated for the loss you have sustained" and that "the people of the United States deem it an outrage in the treatment you...are receiving from Congress." He had, however, little ability to accomplish what she sought. "[T]he men who control the destiny of the whole US....ignore all claims of righteousness and arbitrarily withhold that which justness demands." Speaker Joseph Cannon, "who is nothing less than a Czar, has the power to kill any and all measures." Kuhio shared her frustration and, no doubt, felt it acutely in his daily dealings with other members and as he sought to introduce other bills. Cannon barely spoke to Kuhio but the prince believed he could get Cannon's friends in the House to encourage a hearing on the bill he had introduced in support of the Crown land's claim. His bill for two hundred thousand dollars would be the basis, as he described it to the Queen, for his "fight on your ten million dollar claim." But "I can do nothing else but persevere and hope for the best. You must be patience as I have not the power to force anything."[384]

The Queen increased her travel to the islands including a visit to friends in Hilo. This time her prolonged stay in Hawaii seemed to be a source of rejuvenation; a means of slowing down; and touching the people and places that had deep meaning to her, especially on the islands that she often traveled as queen. She would be certain of a warm embrace and shared memories of a different time and, now perhaps, of old friends with whom she engaged in an epic struggle and would welcome the effort she still was undertaking. She also installed a new kitchen and plumbing at Washington Place and had the house connected to the new sewer system. In February 1907, she decided to auction off some possessions, perhaps to raise money or merely to make some room in her home. They included a few of the books she had in her library, including *The History of the Sandwich Islands* by Rufus Anderson, the one-time director of the American Board of Commissioners of Foreign Missions in Boston, and *The Life of Lucy Thurston* "selected and arranged by herself." In a letter to a friend in Boston, the Queen acknowledged being "conscience stricken" for having failed to respond to her friend's multiple letters, but, she said, "I know you have a big heart and feel already that you have forgiven me." She had, she assured her friend, not been idle but had "taken my affairs in my own hands, and employ one of my retainers to transact my affairs under me, while I tell all that I want done." J.O. Cater had left the Queen's employ.[385]

In April, Prince Kuhio informed the Queen that he had convinced the chairman of the Committee on Claims, Congressman James Miller of Kansas, to consider holding a hearing on his bill. Kuhio would have to go before the committee within the next week to make the request. He informed the Queen that the most significant impediment was the fact the senate had rejected the claim in 1904. He reminded her, in a slight overstatement, that Senators Blackburn and Mitchell, "who were fighting to pass your bill[,] admitted that you had no claim that could possibly be established in a court of law [including] in the Court of Claims." Congress was, in his view, the only place she could get redress. Kuhio dutifully also informed the Queen that he wished she "would realize that I have more personal interest in your claim than in any measure I have had pending before the Congress."[386]

On June 11, Senator John Morgan died suddenly. Testimony to his life in Washington and Alabama recognized with an unintended accuracy the perspective he brought to his treatment of Hawaii. He "examined and decided," one reporter wrote," by only one test — the test of ... archaic principles.... [N]obody ever argued with [him].... The world has moved on, and the very language in which these principles were expressed was foreign in the ears of this generation." The Queen took no special note of Morgan passing away.[387]

Unexpectedly but in a manner that must have engaged her intellectually, the Queen received another offer to provide legal counsel to deal with the Crown lands claim. Francis Harden, a friend from San Francisco, described his conference "with Mr. Lane," a Chicago lawyer, about "your claims against the U.S. government." Mr. Lane believed — as she had for more than a decade — that "the decisions of the Supreme Court of Hawaii render your title clear. The lands are private estate and not public domain." Harden proposed that the Queen consider going to the Hague Tribunal — the Permanent Court of Arbitration in the Netherlands — as "the only court of resort in which your claim can be presented." Harden pointed to a recent claim the Roman Catholic Church brought against the United States for the confiscation of mission lands in California. Harden also lamented that he "would have suggested the Hague years ago if I had had the honor of your acquaintance." The Queen had her own lament. Retaining counsel was no longer within her purview financially. The Harden letter, however, the letter from Crammond Kennedy, and the form of interest taken by the Turkish minister and Schoenfeld affirmed that the fate of the Crown lands warranted a close legal scrutiny by a dispassionate tribunal made by able advocates committed to the Queen and capable of explaining and proving the cultural underpinning of Hawaii law. She had recognized the problem when she wrote *Hawaii's Story*. Such adjudication had not been undertaken. Her frustration and sadness at being thwarted politically in Congress and in Hawaii was well founded.[388]

*

Sidney Miller Ballou came from an old English and Norman family that settled in Rhode Island in the early eighteenth century. He studied law at Harvard. He was raised in a late nineteenth-century New England already tempered by the disquieting intersection of missionary zeal, property acquisition, and the denigration of other people's culture.

When Ballou was admitted to the Massachusetts bar in 1895, Liliuokalani already had been deposed. When Ballou landed in Hawaii, "[he] at once took an active part in the management of affairs under the Dole government that culminated in the annexation of the Islands." He also became a member of the Naval Reserve of the United States. At twenty-five years old, Ballou moved seamlessly into the established legal and governance structure and the cultural characteristics that had provided its dominance. Because of his role in compiling the civil and penal laws of Sanford Dole's Republic for reference in the Organic Act, Ballou understood that the Organic Act included deliberately a formal denial of the Queen's rights in the Crown lands. At a time when, in terms of generational memory and the freshness of evidence, the Queen's property interests were at the height of their ripeness for judicial resolution, those in control of such a possibility denied and precluded it. Ballou had placed himself near the top of that list.[389]

In 1903, Ballou formed a partnership to practice law with Francis Hatch, a signatory of the Organic Act and a powerful opponent of the Queen. As Ballou specially recognized, Hatch was "a member of the Constitutional Convention which framed [the provision]" that declared the Crown lands to be public land and presumably denied the Queen access to the judiciary to protect her interests. In 1905, when Hatch took a position on the Hawaii Supreme Court, Ballou entered into a partnership with William Kinney. Kinney had been chief prosecutor of the Queen in 1895. Kinney denied the Queen had any claim to the Crown lands. By 1906, Ballou's practice included arguments before the Supreme Court of the United States. He was familiar generally with the politics of the nation's capital.[390]

Ballou was appointed an Associate Justice of the Hawaii Supreme Court by President Theodore Roosevelt in 1907. His skill and his loyalty to the Republican Party were recognized formally. In March 1908, Ballou sat on a panel of three judges, including Chief Judge Alfred Hartwell that decided *Territory of Hawaii v. Kapiolani Estate*. Hartwell had a deep, well documented distain for the constitutional monarchy and the Queen. He had drafted her abdication in 1895. Hartwell also was within that generation of Caucasian men who molded and treated the judiciary as an appendage of a council of elders. In the nature of a judiciary, Hartwell and Ballou looked backwards to precedents and a perspective that substantiated the political world both men personally had created and would ensure was unchallenged. They did so with respect to the Crown lands.[391]

In *Kapiolani Estate*, a dispute arose over whether the Territory of Hawaii could require the Kapiolani Estate, which was a tenant or leaseholder of Crown lands, to pay rent to the Territorial government. The land had been leased in 1882, prior to the *coup d'état*. The former leaseholders, who for a period of time included Prince Kuhio and Prince David, periodically sold the lease to others in private transactions. In an opinion written by Hartwell and joined in by Ballou, the Hawaii Supreme Court concluded that the Crown lands were, under "the constitution of Hawaii...declared to be the property of the Hawaiian Government " and now, through "the Organic Act [of 1900] the property of the United States." The Territory of Hawaii was entitled to the rent.[392]

The Kapiolani Estate also argued that if the Republic had acquired the Crown lands it did so illegally or without due process of law or paying compensation for taking it. The court refused to examine the argument. Justice Ballou agreed with the court's conclusion that the "validity of the declaration in the Constitution of the Republic of Hawaii, under which the present title is derived, does not present a judicial question." Put differently, regardless of the argument's merit or the fact that it was not uncommon for courts to examine and decide the merits of such an argument, Ballou and Hartwell declined to do so. To support its position, the court cited to precedents — earlier cases decided by other courts — that supposedly held the same way. Most of the earlier decisions the Hawaii Supreme Court cited actually involved a judicial determination on the merits of the argument presented, not a determination to avoid it. It made no difference. Ballou and Hartwell were engaged in the exercise of raw power. Moreover, the court continued, "[e]ven assuming, but in no way admitting, that the constitutional declaration was confiscatory in its nature [that is, that the declaration was in fact and in the law a taking of private property], this court has no authority to declare it to

174

be invalid. The subsequent derivation of the title by the United States...is clear." The irony in the opinion was that the Republic's constitution no longer existed and the court was bound not by the Organic Act of 1900 but the constitution of the United States. The effect of the opinion was plain. Although not a party to the lawsuit, Liliuokalani could not litigate her claim before the Hawaii judiciary. Ballou and Hartwell had ensured it.[393]

*

Prince Kuhio informed the Queen that although no date was set, the committee on claims had agreed to a hearing. A new strategy was required. Precisely how much or in what manner Liliuokalani and Kuhio negotiated their respective roles and a combined approach is unclear. Some actions were predictable.

On November 8, the Queen submitted a petition to the president-elect of the United States William Howard Taft. Taft's electoral victory a few days earlier against William Jennings Bryan was substantial. Taft brought to the presidency his knowledge of the Philippines and a commitment to continue the growth of American naval strength. The Great White Fleet — sixteen battleships and their escorts with a red, white, and blue banner on the bow and fourteen thousand sailors aboard — was near completion of its circumnavigation of the earth. The Fleet had drawn large crowds in Rio de Janeiro, Auckland, Sydney, Melbourne, Suez, and Honolulu. The Republican Party remained in control of the judiciary. The only noteworthy moment in Taft's ascendancy was at the convention. He had been challenged unsuccessfully by the Queen's friend, Senator Joseph Foraker of Ohio. Taft also counted among those people who shared his values, court of claims judge, Fenton Booth, and the court's chief clerk, Archibald Hopkins.[394]

The petition to Taft reflected the Queen's consistent position since 1893. She was the "rightful owner of all the Crown lands in the Hawaiian Islands;" she had yielded her authority "to the superior forces of the Government of the United States" landed at the request of Minister Stevens; and she "always received and earned my due proportion of the proceeds and income from the Crown lands." Following this summary, she wrote that "it is a painful tale for me to rehearse here how I was deprived of my Government." She set out that history in the remainder of the petition with the appropriate documents and letters attached to substantiate her position. She requested "relief in the lump sum of TEN MILLION DOLLARS...in settlement of all my claims." She affixed her signature — the letters larger, sprawled noticeably but neatly — at the end.[395]

Toward the end of the third week in November Liliuokalani boarded the Pacific Mail liner *Magnolia*. Just before her departure she again used her property as collateral to borrow seventy thousand dollars in part to finance what she hoped would be her last and a successful visit to the United States. The *Magnolia* had begun its voyage "in the Orient" and stopped in Honolulu on the way to San Francisco. Prince Kuhio and his wife accompanied the Queen. Kuhio had been reelected to his fourth term as Hawaii's delegate. When the *Magnolia* landed in San Francisco on November 22, the reporter for the *New York Times* noted that the Queen looked a "frail old women... plainly attired and accompanied by one maid." She had chosen to remain in her cabin during much of the voyage, probably conferring periodically with Kuhio. She had been unrecognized by the passengers. She was not to be deterred. She would not disclose her intention precisely either inadvertently in idle conversation or to a conscientious reporter until she was ready to do so. She was preserving her strength and strategy. One element of her strategy already was certain. Liliuokalani intended to make a personal appearance before the Congress of the United States.[396]

When the Queen reached Washington and settled into the Shoreham Hotel, Associate Justice Sidney Ballou was in California. In late December, he addressed the Los Angeles Merchants Association. He sought to convey to the audience Hawaii's commitment to increased trade and to "American interests." He also spoke directly about the Crown lands. "Under an arrangement with the national government," Ballou was quoted as saying, "the crown lands are now open to settlement under laws similar to the homestead enactments by Congress, and it is hoped to make the country one for white men, as against the proposition of being dominated by the Asians." What he did not say to the merchants — perhaps because it never occurred to him — was that Liliuokalani had taken the position since 1893 that all of the Crown land's income from such "white men" actually belonged to her.[397]

CHAPTER 12. WITHOUT COUNSEL IN CONGRESS: WASHINGTON, DC

Prince Kuhio had more at stake than the fate of the Crown lands. His ability to deliver on his commitment to the Queen would be seen positively among native Hawaiians and, if done properly, among other people who sought either a form of justice for the Queen or a form of tranquility for a disquieting episode in Hawaii's history. Kuhio would have taken the lead in determining who should testify in order to create the best possible image and make the most persuasive argument. In its persuasiveness the argument also had to distinguish the Crown lands claim from the array of other claims before the committee and other demands on the federal budget. The Queen was prepared to create an element in that distinctiveness by being at the hearing in a visible way. She likely insisted on if not relished the prospect. She had sought the hearing. Her presence would signal her seriousness of purpose and in conventional terms put a face to the testimony. She understood Washington's political and social milieu long before Kuhio did and how to create perceptions within it. She was the one person who still could command the press.

When Liliuokalani had arrived in San Francisco, the *New York* Times' observation about her "frail" look was not her only interview. Perhaps more rested but still not revealing a strategy she described to another newspaper that she was in "exceptionally good health, and feeling none of the usual handicaps of years." The reporter noted that the Queen had been preparing a new memoir for publication by the same house that published *Hawaii's Story By Hawaii's Queen*. The reporter also observed that, "As a woman of wide experience among notable people she is said to be more like the late Mrs. Jane Stanford than perhaps any other woman California has known." Stanford had taken control of Stanford University after her husband's death and supported an academic concentration on the arts and the admission of women.[398]

Once the Queen arrived at the Shoreham Hotel in Washington she "declined to see anyone... pleading fatigue. Her secretary refused to discuss her plans but it was learned," the *New York Times* reported, "she will make one last, strenuous effort to have her claim on Congress met." The reporter noted that the Queen will "put aside her exclusiveness and appear personally before the House Committee on Claims." On background, the reporter turned to George B. McClellan, the representative of the Merchant's Association of Honolulu and the Honolulu Chamber of Commerce to confirm the story. McClellan, a lawyer, was among those men who came to Hawaii after annexation. He testified frequently in Congress. He would have known and worked with Kuhio. He also would have been known by the committee members. McClellan was an establishment figure, conservative in his reputation and professional interests. Kuhio wanted him to testify on the Queen's behalf.[399]

The other person Kuhio asked to testify was Francis Hatch. Hatch was formidable, a partisan Republican, and politically connected. Hatch, like Sidney Ballou, was a regular visitor to Washington. He represented the Territory and private interests before Congress. He would have known and worked with Kuhio. He also argued or participated in cases before the Supreme Court of the United States. One case involved "vested rights" to property in Hawaii that Hatch had argued successfully required the court to examine the controversy's underlying Hawaiian culture. Hatch, too, represented the establishment; a former Hawaii Supreme Court justice and a major participant in the *coup d'état* who was prepared to support the claim. Hatch and McClellan also posed risks. Both men had multiple agendas in the nation's capital. They were lobbyists; familiar advocates for particular private and governmental interests. They would be back again for something or someone else. Hatch also brought with him the defensiveness of those men who led the *coup d'état* and he had a first-hand knowledge of the manner in which the Queen had been denied access to the Hawaii judiciary.[400]

Kuhio expected the hearing would be held before the Christmas recess. The committee decided to postpone the hearing until January 14. There was more time to consider strategy. The Cannon building had been constructed. Kuhio had his own office. He and the Queen may have met there. There is no record they discussed the advisability of her testifying. She might have considered the benefit and risks of doing it. Although she had not given a formal speech in some years she had entertained and was entertained frequently and continued to host annual gatherings at Washington Place on her September birthday. Handling the unexpected question or comment was easily within her skill and experience. She had been in Congress to observe debates on numerous occasions and there was little in the temperament of a congressman she had not witnessed. She could give a first-hand recitation of her intention and perspective about the events of January 1893. A woman testifying in Congress, however, would be unusual. She also might have felt too much the supplicant or that the power of the Crown lands story would appear more objectively presented if done by one of the other witnesses. Kuhio opted for a safe and prudent posture. The Queen would not testify. It appears, however, that what the Queen and Kuhio agreed upon, as reflected in the Queen's petition to President Taft, was that the *coup d'état* and the role of the United States would be the central thread of the argument.

*

The day of the hearing, January 14, 1909 — the height of Washington's winter season — must have been viewed with considerable expectation. "It was the first time that a real former queen ever faced a committee of the house." The press was there. The hearing was held in the Capitol. Liliuokalani entered the room. She wore a "brown velvet dress, trimmed in black and partially concealed" by a loose black cloak thrown over her shoulders. She wore tan gloves. She had on "a black hat surmounted by a large white aigrette." Age, it was reported, had "tinged [her] coal black hair with silver threads and wrinkled the kindly brown face, but the former Queen of Hawaii was still queenly in her bearing and dignified in her manner." She was accompanied by Prince Kuhio's wife. They took their seats in a location easily visible to the members of the committee.[401]

There were other perceptions and tones of history within the hearing room. It had been sixteen years since the Queen was deposed. Chairman James Miller came to Congress in 1899. Republican William Graham of Pennsylvania was elected in late 1898 to fill an unexpired term. Republican George Waldo of New York was elected in 1905. Henry Mayer Goldfogle, the senior ranking Democrat entered Congress in 1901. Democrat John Adair of Indiana was in his first term. Democrat Elmer Fulton of Oklahoma was in his first term and would not be returning with the new Congress expected in March. When the Queen arrived on the continent her purpose for coming was described by one observer as "[a]n echo of events which already seem remote." The distance in time also meant the committee members had few, if any, vested interests to protect.[402]

Prince Kuhio's opening presentation set the strategy: The responsibility for the fall of the constitutional monarchy was squarely on the United States. Kuhio's historical recitation relied exclusively on the history set forth in the report submitted by James Blount to President Cleveland and Cleveland's letter transmitting the report to the United States Senate. The Queen, Kuhio concluded, had succumbed not to the provisional government's leaders — including Francis Hatch seated nearby — but to the exercise of military power and the threat of its use by the United States Navy. "There can be no disputing the fact that the former queen of Hawaii was deprived of the income from the Crown lands through the overthrow of her government...and the landing of American troops...was the controlling force that made a successful revolution possible." The critical event that established America's responsibility to compensate the Queen occurred in 1893. Kuhio was unchallenged in creating this context. The Queen's property rights had been extinguished by the exercise of power. Prior to that action "[t] he monarch or the person on the throne had absolute use of the crown lands. You might say," he asserted, perhaps prematurely, "she had a life interest in this crown land. It was originally private property owned by the King."[403]

The committee members were prepared. Chairman Miller and Congressman Waldo were lawyers. They had their own strategy. They cut Kuhio off before he could proceed further. Miller sought clarity about what private interest, precisely, Liliuokalani actually retained. "In which the Queen had a life interest?" he asked. Kuhio: "Yes, sir." With persistence Fulton asked: "On her death to whom would this property descend?" Kuhio: "We are not prepared to discuss where the property would go after her death." Waldo again: "It was annexed to the office and not to the person of the King, is that what you mean?" Kuhio, perhaps recognizing he had gotten beyond his competence, answered: "I would rather not discuss that farther, as Judge Hatch will speak upon that subject." The basic issue was laid bare: Did the Queen have a legally enforceable private interest in the Crown lands?[404]

Before introducing Hatch, Prince Kuhio sought to diminish the relevance of the legal questions now placed on the table. Kuhio stated — perhaps seeking to diffuse another legal argument before it arose — that the "Government [could]... answer [a similar claim] by a technical legal defense under the rules of international law." Whether it was a legitimate statement of the law or not Kuhio wanted the committee to know he and his companions were not there to argue it. Kuhio wanted Congress to act, not a court of law.

Kuhio estimated that the Crown lands "are today worth more than $10,000,000." He pled thoughtfully and passionately "that it is unworthy [of] the dignity and honor of this great nation that it should become, as it has, the beneficiary of this revolution by taking for government use a part of these very lands...and yet refuse to make some reasonable recognition of her claim.... And it is difficult to see how this, or any succeeding Congress, if they refuse to consider the justice of this claim, can be held by history as thereby adding to the renown of this nation for fair dealing and essential love of justice."[405]

Hatch took the witness chair. He was a slender man with a finely cropped mustache and hair. Hatch sought from the outset to base the Queen's claim on two arguments. First, since Kamehameha III the Crown lands had been considered private property; and second, that the unilateral actions declaring that the Crown lands were owned by the provisional government and then the Republic were mere "acts of war" that did not constitute "any sort of legal procedure" capable of denying the Queen her property interest. "I take it," he concluded, "that she has an equitable life interest in the income of these crown lands and has never been deprived of that interest by any sort of legal procedure. She was deprived of her throne by acts of war. There was a revolution, and an actual state of warfare existing for over three years."[406]

"The Constitutional Convention," Hatch continued, "declared by resolution that the crown-land estate was public property. There was no decision of a court... It was merely a *pronunciamento*, without any consideration of her interests." The interest of "both parties were [not] heard." The Hawaii Supreme Court had ruled in 1864 in the *Estate of Kamehameha IV*, Hatch contended, that "The portion which [Kamehameha III] reserved as his private estate [in 1848] is the domain which is now in question. It has been considered to have a quasi-public character; I deny that it has ever lost its character as a private estate. It was a private estate separated by deed from the public domain and has remained a private estate down to this day as I contend." The commissioners created by the legislature in 1865 and later to ensure that the Crown land was not sold acted as private trustees paid by the rents from the land. They were not government employees paid by the government. The United States, Hatch concluded with an element of fiction, may have accepted the Crown lands in "ignorance" of the Queen's "private rights" and "should hasten to undue that wrong." Hatch's position was a dramatic departure from the position his colleagues had taken in the past. He also sought to carve a fine line. The lands remained a private estate but the Queen had an "equitable life interest" only in the income. Listening to him, the Queen must have felt a vindication. Hatch may have drawn a fine line with respect to her interests but he read the law — the 1864 decision and the 1865 Act — as she did.[407]

Members of the committee sought to enlarge the fine line. Had Hatch opened an issue unnecessary to the attainment of the Queen's objective in Congress? Congressman Graham of Pennsylvania probed carefully with respect to what, precisely, the court intended in its 1864 decision in *Estate of Kamehameha IV* and how that decision may or may not support Hatch's position. Hatch had no certainty in his answers. "Do you maintain that this private estate vested in the person as an individual or as a sovereign?" Graham asked. "It could not have vested in her unless she had been sovereign," Hatch replied. He provided no clarity that seemed to ensure comfort or acceptance of his position.[408]

Chairman Miller also was not distracted by Hatch's "*pronunciamento*" characterization of what was, in fact, a Constitutional provision approved by him and others or the hypocrisy in such a characterization being evoked by the person who wrote the provision. Miller: "I understand as a member of the [Republic's] constitutional convention you took the position that the members of the constitutional convention had a right to declare that these lands were public lands?" Hatch: "Yes." Miller: "Since that time, as a lawyer, you take the position that they were not public lands, but private lands belonging to the Queen?" Hatch: "I say that that declaration cannot be given the effect of a decision of a tribunal where the interest of both parties was heard." Miller: "Did you take that position in the constitutional convention?" Hatch: "No, I did not." The down side of Hatch as a leader in the *coup d'état* and the fine line he had drawn were now apparent. Matters got worse. Graham asked Hatch, "When the Americans occupied the country, was the system of judiciary continued?" "Yes, sir," Hatch replied. He was trapped. Graham: "But all your domestic questions were to be settled in your courts?" Hatch: "Yes, sir." Graham: "If that land is private property, why have you not attempted to enforce her rights in your courts?"[409]

Hatch had articulated a good legal argument. He could not defend, however, a system of governance that had denied the legitimacy of the Queen's rights or even provided her a judicial forum within which her arguments could be heard. He and his friend Sidney Ballou had ensured those conditions. Hatch sought to move away from accountability. "I came here as a private individual," he said. " I have never been retained by the Queen. The question I have argued to-day, I think it is a good, fair, legal question which could be presented in any court." Perhaps simply to get out of his personal quagmire, Hatch added: "I have no responsibility about the conduct of the case." Congressman Adair then asked the obvious: "There never has been any suit in Hawaii?" Hatch: "There never has been any suit brought, no." Chairman Miller drove the point deeper. He would not let Hatch escape his own history or testimony. "Is not this a legal question," Miller asked, "and one that ought to be submitted to a court rather than to Congress?" Hatch sought to shift the failure for not providing the Queen with some form of compensation to the United States. "The Queen is asking for an equitable settlement," he replied, not a legal one. Whether the colloquy between Hatch and members of committee gave comfort to the Queen is unclear. She might have asked the same questions. [410]

George McClellan took the witness chair. He sought at the outset to make clear that neither he nor Hatch were "retained as counsel for the Queen in this claim. We have absolutely no financial connection with this claim and we appear simply as citizens of Hawaii." McClellan suggested another way that he thought demonstrated the prudence of a legislative settlement. The Queen would agree to have that portion of the Crown lands actually being used by the United States, which included the entire naval station at Honolulu, appraised or condemned by legal process. This approach would yield the Queen "compensation of about four times the amount which is covered by the pending bill." McClellan's argument was based on the certainty the Queen had a private interest in the Crown lands. McClellan's threat of an alternative provoked no apparent apprehension from the committee's members.[411]

McClellan proceeded to his basic argument, the one started by Prince Kuhio: The United States "was responsible as the moving force in the downfall of the monarchy." No one on the committee seemed to doubt or disagree with his detailed historical recitation. He relied on original documents, the Blount report, and President Cleveland's position. McClellan focused especially on Minister Stevens' reference in a letter to the need to "Americanize the Island and assume control of the crown lands." Miller interrupted him and perhaps looked at Hatch directly. "Judge Hatch and these other revolutionists must have been keeping the Government of the United States pretty closely in touch with what was going on," Miller stated. McClellan: "I did not say Judge Hatch was there, but possibly there were other gentlemen there in close touch with this ardent American Minister."[412]

Miller may have engaged in an act of provocation or good natured banter. The relationship between the United States and the *coup d'état* seemed settled. Chairman Miller indicated that he needed to bring the hearing to a close for the day. Because the next hearing was not scheduled for a week, Miller asked if "there is anyone here from Hawaii that wants to speak?" Miller may have been thinking of the Queen. Hatch wanted to be heard again. Chairman Miller allowed it. In fact, it appears as if he welcomed it. Kuhio could have been only discomforted at the prospect. The hearing had gone well. Kuhio had created a record upon which he could discuss the claim further with Miller and the other leaders of the House.[413]

Hatch moved to the center of attention. "I want to state at this time," he said, "that I am unable to agree with the contention of Mr. McClellan. I was present and took part in that revolution. I want my statement to go on the record most emphatically that we revolutionists received no advice, aid, or comfort from any officer of the United States." Back to 1893. Miller knew what he heard and had read. "The disclaimer is all right," Miller replied, "but I think in view of the letter, Mr. McClellan is justified in making the statement." Hatch could not allow the *coup d'état* to be suspect in its origins or reason for success. He persisted as if the purpose of the hearing or the power of the committee chairman was irrelevant to a larger cause. Dole, Smith, and Thurston could have been seated aside him. "But I deny any connection with any former minister of the United States on the part of the revolutionary government," Hatch added.[414]

Miller was not going to let Hatch's unnecessary arrogance pass. Miller: "I think there is no desire of the committee to connect you to it. But I want to ask a question or two of you, Judge Hatch, before you go. I want to ask you whether it is possible for this lady to maintain an action under the laws of Hawaii in reference to these crown lands for the purpose of determining title?" Kuhio must have moved to the edge of his chair to hear the answer. The Queen must have wondered whose interest Hatch was now serving. "I suppose she could only maintain an action for the income for the last six years," he stated authoritatively. "It strikes me that the statute of limitation would deprive her from going back of six years." Six years was, generally, the accepted time period within which a law suit in the court of claims could be filed following the event that the law suit claimed was illegal. Hatch had implicitly agreed a law suit was available and could be successful. Kuhio's strategy was being torn asunder. Miller asked Hatch: "That is why I ask you the question . . . . If she can under the laws now maintain an action, I do not know why she should not maintain an action. And it might be better for the Government of the United States to adjust the claim [after the court decision]. . What would you think of the suggestion . . . that the case should be sent to the Court of Claims . . . to hear and determine all matters growing out of this matter?"[415]

McClellan intervened. He knew Hatch had caused harm. "Would not the result of that be that it would require one or two years to get the legislation permitting that?" he asked Miller more in the nature of a plea than a question. Miller, perhaps for a range of reasons including Hatch's testimony, put the matter to rest from his perspective. Miller: "But let me suggest this. Suppose this case were sent to the Court of Claims giving jurisdiction to that court to hear and determine all matters arising out of the revolution down there, so far as the rights of the Queen are concerned. Do you think that if it came back from the Court of Claims to Congress with a favorable report from the court in her favor, that there would be very much more liability for a bill of relief passing Congress than it would be now?" McClellan tried to dissuade him. "I think that would undoubtedly be the case," McClellan stated with a politeness, "but from the standpoint of time," and the Queen's age "it would no longer be an act of grace to this claimant, and Congress can in the first instance do justice." McClellan's argument had no converts on the committee. Chairman Miller would not allow Hatch out of his own history or the provisional government and the Republic out of its obligations or the Hawaii judiciary out of its duty. Hatch, it appeared, had provoked the committee chairman to do precisely what the Queen and Prince Kuhio sought to avoid.[416]

At the hearing's conclusion it would have been customary for the members to be introduced to the Queen by Prince Kuhio. Kuhio made a grander move. The "former queen held an informal reception" in the Capitol building. "All the members of the committee were introduced to her." In the small talk that followed and in the special moment the members had to meet the Queen, Kuhio, McClellan, and Liliuokalani had a tough political task to accomplish.[417]

On January 21, the claims committee held a second hearing. The Queen did not appear. There is no indication Kuhio was there. McClellan was the only witness. He devoted the entirety of his testimony to re-establishing the historical record he and Kuhio thought essential. The committee members, although probing for more facts, never questioned the fundamental premise: The United States Navy and Minister Stevens largely caused or aided the fall of the constitutional monarchy. This time, however, when McClelland testified he made clear those sentiments belonged to James Blount and President Cleveland, not to him.[418]

*

Liliuokalani's skill as a publicist now was critically essential to attaining the goal she sought. The *New York Times*, the *Chicago Daily Tribune*, the *Los Angeles Times*, and the *Honolulu Semi Weekly Star* wrote about the hearing and the Queen's presence. The articles were not always accurate or complimentary. Articles written in more depth and with reflection also appeared. On January 23, the *Christian Science Monitor* wrote about the need for "Fair Treatment for Liliuokalani." The editors did not endorse compensation. They would welcome her explanation not with respect to the *coup d'état* but to the editor's recognition "that she was misrepresented in her intentions [to behead] Sanford B. Dole and his associates." The Queen had succeeded through more than a decade of presence in the United States in finally dispelling the certainty that some in the press had embraced uncritically when it mattered to Hawaii's fate. The *Washington Post* also editorialized. With an appropriate tinge of irony they chastised the Queen for her "Queen's Mistake." "She yielded too easily," the *Post* wrote. "Hers was a peaceful kingdom... and she had not the heart to see bloodshed over the control of her islands. Had she refused to abdicate...landed a few cannons...and marched out to the jungles about Mauna Loa under a flag of insurrection, she would probably have been able to sellout all her right[s]...at a fat figure.... But having admitted herself a person not to be feared, she is no longer in a position to expect justice." The *Post* also recognized "incidentally" that "the Hawaiian Islands constitute the only bit of territory belonging to the United States which never cost this government a dollar to acquire."[419]

The *Boston Daily Globe* wrote a story that included a photograph of the Queen taken recently. She was seated in a high back chair, her hair pushed up and wrapped tightly around her head, dressed in a fitted high button dark suit with what appears to be an emblem or decoration — perhaps belonging to her husband, John — pinned on the left side of her dress lapel. She was looking downward seemingly studying a document perhaps related to the planned hearing. The photograph was a deliberate pose of seriousness of purpose. On February 14, the *Boston Daily Globe* ran another photograph "taken in Washington." The Queen was seated in a large armchair in what appeared to be the Shoreham's lobby. Her hair continued to be finely shaped atop her head; her dress slightly more regal; her face — directed to the reader — appeared weathered by experience but reflective of a confident serenity about life and her choices. The article contained a detailed story that she wrote exclusively for the Boston newspaper. At the story's conclusion she added that "she had reconciled to the change in government in Hawaii; but I am too loyal to the United States to be willing to be the occasion of reproach to this great nation when future historians shall tell how the government was enriched by accepting without compensation, land it had assisted in taking from a weaker sovereign." In taking the long view, which she had done throughout her life especially since the day of the *coup d'état*, she added that, "I do not want to end my days knowing that my Hawaiian people will always feel that this nation respects only the right of the armed force."[420]

No formal committee decision was made perhaps out of deference to Kuhio but the outcome was clear unless Kuhio could undo it. On March 2, the Queen paid a "farewell call" to Theodore Roosevelt. She was accompanied by Prince Kuhio. She gave the departing president a copy of her book, *Hawaii's Story by Hawaii's Queen*. On March 16, Liliuokalani departed Washington. She said her farewell to Prince Kuhio and his wife from the newly opened grand railroad station that Daniel Burnham had designed. She traveled to Chicago. She had choices to make.[421]

*

The recrimination or certainly the discussion that followed the hearing of January 14 must have been intense. Kuhio could not have been pleased with Hatch. The hearing on January 21 revealed that McClellan was quite careful not to offend Hatch or anyone else involved in the *coup d'état*. The burden on Kuhio to ensure a favorable outcome became heavier. Hatch also succeeded in limiting the Queen's choices if Kuhio could not deliver: Abandon the claim or go to the United States Court of Claims.

The closing admonition from Chairman Miller — go to the court of claims — needed to be taken seriously. Hatch would have sought to assure the Queen that a meritorious claim existed in order to rationalize the result of his unnecessary provocation. Given his professional and personal relationship with William Kinney and Sidney Ballou and Hatch's continued interest in the Queen's legal argument, Hatch may have recommend either himself or one of his colleagues to actually undertake the preparation and filing of a law suit at the court of claims. Ballou was only a few months away from bringing his judicial career to an end. The Queen had additional resources from her loan but with Miller's admonition a dimmer prospect of successfully paying the loan off with ease. She returned to Hawaii on April 2.[422]

*

Curtis Iaukea had served as an ambassador and in the cabinet of Liliuokalani's brother, King Kalakaua. He had kept his distance during the *coup d'état* and the counter-*coup* lead by Robert Wilcox and others. Iaukea was not supportive of the Queen's position on the Crown lands during the senate hearings in 1902. He also challenged Kuhio for the position of delegate in 1904 and then challenged Kuhio's victory unsuccessfully in court and Congress. He had become close to the men who led the Republic and now the Territory. Iaukea had, it might be said safely, acquiesced dutifully into the new order. Iaukea had two virtues. The Queen respected his skill professionally. They also shared remembrances. She requested Curtis Iaukea to take on the task of representing her interests. With-

186

in a few months he also assumed responsibility for managing her finances and property.[423]

In early May of 1909, Sidney Ballou left the Hawaii Supreme Court in order to re-enter private practice with William Kinney, Mason Prosser, and Robbins ``. The new firm appears also to have included Francis Hatch and, eventually, Alfred S. Hartwell. Ballou had considerable financial success and moved comfortably among the sugar planters, industrialists, their lawyers, and investors. On July 13, Liliuokalani retained the law firm of Kinney, Ballou, Prosser, and Anderson. It was responsible for "the claim for income of the Crown lands in Court of Claims and the Supreme Court Washington, DC." She paid the law firm two thousand five hundred dollars. Precisely what the payment would cover — fees, expenses, or a flat amount for everything — was unspecified. She would have expected that Ballou would make the legal argument that Kuhio, McClellan, and Hatch had made in Congress only with all the research, acumen, and resources of the firm and with whatever evidence was necessary.[424]

On or prior to November 20, the Queen was presented with a type-written original of the petition that Kinney, Ballou, Prosser, and Anderson intended to file in the court of claims. No lawyer within the firm affixed his signature to the petition or took individual accountability for its content. Curtis Iaukea would have seen and presented the petition to the Queen. Under the rules governing the court of claims she was required to sign the petition. In a broad and clearly crafted script with the uneven lines and awkward curvature reflective of her seventy-one years Liliuokalani affixed her signature at the end of the petition. Whether she understood fully and correctly what the petition represented or the thoroughness of the research that should have preceded its preparation or the accuracy of the facts it alleged or what evidence the firm intended to present to support the allegations or the import and persuasiveness of the legal argument included — or not included — in the petition or the risks she was taking in an unfavorable outcome was another matter altogether. The petition was held in abeyance. She had authorized and now held an alternative to Congress.[425]

In late October or early November 1909, it was apparent that "[p]overty [had come] to live with Liliuokalani. People who had been willing to lend her money on the hope of a rich inheritance from the government — the United States or the Territory — [had begun] calling in their loans." She retained the major encumbrance on her property from money borrowed to finance her visit to the continent and to finance the work of Kinney, Ballou, Prosser, and Anderson. Some of her lands were not defined with care from the boundaries of the Crown lands. She was entangled in numerous, often costly disputes over boundary lines. Portions of her property leased to poor native farmers and families were not producing rent. She refused to insist upon receiving it. Liliuokalani decided to create a will to leave her assets, largely real property and some financial reserves, for the benefit of native Hawaiian children who were orphaned, and determined to further discipline her spending to attain her goal.[426]

At the suggestion of Curtis Iaukea, she sought the legal advice of A.S. Humphreys, who had represented her along with Clarence DeKnight during the 1902 Congressional hearings in Hawaii. Either through Humphreys or at Curtis Iaukea's request, William O. Smith was invited to aid Humphreys and meet with the Queen. The meeting was later described by Smith only as to the fact it occurred and the advice that was given. He, Humphreys, and Iaukea convinced her to create a trust instead of a will. Smith's law firm drafted the trust agreement and became legal advisor to the trust. Three trustees would control and manage the trust's assets — her real and personal property — and provide her guidance, including with respect to her legal choices and the costs associated with each. In the trust she also granted to Curtis Iaukea some of her property located in Waikiki. [427]

She already had decided that Archibald Cleghorn, her brother-in-law, would be the chairman of the trust and Curtis Iaukea the managing trustee and treasurer. Iaukea's responsibility was to manage daily affairs, make monthly reports to the Queen, and provide her with her monthly allowance and other expenses. Smith, Humphreys, and Iaukea dissuaded her from choosing anyone other than Smith as the third trustee. On December 2, 1909, Liliuokalani approved and signed the will and deed that created the Liliuokalani Trust. She would now live off its modest proceeds at an amount of one hundred dollars per month. Her commitment to native Hawaiian children was highly praised in Hawaii and in the United States. Prince Kuhio and others were aware fully of the details, which were published. Kuhio received nothing under the trust.[428]

Liliuokalani chose Smith on Iaukea's recommendation. The choice of Smith was fraught with risks. As a practical matter Smith certainly had personal and political connections including in his relationship with judges who would have to approve various aspects of the trust's decisions. Smith also had experience in real estate and trust matters. It was not apparent, however, that the fact Smith represented the estate of Bernice Bishop, the Queen's sister, was a factor to the Queen. The Bishop estate had been created more than twenty years earlier. The Queen had expressed her dislike for the religious discrimination that determined the estate's beneficiaries and Charles Bishop, who managed his wife's trust, was very supportive of annexation from the outset of the *coup d'état*. The Queen may have believed Smith would stop opposing her claim as he had done so frequently in the past. Her property would have been unencumbered if she had not needed to borrow money to finance her personal obligations and continued pursuit of the claim after 1904, when success in Congress seemed imminent. Smith had done discernable harm to her, including financially. If Congress approved the Crown lands claim, two hundred thousand dollars would be a considerable addition to her trust. The alternative — the proper presentation to the court of claims of her argument even in the form presented to Congress — also had the potential to add to the trust. Allowing those actions to occur unimpeded by Smith might be worth the risk of having him know as much as he would in his new position.[429]

William O. Smith now had control of the trust and an intimate knowledge of the Queen's finances, property, and legal decisions that could affect the trust's viability. In the proper fulfillment of his responsibilities and in his personal relationship with Curtis Iaukea and Sidney Ballou, Smith would have known and reviewed the content and purpose of the petition prepared by Kinney, Ballou, Prosser, and Anderson and signed by the Queen.

*

On December 4, Liliuokalani boarded the *Magnolia* for San Francisco. Receiving compensation from Congress would obviate the need for the lawsuit in the court of claims. She certainly might have believed that Kuhio would need encouragement. The Queen also wanted to visit her friends in San Francisco and Washington, DC, and her relatives in Boston. Perhaps she sensed within her body and her financial constraint an impending finality; the need for completion with regard to saying farewell to people who had welcomed her without reservation or complication. On the day of her departure Iaukea wrote her. He focused on the law suit, not Congress. Implicitly he recognized the one action he could influence that Kuhio could not. He felt "confident," he said, that "success will crown your majesty's efforts....I feel that your claim will receive due consideration because it is in proper and responsible hands -In the hands of a man like Ballou, there is no doubt that it will obtain a respectful hearing and adjudication, and unless all signs fail, I believe your claims will get proper recognition at last." Iaukea also commended the Queen for "placing control and the management of the estate in the hands of such men as Cleghorn and W.O. Smith. They are men above reproach and honorable in business matters. Men that you can trust fully and have confidence in. These are men that I have been trying for years to bring around you and who will be glad to serve you in every way they can — Already, the good impression by this simple act of yours will go far towards establishing the confidence and respect that your majesty should enjoy in this community as the First Lady in the land." Iaukea's solicitousness toward Smith coincided far more with his own need for legitimacy than it did with establishing Liliuokalani's "respect... in the community." He was still trying to convince her of the propriety of her action.[430]

No one was more discomforted with the choice of Smith and the influence exerted by Iaukea than Prince Kuhio. A disruptive clash of temperaments and motives, personal, political and financial, emerged with an insidious pervasiveness. When she arrived in San Francisco, Liliuokalani stayed at the Stewart Hotel on Geary Street near Union Square. The Stewart had survived the 1906 earthquake and fire with only modest damage. Kuhio visited her. They discussed the trust. Kuhio may have threatened to withhold any support for the claim in Congress unless he was made a beneficiary under the trust. On December 8, Iaukea informed the Queen the trustees had met on December 7 and adopted by-laws for the trust, which he enclosed for her review. He assured her that her interests would be handled property "as long as your affairs are under the control of such men as W.O. Smith and A.S. Cleghorn." The Queen's personal challenge was to preserve her equilibrium and to take the long view.⁴³¹

On December 18, Cleghorn wrote the Queen about the manner in which he was organizing the trust. She was still in San Francisco. Cleghorn came to his closing comments. "I hope you will take the best care of your health and keep your mind at ease with regards to matters here," he wrote, "as everything will be done for your interests. I trust that there is no truth in the report that your lawyer is going before the Court of Claims at Washington, as I think it would be the worst step you could take. Your best policy being to deal directly with the Government, Senate and Congress." The existence of the petition to the court of claims, the Queen's decision to sign it, and an opportunity to review and comment on its content was kept away from Cleghorn. He was neither consulted nor advised despite his chairmanship of her trust.⁴³²

When she arrived in Washington, DC, the Queen stayed in the Arlington Hotel near Lafayette Square. Kuhio visited her again. The effort in Congress had failed. The committee either informed the Queen informally that it would not approve Kuhio's bill or Kuhio indicated he would no longer support it. In a letter to Liliuokalani of January 14, 1910, Iaukea informed her that he is "sending under separate cover...a package containing the Briefs... which Mr. Ballou brought to my office yesterday. The Petition is printed in book form and intended for circulation at Washington where it will do the most good.... Mr. Ballou will leave for Washington about the 15ᵗʰ of next month [February] to represent Your Majesty before the Court of Claims when the matter of your Petition comes up for a hearing. I have read the claim over carefully and it seems to me that Your Majesty has put up a strong case, and if there is any sense of right and justice in those composing the Court of Claims, it should be meted out to Your Majesty. Let us hope that success this time will crown your efforts." In the same letter of January 14, Iaukea referred to a recent meeting he held with the two other trustees, Cleghorn and Smith. He made no reference to whether the petition or the retention of Kinney, Ballou, Prosser, and Anderson to file it had been discussed. ⁴³³

On January 28, Cleghorn again wrote the Queen in reply to letters he received from her of January 3, from San Francisco and January 9, from Chicago. After he assured her that she would receive "a statement of Iaukea's stewardship at the end of each month," he added that "[a]s you do not acknowledge my letter of December 18, I enclose a copy as the original may have miscarried." Whether

Liliuokalani deliberately or inadvertently chose not to respond to Cleghorn's admonition about the court of claims or whether, in fact, his letter of December 18 "miscarried," Cleghorn seems not to have participated directly in determining the wisdom — legal or political — of filing the petition in the court of claims.[434]

In the end, the Queen decided on legal action. The petition, in its typewritten form with the Queen's boldly crafted signature attached, was filed on January 20 with the clerk of the United States Court of Claims, Archibald Hopkins. It was likely the Queen had walked or carriaged by the court house many times. She may have visited it when, in its earlier iteration, the building housed the Corcoran art collection. It would have been like her to visit the building again; to walk up its steps and, in the moment, reflected upon the journey she had taken and what she now had authorized. Inside the clerk's office, someone reviewed the petition's content and with the care of experience neatly docketed the date of the petition's submission and the petition's title plainly in script in the court's record book: *Liliuokalani v. United States of America.*

WASHINGTON, DC, APRIL 7, 1910

The United States Court of Claims was established in 1855. The court was necessitated in part by war and the acknowledgement by Congress that it could not determine impartially individual petitions for compensation against the United States. During the British occupation of the nation in 1812 and the war against Mexico in 1848 the United States used, destroyed or occupied personal property and exploited, impeded, and harmed livelihoods. Congress decided to share the responsibility for judging those claims with a court of law. In the early moments of the Civil War, President Abraham Lincoln described succinctly the court's obligation as "the duty of the government to render prompt justice against itself, in favor of citizens."[435]

The court of claims' duty remained the same in 1910: To hear "all claims upon the Constitution [that]... would be entitled to redress from the United States, either in a court of law [or a court of] equity." To accomplish its purpose the court was authorized to take testimony from individuals under oath wherever the wrongdoing allegedly occurred and allow the parties to submit expert testimony and documentary evidence to support their claim. The process began, as it did in *Liliuokalani v. United States of America*, with the submission of the petition. It is the opening move; the most critical document; the first and freely crafted explanation of precisely what rights the petitioner possessed and how the conduct of the United States violated those rights either in law or by unfair — inequitable — treatment.[436]

When the clerk of the court, Archibald Hopkins, entered the courtroom and directed those in attendance to rise as the judges' entered, Sidney Ballou instinctively must have felt discomforted if not embarrassed. He was on the defensive. The petition his law firm submitted was prepared inadequately. Normally, as the petitioner, Ballou would have argued first about the facts and the legal questions in the case as he had presented them in his petition. Presumably, he also would argue about the testimony or evidence he had submitted. Instead, Samuel Ashbaugh, the Assistant United States Attorney, had taken the initiative away from Ballou. Ashbaugh was on the offensive.

The courtroom added its own source of solemnity to the importance of the court's duty. The courtroom's ceilings were forty feet in height. The doors of its entranceway were made of black walnut with bronze knobs. Behind Ballou were benches for spectators that were used in the original Hall of Representatives in the United States Capitol. A polished wood railing separated Ballou from those people who had come to observe. Before Ballou was the noticeably elevated bench in elegantly crafted polished woods long enough to accommodate the five members of the court seated in wood-framed black leathered chairs. From Ballou's perspective, the bench's backdrop was framed by four Ionic columns interspersed with black draperies. Atop the columns and properly centered was a large, tastefully-carved eagle head adjoined to a shield in embossed stars and stripes. Between the lawyers and the judges' bench were two tables for counsel. Ballou's table was to his left. In the center was the podium behind which each man would stand to make their argument to the judges. It appears that this case was Ballou's first in the court of claims. Ashbaugh was in regular attendance.[437]

The petition submitted by Kinney, Ballou, Prosser, and Anderson failed in the most elementary way. The firm never asserted the Queen had any rights in the Crown lands or that the United States committed any wrongdoing against her. In its allegations, the petition merely recited the existence of the 1848 action of King Kamehameha III that created the Crown lands, and the 1865 Act and subsequent acts of the Hawaii legislature, which — as Ballou characterized them in the petition — were intended to prohibit the sale of the Crown lands by the sovereign and restrict their use and benefit only to "the reigning sovereign." The petition provided no excerpt from the acts or a description that indicated the acts served other purposes or that even with the passage of the acts the Crown land retained its private nature.[438]

In setting forth the description of the action by the Hawaii legislature that responded to the sale by Princess Ruth of her interest in the Crown lands, the petition nowhere stated the transaction indicated the Crown lands retained a private character. The petition also stated that when Liliuokalani became queen in 1891, she "became vested with a life interest in and to all the rents...derived from the Crown Land" with no factual statement or reference to a document or transaction to support how she derived that vested right or why that right was based on a private interest in the land. The petition also stated that the Queen "was deposed by a revolutionary government and on said day of January 17, 1893 and yielded her authority to said Provisional Government under the following protest duly signed and transmitted to said Provisional Government." Although the petition included the protest she actually prepared, there was *no* reference in the petition to the actions of the United States Minister or the Navy or the Queen's expectation — realized fully in fact — that the United States would examine the circumstances of the *coup d'état* and the decisive and inappropriate role the United States played in it. Ballou had disconnected the United States from any wrongdoing or unfairness against Liliuokalani or the constitutional monarchy she headed. Ballou had yielded the Queen's legal and moral high ground — her right to due process and fairness.[439]

The petition referenced the formation of the Republic but merely recited the constitutional provision that "declared" the Republic's ownership of the Crown lands. The petition made no reference to the fact this declaration was unilaterally made — Francis Hatch's "act of war" — or what effect it had on the Queen's private interest in the Crown lands or that either the provisional government or the Republic had engaged in wrongdoing. The petition recited further that in 1897 the "Republic...signified its consent in the manner provided by its constitution to cede to the United States...the absolute...ownership...of all [the] Crown land," which the United States accepted through annexation in 1898 and was now vested with legal title because of the Organic Act in 1900. Wrongdoing against the Queen by the United States, according to Ballou, did not occur until six years after the *coup d'état*.[440]

Through the Organic Act in 1900, the United States "extinquish[ed]" the Queen's rights and engaged in "a taking of [Liliuokalani's] property without due process of law, contrary to [*sic*] 5th Amendment of the Constitution of the United States." The United States, the petition stated, now held the Crown lands in trust for the Queen; an assertion of law or a conclusion that stood without any support from the allegations of fact that preceded it.[441]

The petition contained two more allegations that made it vulnerable to an attack by the United States. The petition stated that a "claim has not been presented to Congress or any Department except that bills for relief...have been introduced in Congress from time to time." In fact, Liliuokalani had raised the illegality of taking the Crown lands through her lawyers and personally with Congress or the president in 1893, 1897, 1898, 1900, 1902, 1904, during a congressional hearing in Hawaii, 1905, 1908, and during the congressional hearing in 1909. Congress also had acted on the petitions and requests. Each time she had tied the illegality of taking the Crown lands to the illegality of the *coup d'état*. The drafters of the petition — who actually had months to prepare it — either were pathetically ignorant of the facts or thoroughly entombed in the need not to expose the illegality of *coup d'état* in which Kinney and Hatch had engaged and Ballou as a judge ensured would not be examined. The Queen, according to Ballou, had sat idly on her rights from 1893 through the filing of the petition in 1910. Worse still, the assertion in the petition exposed to the attorney representing the United States that Ballou was not thorough or not much of an advocate for his client and her cause or he had something to hide.[442]

The second allegation that enhanced the petition's vulnerability to attack was that Ballou claimed the Queen was entitled to only six years worth of rent estimated at four hundred and fifty thousand dollars. This allegation was based on the assumption that the court of claims only had authority to consider a claim that arose from an event six years old. The petition could have contended that the wrongdoing by the United States against the Queen began in 1893 and had continued in different forms until the filing of the petition. Instead she was made to appear, once again, as if she sat idly on her rights or that she did not believe she had any rights that were harmed until 1904; that is, six years prior to the filing of the petition.[443]

Many of the allegations in the petition would have benefited from reference to facts and the attachment of documents to the petition. The Queen's letters and petitions to Congress and the president; the facts set out in the *Hawaii's Story By Hawaii's Queen* demonstrating the common understanding by the royal family that a private right existed in the Crown lands; the fact of private transactions engaged in by leaseholders on the Crown lands between 1864 and 1893 when Liliuokalani was deposed; notes or a transcript of the debate when Hatch, Smith, Thurston, and Dole ensured inclusion of the constitutional provision that declared the Crown lands belonged to the Republic; the facts to support the proposition that Hatch asserted in Congress that the commissioners created in the 1865 Act were private trustees of the Crown lands; or the fact that legal opinions were used persuasively in 1882 to show that Princess Ruth had a private right to the Crown lands that she could sell, were available to Ballou and could have been included or referenced in the petition. From November 20 — the day the Queen signed the petition — through January 20 — the day the petition was filed — and further still through March 23, Ballou had the opportunity to revise or to formally amend the petition to include these facts or others. He did not.[444]

Samuel Ashbaugh recognized the petition's flaws. On March 23, he filed a "demurrer," a statement that even if every one of the allegations in the petition was accepted as true and unchallenged they "are not sufficient to constitute a cause of action [i.e. a claim]" against the United States. Ashbaugh treated the petition cavalierly and sought to convey to the court that it should hold the petitioner — really the lawyer — to the precise words the law firm had written. There also was a penetrating confidence in the government's brief in support of the demurrer. "The facts alleged in the petition are simple and of easy comprehension," Ashbaugh wrote. Relying on the plain meaning of the expressed words used in the constitution approved by the Republic and the expressed words used by the Republic in approving its acceptance to become a Territory of the United States — all quoted without qualification or explanation in the petition — Ashbaugh stated the "property was transferred to the succeeding" governments "in fee simple, free and unencumbered," including "to the United States unencumbered with any claim of any person whomsoever."[445]

"The Crown lands referred to were in no sense private lands," Ashbaugh wrote, "and no personal rights of such person so occupying the throne are alleged in the petition." Moreover, reading the petition literally, Ashbaugh also stated that the Queen's protest of January 17, 1893 was the "abdication of the claimant" to the provisional government and that the petition made no connection between the United States and the harm suffered by the Queen. With a special irony, Ashbaugh relied on only one document to support his argument: The memorandum that William D. Alexander had prepared for William O. Smith in 1893 and submitted by Alexander to Commissioner James Blount to justify the acquisition of the Crown lands by the provisional government without regard to the Queen's rights. "The facts set out in the petition," Ashbaugh wrote," are not only fully sustained but somewhat elaborated in the opinion of Mr. Alexander, the surveyor general of the Hawaiian government." A copy of Alexander's memorandum to Smith was submitted later to the court.[446]

When "the sovereignty of the Kingdom of Hawaii was destroyed by that revolutionary government, as alleged in the petition," Ashbaugh explained as he came to his conclusion, and "the claimant . . . abdicated the throne, as is also alleged, the sovereignty ceased, and at that same moment the emoluments of that office were also extinguished. If the claimant in this case had alleged that she had retained certain private rights that were susceptible of support in law or equity, such claim might be beyond the reach of a demurrer." Put differently, if Ballou had submitted a petition of elementary quality properly crafted with reference to facts available easily, Ashbaugh acknowledged he would have been unable to file his demurrer.[447]

There was no surprise in the content of Ashbaugh's demurrer. The questions raised by Ashbaugh were similar to the questions raised in Congress by members of the committee on claims about Francis Hatch's legal arguments, which were presented with more specificity than Ballou's petition and without the benefit of the resources available to Ballou or the duty Ballou had to represent his client. In fact elements of Ashbaugh's argument could be traced back to all the events critical to the history of the Crown lands. A modestly serious effort at research and analysis by Ballou would have yielded the facts necessary to write an adequate petition. Even after the filing of the demurrer by Ashbaugh, Ballou could have amended the petition. Still, he did not.[448]

*

At the time Ashbaugh submitted his demurrer and brief in late March, Lili-uokalani had just departed San Francisco to return to Hawaii. She had visited Boston and taken a train directly to Chicago, where she laid over for one night before taking the Northeastern railroad to San Francisco. Her last effort to get Congress to act had failed. Her last hope was in the court of claims. "Discouraged in her mission and broken down in health, the former ruler," it was reported, "is going back to the land of her former splendor, where the people still call her Queen." She is now a poor woman "unable to take a cab to the hotel." Boarding a commuter bus she was unable to find a room downtown and "had to put up at a small hotel on the South Side." She told the reporter that "'I am going back to my people to spend my declining years,' as tears rolled down her checks." She added that "I am still the Queen of my people. This sovereign right cannot be taken from me." She was confident that the "loyalty of the Hawaiian people" will ensure that "I can end my days without actual want."[449]

As the Queen moved westward toward Honolulu, Sidney Ballou moved east-ward toward Washington. Ballou apparently left Honolulu for the continent in mid-February for the April 7 oral argument. Perhaps he stopped in Los Angeles, where his new wife Lucia had family. As reported in the *Washington Post*, Ballou arrived in Washington, "to argue a claim in favor of former Queen Liliuokalani before the Court of Claims" in mid-March.[450]

Ballou had an evolving ambition that no longer included a permanent resi-dence in Hawaii. He gave a talk at the Shoreham Hotel on March 18 on how "the Japanese of Hawaii ... might prove a serious menace to the government...and the sugar plantations." He was concerned about labor unrest and the demand for higher wages. "[T]he facility with which the Japanese were organized," he told the audience, "demonstrated that the yellow men might prove formidable in case they were inclined to rise against the government." Ballou was transforming his practice of law toward lobbying in the nation's capitol in support of the same sugar plantations. When he arrived in Washington, in March, Sidney Ballou was a man in the midst of a professional, personal, and geographic transition.[451]

Ballou's seriousness of purpose and the goal he sought to accomplish on his visit to the continent were no match to the purpose and goal of his client or the longer term native Hawaiian interests that underpin it. The Queen's case before the court of claims had emerged as less hers and more of an exercise in seeking — once again — to bring finality to any challenge to the *coup d'état's* legality and to ensure the legitimacy of the Republic's and now the Territory's ownership and control of the Crown lands.

*

Into the courtroom walked the five members of the court of claims dressed in the black robes reflective of their stature. Stanton Judkins Peelle was from a small farm in Richmond, Indiana. He had fought in the Civil War and later served as a member of Congress. He was appointed by President Harrison in 1892 and elevated to chief judge by President Roosevelt. Peelle was sixty-seven years old. Charles Bowen Howry was from Oxford, Mississippi. Howry served in the Confederate Army. He had fought in the battle of Chickamauga with Senator John Morgan of Alabama. He was appointed by President Cleveland in 1897. His colleagues considered him a "southern gentleman whose kindness, patience, and courtesy was much appreciated." He was sixty-six years old. George Wesley Atkinson was from Charleston, Virginia. He was the former governor of West Virginia. Atkinson was sixty-five years old. Samuel Stebbins Barney was from Washington County, Wisconsin. He, too, was a former member of Congress; appointed to the court by President Roosevelt in 1905. Barney was sixty-four years old. Seated to one end of the five-member court was Fenton Booth, its youngest member. Booth was now forty-one years old. In addition to his judgeship, Booth also taught law four nights a week and served, without pay, as the Dean of Howard University Law School.[452]

Generally, the court of claims reflected a particular breath of America, certainly its Republican, mid-western perspective and character. The chief clerk, Archibald Hopkins, maintained a similar perspective although decidedly oriented toward the subtle constancy of the Washington insider's view of the world. He also may have shared with the members of the court his experience concerning the 1893 *coup d'état* and his work for Lorrin Thurston or his friendship with William O. Smith or, perhaps, those connections were common knowledge. The cultural perspective or mindset or conservative view of the law's purpose held by Judge Booth or the other members of the court were radically different than the experience of Liliuokalani or the cultural characteristics that underpin the history of the Crown lands necessary to understand and decide the case.

Booth wrote some years later, after leaving the court, that he "discovered that lawyers of great ability and enviable reputations are as likely to be wrong as more inexperienced and ones little known to the profession." Whatever personal stature Sidney Ballou had in Hawaii was of little consequence to Fenton Booth. Booth and the other judges relied on their reading of the petitions and the briefs and whatever other forms of evidence the lawyers sought to bring to their attention before they walked into the courtroom to hear the oral argument. Booth, like his colleagues, had decided cases and written opinions in cases involving Indian reservations and claims. They also had available to them the way the United States Supreme Court dealt with the cultural characteristics of native Hawaiian cases when those characteristics were brought to its attention. The courts of claims' cultural disposition would — in this case especially — place the burden for educating each of the court's members onto Kinney, Ballou, Prosser, and Anderson beginning with the content and thoroughness of the petition. There is no indication the firm recognized or sought to meet its burden.[453]

*

Before he entered the courtroom with his colleagues, Judge Booth would have read Sidney Ballou's response to the demurrer filed by the United States. Much of the answer to the argument made by the United States lied, according to Ballou, in the Hawaii Supreme Court's 1864 decision in *Estate of Kamehameha IV*. In fact, significant portions of the decision were reproduced in the brief. "[W]e can do no better than refer the Court to the leading case," Ballou's response stated. But Ballou provided little of his own explanation of the decision's meaning or the correctness of the decision's recitation of Hawaii's history or the ambivalent outcome of the decision — Queen Emma could inherit Crown land as if it were privately held by her husband the king and, at the same time, the king could no longer do what the court had said he had done legally with his private property. Ballou also could have explained the political dilemma the Hawaii Supreme Court sought to resolve by not offending either the deceased king or his wife, or demonstrated why some or all of the Hawaii Supreme Court decision was incorrect. His meager explanations, instead, were easily noticeable and left the court and Ashbaugh the freedom to read the 1864 opinion without much guidance from Ballou.[454]

Ballou also acknowledged that William. D. Alexander's report to Smith relied upon by the United States "is accurate as to its historical facts," a remarkable admission and hardly the Queen's position. Ballou's subsequent effort to discredit the report — it "was made two months after the overthrow of the Queen and ... is a statement of the officials of the revolutionary government under which they sought to justify to Mr. Blount the confiscation of the Queen's interest" — described only the motivation for the report, not why it was factually incorrect. Ballou had supported Alexander's and Smith's position in 1893. Ballou was at war with the Queen's interests.[455]

With respect to the Republic's unilateral declaration that it owned the Crown lands, Ballou wrote that it was "an attempted confiscation of the interest of the petitioner," and "absolutely opposed to every fact in the history of the Crown Land." The Republic's action, Ballou added, was a "deprivation of property without due process of law, contrary to the constitutional provision, [which] is so obvious that . . . we are content to leave it without argument." Having just acknowledged the accuracy of William D. Alexander's report to Smith, it was easy enough for the court to regard this statement as a mere assertion by counsel for which he had provided no support. Ballou did include reference to Francis Hatch's testimony before Congress in support of his argument as if Hatch's testimony was a substitute for factual statements in the petition filed in a court of law. The gap in the logic of Ballou's reasoning and persuasiveness created by the failure to submit an adequate petition was insurmountable.[456]

At no point in his brief did Ballou attribute wrongdoing to the United States. The failure of Hawaii and its judiciary to consider the Queen's claim Ballou attributed to "fear;" and, recognizing the error in the petition about the Queen's protests before Congress, Ballou acknowledge only one of them, the congressional effort in 1904. Ballou did not correct the statement by Ashbaugh that the Queen had abdicated in 1893, a fact the court now could assume was not disputed by Ballou or his client.[457]

Within seven days of Ballou's submission to the court, Ashbaugh replied. The court, he wrote, had to decide only one question to bring the case to an end: "At the time of the [the *coup d'état* in 1893], did the claimant have any personal rights or private interests in the Crown Lands in question?" Ashbaugh prefaced his answer by stating that "[f]rom what had appeared in the public prints...one would have been warranted in believing that in the forum of conscience these claims of the deposed Hawaiian Queen . . . would demand a settlement even if they could not be supported by law. The brief, however, of counsel for the claimant has dispelled all this. It now appears from the facts and the law, and from the solemn enactments of four different governments, that these claims are without any foundation whatever." The answer to the question Ashbaugh had posited was simple: "[T]he sovereign of the Hawaiian Islands had had no personal interest or private rights in these Crown Lands since" 1865, "long prior to the claimant's ascending to the throne," and "this position is not controverted in the least by the decisions of the courts of the Hawaiian Islands."[458]

In his last submission to the court on April 2 — just five days before the oral argument — Ashbaugh filed a "Supplemental Brief." He wrote that "if we should admit for the sake of argument...that [Liliuokalani] had a valid legal estate in the crown lands," that estate was "entirely extinguished" by the adoption of the constitution of the Hawaiian Republic. "If the [Queen] could not dispute the constitutional declaration of her own government, much less could she set up a claim as against the United States Government in this case. The courts of this country could do no more than the courts of the Hawaiian Republic.... [Liliuokalani has] no legal rights in the [Crown lands] which could be decreed in her favor by the Hawaiian courts."[459]

Who sitting or standing in the court of claims did not know that the lawyers who led the *coup d'état* and who controlled the Hawaii judiciary were unwilling to match their skill against Liliuokalani in a court of law? When Sidney Ballou was viewed by Fenton Booth and his colleagues as they entered the courtroom to hear the oral argument, who among them could respect the use of coercion and raw power that Ballou represented to deny — for more than seventeen years since the *coup d'état* — Liliuokalani's right to petition her own government?

*

Samuel Ashbaugh stepped to the podium to make his argument. He was from Illinois. He was a Republican who came to Washington during the Roosevelt

Administration. Ashbaugh also was a well know Shakespearean scholar and lecturer. He was fifty-nine years old.[460]

Ashbaugh's argument was straightforward and apparently brief. His critical challenge was to keep the controversy away from the role of the United States in the *coup d'état* and to keep the argument simple. Everything after 1865 did not matter. In that regard he had Ballou's implicit agreement. Ashbaugh argued as if the case was based on Anglo-Saxon principles of law and nothing more. Ballou's petition and brief gave him the freedom to argue it that way. The 1864 Hawaii Supreme Court decision, Ashbaugh told the court, "vested [the Crown lands] in fee simple in the Crown as distinguished from the personality of the sovereign." The Hawaii court so restricted the right Liliuokalani now claimed so as to ensure whatever her interest in the Crown lands it "was abhorrent to an estate in fee simple absolute." She could not sell the land or pass it on to a descendant. The Queen could have a legal right in the Crown land, Ashbaugh contended, only if it was free of any restrictions. Through the 1865 Act the Hawaii legislature "divested the sovereign of whatever legal title he had." When the *coup d'état* occurred in 1893 the monarchy ceased and the land passed to the Republic and, with annexation and the Organic Act, passed without restrictions to the United States.[461]

Ballou was in a bind. He was constrained by his own political and ideological imperatives. To get pass the demurrer he had to argue that, in fact, the Queen had legal rights in the Crown lands, the Republic acted illegally in declaring ownership in them, and that the United States had played a role in the *coup d'état*, none of which he had pled in the petition. He also had not pled in the petition or written in his brief anything about some unique character of the Hawaiian culture that the court should consider. When he took his place behind the podium and looked up at Judge Fenton Booth and Booth's fellow judges, Ballou also had to ask the court of claims to examine and determine precisely what he concluded he would not examine as a judge.

Ballou reiterated orally the position he took in his brief. The Crown lands were always considered private property and the intention of King Kamehameha III was "to reserve to the King certain lands which could not by any possibility be treated as the property of the Government." He also stated that there "has been no pretense that the declaration of the constitution was...anything other than arbitrary confiscation" of the Crown lands. He had been unwilling to provide any factual assertion in his petition and was unable to cite to a Hawaii Supreme Court decision that supported his argument. The remainder of his argument was based on the assumption the Queen had a legal interest in the Crown lands. He described the precedents in court decisions that established that when a nation was conquered the private rights of individuals in property could not be confiscated and annulled. He was referring to the United States government's acquisition of the Crown lands in 1900, although he made no allegation in the complaint the United States had acted the conqueror. He also emphasized that because the Queen had a legal interest in the Crown lands, any government that had notice of the existence of the Queen's legal interest or had notice the government from which it took the land already held the land in trust for the Queen, the new government had to assume that same responsibility. Ballou did not mention — and it was not in his petition or brief — that neither the provisional government nor the Republic had acted as a trustee for the Crown lands with respect to the Queen. Since 1893, she had received none of the rents or proceeds from their lease or sale. Ballou acknowledged that "strenuous efforts have been made to deprive her of this right [to the Crown lands], legally as well as in fact," including by the Hawaii Supreme Court. Nonetheless, Ballou wanted the court of claims to exercise "good conscience" to recognize the Queen's rights.[462]

*

On May 16, the court of claims entered a unanimous decision. Judge Booth wrote the opinion for the court. He denied the claim. He accepted Ashbaugh's characterization of the legal issue: Whether, in the "absence of [a vested life interest], the crown lands [were] subject to the usual transmission of title appurtenant to a change of sovereignty." Booth noted that this characterization was "conceded" by Ballou. The "solution of this question," Judge Booth wrote, "involves a detailed examination of the various acts of the Hawaii legislative body and reference to various sections of the Hawaiian constitutions."[463]

To Judge Booth, reliance on the 1864 decision in *Estate of Kamehameha IV* — the mainstay of Ballou's argument — was of little help to Ballou because "it is clear from the opinion that the crown lands were treated not as the King's private property in the strict sense of the term." Booth also found comfort in the "system of land tenure" in Hawaii which, he wrote, was akin to the "feudal system" of Europe, with rules he understood and that also were reflective of the same perspective contained in Alexander's report to Smith. Ballou had conceded the accuracy of that perspective as well. "In January, 1865," Judge Booth continued, "the unlimited latitude allowed in the control of the Crown lands" came to an end. Judge Booth viewed Princess Ruth's private sale of her alleged interest in the Crown lands as supportive of the same view. Because the legislature "stepped in to resolve the dispute" the Crown lands were not Princess Ruth's private property to dispose as she wished. The underlying history of Princess Ruth's transaction was viewed by Booth through the conventional Anglo-Saxon rules governing property law.[464]

Booth concluded that the "Crown lands acquired their unusual status through a desire of the King to firmly establish his Government by commendable concessions to his chiefs and people out of the public domain. The reservations were made to the Crown and not the King as an individual. The crown lands were the resourceful methods of income to sustain . . . the dignity of the office to which they were inseparably attached. When the office ceased to exist they became as other lands of the Sovereign and passed to the [United States] as part and parcel of the public domain."[465]

Having resolved the case in this way, Judge Booth concluded that it was unnecessary to discuss the Republic's declaration of ownership and the similar declaration in the Organic Act that ensured ownership of the Crown lands in the United States. "It is, however, worthy of note that the Organic Act of 1900 put an end to any trust — if the same possibly existed — and the petition herein was not filed until January 20, 1910," ten years after the event Ballou claimed gave rise to the connection between the United States and the Queen. Ballou had not given the court any reason to examine the conduct and unfairness of the United States.[466]

*

The court of claims did not dismiss the case or bring it to an end. Part of the unanimous decision was to provide the Queen — and Ballou — another opportunity to present her case. Booth gave Ballou ninety days "to amend her petition" in order to correct the deficiencies identified in the court's opinion and proceed with the case. The firm took no further action. Perhaps the Queen simply ran out of money. Perhaps she was assured by her trustees, William O. Smith and Curtis Iaukea, and her lawyer, Sidney Ballou that everything had been done with considerable skill and she had no further recourse. Perhaps in her wisdom she realized that Sidney Ballou was unwilling or incapable of representing her interest and advocating her position.[467]

Epilogue. Outraged Agony: The Embattled Soul of Sovereignty

When Liliuokalani departed Washington for the last time in January 1910, she was weary and financially depleted. She was looking forward to the simple quietude of Washington Place and her property along Waikiki, to special moments with her friends and being alone in her garden. She also planned changes to her home. Her legacy of grace and persistence and intellect was settled long ago. She had created a trust to provide for the children of native Hawaiians. She had crafted songs and poetry of enduring meaning that she heard sung and said and repeated in subtle variations while she was still alive. She had written a biography and letters and notes and diary entries. The love and respect with which she was held would endure through the memory of those who knew her, saw her, watched her reign and counsel, take risks and embody what they believed. The memories would flow through the children and grandchildren of those people who could share stories from a parent or uncle or aunt or friend.

The memory was related not only to a past way of life or to adherence to a custom or ritual or the moment of a meeting. At seventy-one years old Liliuokalani had sued the United States of America. The suit was filed in a building that still remains, located only a few yards from the home of the president of the United States. She had stood "shoulder to shoulder, heart to heart" in the nation's capital in a way that Emma Nawahi could imagine easily when she asked the people of Hilo to affix their names in support of independence for which the Queen was fighting at precisely that same moment. The wrongdoing of the leaders of the *coup d'état* and the decisive role played by the United States Navy was a judgment she gave life to into the twentieth century.

When she boarded the steamer in San Francisco to return home, the *Tucson Citizen* of Arizona — far distance from the Pacific's currents and winds or the volcanic eruptions that characterize Maui or the town of Hilo — had written about the Queen and native Hawaiians and Hawaii in an editorial. The paper's editor had followed the evolution of the Crown lands claim and understood the Queen's intention in filing it. "One of the most persistent and perhaps remarkable women in the United States is now in San Francisco," he wrote. The "long pilgrimage of this lady from Honolulu to Washington" reflected "one of the unique stories in our national history." The editor searched for a prophecy. "That the claim is to be paid is scarcely to be expected," the editor wrote, "though the United States recognized a more unreasonable demand, perhaps when it 'paid' Spain $20,000,000 for the Philippines. But there is still something striking and interesting about the long journey of the former queen, and her visit to America that will serve to impress on our minds again with the vastness and diversity of our possession. For a more strange and alien region than that which was discovered by Captain Cook has never been 'assimilated' by any of the nations of Europe with all their experience and experiences in colonization."[468]

The *Tucson Citizen* editorial distilled in the Queen's action her insistence on taking the long view. She had created unsettledness, a circumstance, an attitude, a temperament about Hawaii and its native people and their identity that no one but they could define when they were ready.

In 1912, Sanford Dole was still a United States District Court judge. His service on the bench was admirable and without special distinction. The Hawaii legislature and the new governor recognized the need — financial as well as historic — to provide Liliuokalani with something in the nature of a pension of twelve thousand dollars a year. She accepted the money. It allowed her a modicum of material comfort and an ability to care for people she loved. She also could reduce her debt and add to her Trust. The money was authorized without recognition in law that it related to the *coup d'état* in 1893 or the acquisition of the Crown lands by the provisional government or the Republic. William O. Smith and Lorrin Thurston could only support it. Sidney Ballou was, within the year, a permanent resident of Washington, DC. The United States remained silent.[469]

All four men had done irreparable harm to the legal rights of the Queen and the fate of native Hawaiians in a court of law. Dole, Smith, Thurston, and Ballou had used their power to ensure the Queen did not get judicial review of her rights to the Crown lands or any financial benefit associated with their loss. All four men also diminished the unique importance of the Hawaiian culture in understanding the meaning of land and the common duty that imbued the land's purpose. In the federal judiciary the underlying meaning of *Liliuokalani v United States of America* had been set: Anglo-Saxon jurisprudence and the history of Hawaii as viewed through that lens would be difficult to surmount. Throughout the remainder of her life the Queen "never ceased to hope that the rights she claimed would be recognized by the government of the United States." In a way that she may have understood, her persistence ensured the fate of the Crown lands would remain unsettled. Her arguments have never been properly and fully made in a court of law.[470]

On April 21, 1917, the frail, fully white-haired Liliuokalani walked alone across the grass and flowers of the front yard of Washington Place. She was still "straight backed and firm in resolution;" a women who had known and still preserved the countenance of a queen. She was seventy-eight years old. Her holoku dress was black. It had become the color of dissonance; a stigmata she wanted others to feel. She wore black with comfort and knowing. Five native Hawaiians, it was reported and she was told, had been killed during a German submarine attack upon the naval ship *Aztec* then engaged in fighting in the broader European campaign. Once again, in a cause of liberating people subject to denigration that certainly the young Hawaiians believed important, she recognized a purpose worthy of recognition and tribute that had been displayed by young people with whom she shared a culture. "She ordered the American flag raised over Washington Place for the first time since her mother-in-law's death a quarter of a century earlier." There was no "reconciliation" with the harm that had been done to a culture that she had witnessed and loved or the display of a gesture that implied she had reconciled herself to the stain of wrongdoing engaged in under the same flag in 1893. Raising the flag of the United States was an act in support of the choice and the sacrifice the soldiers had made and the mourning that now should follow. It was reported later that she said "In the past one hundred years Hawaiians have never shed — nor caused blood to be shed — for their own desires. If now their lives are lost it is to be under a different flag." She had done her duty when the responsibility was hers through her final action in the court of claims. Her gesture that day was intended to reflect the dignity with which she still held the right of her people to choose their own fate long after she was gone.[471]

In the latter weeks of October and into early November, the Queen's illness captured Hawaii's attention. She died at Washington Place on November 11. The "St. Andrew's bells tolled, and Honolulu knew it had come — the passing of Hawaii's last and most gracious Queen." Her body was lain "on an open bier, canopied by a royal yellow pall," as it left Washington Place. The outer shell of the coffin was made of koa wood. Black silk laid over it. The hearse moved gently between "a double line of kahili-bearers, led by two royal torch-bearers" in front and by "two long lines of Hawaiian men and women bearing other kahilis and torches" that followed. All were dressed in black. The women "escorts chanted the sacred *olis* — the songs — to the royal dead." No word or smile passed between them. Forty thousand people came to Honolulu to pray and mourn and witness.[472]

The Queen remained for a time in the large Kawaiahao Church. It was chosen because of its size; it was spacious enough to accommodate all the accoutrements of a royal funeral and the people who came to genuflect to her grace or merely, with an ambivalence and discomfort, to say they had been there. The "pall was lifted and Her Majesty lay at full length, and in attitude of peaceful repose, as though asleep in her favorite bedroom, a stone's throw away." Songs that she had written that had moved the nation and would for a century to come were sung in "a tender rendition" in homage to her life. The "favoring omens [were in] perfect accord." Rain had fallen, which signified "that the spirit of the departed *ali'i* has found favor in the heavens, and that a place has been fittingly prepared" for the Queen.[473]

The entrance to Iolani Palace was "crape-festooned...with the catafalque drawn up to the foot of the steps," when the Queen's coffin was brought into the throne room on the palace's first floor. "All throughout the long night the Queen lay in the Throne Room of the palace, the kahili watches were made eloquent by the unforgettable Hawaiian wail for the dead. ... [N]o other sound could possibly have within it the same wild, weird note of outraged agony that refuses to submit to the onrushing ages and their ever-advancing changes." Emma Nawahi had survived her queen. They had witnessed the loss of Hawaii sovereignty. Together they had endured unique and hard moments shared through a culture they both valued and lived. They retained with each other stories of life, some publicly known and many others privately expressed, that in this moment of death would take on a new and enduring meaning for others to discern and, if they choose, to provide their own form of inspiration.

When the coffin was taken from the palace to be laid to rest in the Royal Mausoleum, the procession took on a noteworthy character recognized by those present. In the "procession were several men who, as prominent figures in the revolutionary days of the monarchy, had suffered imprisonment in the cause of the Queen to whom they now paid their final earthly respects." Singular in their devotion, their names were known to those adults assembled and standing along the thoroughfare as the coffin passed. Together they had known the independence of a nation. Now, in their own way, they marched and stood with a dignity that would penetrate subtly the memory of the children who watched in silence and respect.

Acknowledgments

I visited Hawaii for the first time in 1976. My parents, Matthew and Celeste Proto, were celebrating their thirty-fifth wedding anniversary in Honolulu. My mother's two brothers, Thomas who lived in Honolulu and Dan who lived in Kikei, Maui, introduced me to the distinctive nature of the Hawaiian culture. Both men had served in the United States Army during World War II. Dan understood the geography of Hawaii and showed me places of special meaning in its history. Thomas understood the native Hawaiian culture and gave his time freely to native Hawaiian charitable organizations. When, in 1992, I was asked by my colleague Denis Dwyer, with whom I practiced law, to write the bill that would become the law that transferred Kahoolawe from the United States to Hawaii to be held in trust for native Hawaiians, I appreciated the introduction to the culture and the islands provided by both my uncles. I would be remiss if I did not acknowledge their role.

I read the 1910 decision in *Liliuokalani v. United States of America* in 1992. I was engaged deeply in my representation of Hawaii — Governor John Waihee had made the transfer of Kahoolawe an essential imperative during his term of office — and wanted to understand more than the history of the islands, the missionary influence, the Navy, and the native Hawaiian culture that I did learn over time. I wanted to know how the federal judiciary examined cases involving the intersection of law and a culture imbued with values and perspectives that were not Anglo-Saxon and not part of the continental United States. That education, which grew beyond the United States Court of Claims decision in *Liliuokalani v. United States of America*, opened the experience with Kahoolawe into a much deeper inquiry about Liliuokalani and the Crown lands claim that brought her frequently to the United States before and after annexation. Although some of the documentation concerning her periodic and often lengthy stays in San Francisco, Boston, and especially Washington, DC, was contained in the archives in Hawaii, most of the essential information existed here. I found that I was on totally new ground; examining a history and discerning a temperament, in her and in others, not explored previously. The single factor that emerged with a disquieting and powerful force was the harsh remnant of the Civil War and the failure of Reconstruction; the domestic meaning of race and cultural and religious condescension in the United States that provided the deeper underpinning for what has been viewed, until now, as American foreign policy toward Hawaii and native Hawaiians. What also emerged was the continuity in the economic imperatives and spiritual tenets of the Calvinist missionaries and the attitude and political perspective of those among their progeny — all lawyers — who led the *coup d'état* in 1893 and succeeded in making Hawaii a Territory of the United States. My own experience in the law allowed me the scrutinize, with a practical insight, the role played by those lawyers, including through the United States Court of Claims case in 1910. Other historians also have documented, with special care and of great benefit to me, the role played by native Hawaiian women in this history; documentation that my own research, before and after annexation, showed warrants even more attention than I was able to document further in this book. In the depth of Liliuokalani's cosmopolitan character and foresight — taking the long view, as I characterize it — was, I came to appreciate, the continuity of purpose and resilience that seemed to imbue, in part, those men and women who occupied Kahoolawe in 1976 and brought its fate to the attention of a larger world and, with additional discernment, may provide further guidance to others.

Guiding me throughout this inquiry in gathering documents and engaging the depth of archival records throughout the continental United States and into Hawaii was Dr. Peggy Ann Brown. We received cooperation from the archivists at the Bernice Pauahi Bishop Museum and the State Archives of Hawaii. Dr. Brown's effective skill at penetrating the depths of the National Archives here in Washington, DC, and eliciting their cooperation was invaluable and timely. I also benefited from conversations with Corinne Chun-Fujimoto, the director of Washington Place, the Queen's residence in Honolulu and Corinne's special interest in exploring the Queen's life after Hawaii was annexed to the United States. I also received valuable insights into the Hawaiian language and Hawaii's culture from Stanton Enomoto and Kala Enos, both of whom I met and befriended during our collective effort to give new life to Kahoolawe.

Insightful and at times properly cutting comments were received from those people who agreed to read portions of the manuscript. They each undertook the task with grace and endurance and a candor that I especially appreciated and welcomed. They included Dr. Philip Piccigallo, Thomas Bolle, Martin Mendelsohn, Dessa Dal Porto, Virginia Price, and Steven Ebbin. My law firm, Schnader

Harrison Segal and Lewis, also was supportive of my effort and the time it took away from my duties. The encouragement from Schnader's chair Ralph Wellington and the lead lawyer in the firm's Washington office, John Britton, was critical to my ability to approach the research and writing with the intensity I felt necessary for the task. My colleague Joan DeCarli served as my assistant and confidant throughout this process. The firm's librarians, Annemarie Lorenzen and Lisa Kelsey, and paralegal Kristine Rawls, were diligent and timely in their effort to locate some obscure court decisions and articles that made a critical and supportive contribution to my work. I also had to forgo my regular teaching rotation as an adjunct professor at Georgetown University's Public Policy Institute. I am grateful for the Institute's patience.

The responsibility for the content of the book is wholly mine. I do feel, however, that because of the constant inspiration and fine tuning in thinking and writing I received from my sister, Diana Proto Avino, and from the conversations I had with my brother, Richard Christopher Proto, before his death in July of 2008, any credit or praise for this effort is shared lovingly and appropriately with them.

Neil Thomas Proto
Washington, DC

ENDNOTES

1   William Hodges, Jr., *The Passing of Liliuokalani. Honolulu Star Bulletin*: Honolulu (1918) 55. "Weather," *The Evening Star* (April 7, 1910 and April 8, 1910) 1.

2   See, generally, "The Corcoran Gallery of Art," *The Aldino, The Art Journal of America*. Vol. VII, No. 6. James Sutton Publishers, New York, New York (June 1874)120; and personal review of photographs by author in Renwick Gallery archives.

3   Theodore Roosevelt, *An Autobiography*. New York: DeCapo Press (1985) 563.

4   "Queen Lil Now A Poor Woman," *Los Angeles Times* (February 10, 1910) 18.

5   "Died," *Washington Post* December 2, 1928) 3; "S.S. Ashbaugh Dies of Paralysis, Well-known Shakespearean Collector Also Lectured," *Washington Post*, (December 3, 1928) 3; "Told In Department," *Washington Post* (September 26, 1908) 7.

6   William C. Widenor, *Henry Cabot Lodge and the Search for an American Foreign Policy*, Berkeley: University of California Press (1980) 3.

7   On December 11, 1912, President Taft announced his nomination of Judge Booth to be chief justice of the court of claims. "Boutell For Claims Court, Minister to Switzerland Will Fill Vacancy to Be Caused by Promotion of Judge Booth," *Boston Daily Globe* (December 12, 1912)11. The senate declined to confirm Booth. "Has Places for 1,400, Wilson Must Fill Those Held Open By the Senate," *Washington Post* (March 4, 1913)4.

8   Helena Allen, *The Betrayal of Liliuokalani, Last Queen of Hawaii*. Mutual Publishing: Honolulu (1982) 280.

9   *The Betrayal of Liliuokalani*, 280, 285.

10 Liliuokalani, *Hawaii's Story by Hawaii's Queen*, Charles E. Tuttle Company, Inc. (Rutland, Vt.: 1964 ed.) (Originally published in 1898) 75–92, 206–209.

11 *Hawaii's Story by Hawaii's Queen*, 79–99; 202–207; *The Betrayal of Liliuokalani*, 73–74; Davianna Pomaika'i McGregor, *Na Kua'aina, Living Hawaiian Culture*. University of Hawaii Press: Honolulu (2007) 9–12, 23–25, 30.

12 *Hawaii's Story* 181; Jon M. Van Dyke, *Who Owns the Crown Lands?* University of Hawaii

Press, Honolulu(2008) 124–126; *The Betrayal of Liliuokalani*, 141–142, 216.

13 Ernest Andrade, Jr., *The Unconquerable Rebel, Robert Wilcox and Hawaiian Politics, 1880–1903*. University Press of Colorado: Niwot, Colorado (1996) 15–16

14 *The Betrayal of Liliuokalani*, 266; *Aloha Betrayed*, 124; *Hawaii's Story by Hawaii's Queen*, 230–23; Jack Beatty, *The Age of Betrayal, The Triumph of Money in America, 1865–1900*. Vintage: New York (2008) 198 (use of the full poll).

15 Merle Curti, *The Growth of American Thought* (3rd edition) Harper & Row Publishers. New York (1964) 46, 107; David W. Kling, "The New Divinity and the Origins of the American Board of Commissioners for Foreign Missions, 1810–1914." *Theology, Theory, and Policy Studies in the History of Christian Missionaries*. William B. Eerdmans Publishing Co. Grand Rapids, Michigan, Cambridge, U.K. (2004) 18.

16 *The Growth of American Thought*, 29 (Samuel Hopkins); Kline, David W. "The New Divinity and the Origins of the American Board of Commissioners for Foreign Missions," in *.North American Foreign Missions, 1810–1914, Theology, Theory, and Policy Studies in the History of Christian Missionaries*. William B. Eerdmans Publishing Co. Grand Rapids, Michigan, Cambridge, U.K. (2004) 19.

17 "The New Divinity and the Origins of the American Board of Commissioners for Foreign Missions," 35; William A. Kinney, *Hawaii's Capacity for Self Government All But Destroyed*. Frank L. Jensen, Publishers: Salt Lake City, Utah (1927) 16–17 (quoting the letters of ABCFM to its mission in Hawaii.).

18 Warren Zimmerman, *First Great Triumph, How Five American's Made Their Country A World Power*. New York:Farrar,Straus and Giroux((2004)127–128; Wilbert R. Shenk, *North American Foreign Missions, 1810–1914, Theology, Theory, and Policy Studies in the History of Christian Missionaries*. William B. Eerdmans Publishing Co. Grand Rapids, Michigan, Cambridge, U.K. (2004) Introduction at 3 and related footnotes. See also Christopher Lasch, *The True and Only Heaven*. Norton: New York (1991) 52–63 (Adam Smith, acquisitiveness, and how to restrain it).

19 Philippa Strum, *Louis D. Brandeis*. Cambridge: Harvard University Press (1984) 15.

20 "The New Divinity and the Origins of the American Board of Commissioners for Foreign Missions," 20–21, 33–34; *.Missionary Album, Sesquicentennial Edition 1820–1970*. Hawaiian Mission Children's Society: Honolulu (1969), 17; Vernon Parrington, *Main Currents in American Thought, An Interpretation of American Literature From the Beginnings to 1920*. Harcourt, Brace and Company, New York (1930) 122.

21 *North American Foreign Missions, 1810–1914*, Introduction, 3, and related footnotes; see also *Louis D. Brandeis*, 15.

22 Dole is credited with supporting a continuation of the monarchy through regency held by Princess Kaiulani under control of the cabinet. See *The Betrayal of Liliuokalani*, 291, but see also Helena Allen's more detailed description of Dole's mere passing thought about regency in the negotiations of what he might expect as president, which he accepted in less than a day. *Sanford Ballard Dole, Hawaii's Only President, 1844–1926*. Arthur Clark, Glendale, California (1998), 49,188; *Hawaiian Kingdom, 1874–1893*, 596–597, and 588. There also was no indication Thurston ever considered or expressed an interest in the presidency. His concern was how to enhance his business interests. *Betrayal of Liliuokalani*, 289; *Hawaiian Kingdom, 1874–1893*, 596–597.

23 *The Betrayal of Liliuokalani*, 269, 282.

24 *The Betrayal of Liliuokalani*, 304; Evelyn E. Cook, *100 Years of Healing, The Legacy of a Kauai Missionary Doctor*, Halewai Publishing. Kauai (2003) 93–95; and *Hawaii's Story by Hawaii's Queen*, 78 ("We know now what imported or contract labor means.") and 361("The poor Hawaiians, strangers on their native soil, excluded from their own halls of legislation, have had their experience; alas, a bitter one. The Japanese, urged and inveigled and brought to come to Hawaii while they were needed to increase the foreigners' gold, have had theirs...;" and "Right or wrong, Liliuokalani...thought the 'slave labor' on the [sugar] plantations was 'inhuman.'").

25 Thomas Coffman, *Nation Within, The Story of America's Annexation of the Nation of Hawaii*. Epicenter Press: Hawaii (2006) 148; see also *100 Years of Healing*, 110, 116.

26 *The Betrayal of Liliuokalani*, 286. The queen had only two hundred and fifty modestly trained and armed soldiers. Stevens made plain he would protect the Caucasian vigilantes and the *coup* leaders with the use of force.

27 *For Whom Are the Stars?* 12.

28 David F. Long, *Gold Braids and Foreign Relations, Diplomatic Activities of U.S. Naval Officers 1798–1883*. Naval Institute Press: Annapolis (1988) 272–284.

29 Robert Johnson, *Thence Around Cape Horn, The Story of the United States Naval Forces on Pacific Station, 1818–1923*. United States Naval Institute: Annapolis (1967) 162–163.

30 Alfred Thayer Mahan, *The Interest of America in Sea Power, Present and Future*. Boston, Little, Brown & Company (1897), "United States Looking Outward" (essay, 1890) 15. See also, 22, 33–35, 43–44, 50, 52, and reproduction of letter to the editor, January 30, 1893, "Hawaii and Our Future Sea Power," written in response to the *Time's* request.

31 *The Betrayal of Liliuokalani*, 141–142; 216. The 1887 treaty that ensured control of Pearl Harbor, was finalized at the height of her brother's vulnerability to coercion and the threat of assassination, while a United States Navy vessel sat vigilantly in the harbor.

32 *Who Owns The Crown Lands of Hawaii?* 124.

33 See *L. Ahlo v. Henry Smith et al*, 8 Haw. 420 (decided January 28, 1892). See also *Who Owns Hawaii's Crown Lands?* 142; Alexander Liholiho, *The Journal of Prince Alexander Liholiho, The Voyages Made to the United States, England and France in 1849–1850*. University of Hawaii Press (1967) 108. Prince Liholiho — later King Kamehameha IV — was asked to leave his compartment on a train in Washington, DC, because the conductor believed he was black. *Hawaii's Story by Hawaii's Queen*, 179 (Kalakaua's meeting with Grant).

34 *Hawaii's Story by Hawaii's Queen*, 348–350.

35 *Hawaii's Story by Hawaii's Queen*, 358–360.

36 *Na Kua'aina*, 2; *Hawaii's Story by Hawaii's Queen*, 38, 177–178 ("The proposition ... was vehemently opposed by those of native birth; for patriotism, which with us means the love of the very soil on which our ancestors have lived and died....").

37 *Nation Within*, 116–117; *The Hawaiian Nation, 1874–1893*, 534.

38 "The New Divinity and the Origins of the American Board of Commissioners of Foreign Missions," 35; *Sanford Ballard Dole and His Hawaii*, 65–67; "Archibald Hopkins Dies In Washington," *New York Times* (June 19, 1926).

39 "Archibald Hopkins Dies In Washington," *New York Times* (June 19, 1926).

40 "Archibald Hopkins Dies In Washington," *New York Times* (June 19, 1926).

41 *Hawaiian Kingdom 1874–1893*, 564.

42 *Hawaiian Kingdom 1874–1893*, 554–566; *Hawaii's Story by Hawaii's Queen*, 177–178.

43 *For Whom Are the Stars?* 19–20; *Who Owns the Crown Lands?* 163.

44 *For Whom Are the Stars?* 21–23; *The Betrayal of Liliuokalani*, 268.

45 *For Whom Are the Stars?* 21–23; *The Betrayal of Liliuokalani*, 268.

46 *The Betrayal of Liliuokalani*, 56–59. There is little probative evidence the Queen thought the 1843 Paulet incident was of paramount or exclusive guidance in 1893. Also, the Queen kept no notes or diary entries during these three days. *For Whom Are the Stars?* 22.

47 *Hawaii's Story by Hawaii's Queen*, 259–260. ("No one, outside or inside the Hawaiian Islands, has contributed a cent to the repeated outlays I have made for the good of the Hawaiian people.")

48 *For Whom Are the Stars?* 21–23

49 *For Whom Are the Stars?* 21–23

50 *Washington Place, Historic American Buildings Survey*, National Park Service, (Washington, D.C.), by historian Virginia B. Price for the Washington Place Foundation and curator, Corinne Chun-Fujimoto. References are to the Survey's Addendum, No. HI-6 (2006) ("HABS").

51 HABS, 65; A "feathered symbol of royalty," made from rare bird features atop a standard or pole carried in processions and funerals. HABS, 143; HABS, 108, 114.

52 *Hawaii's Story by Hawaii's Queen*, 388(Harrison), 389(Cleveland).

53 *Hawaii's Story by Hawaii's Queen*, 388–389 (Cleveland).

54 "Paul Neumann is Dead of Paralysis of the Brain," *Hawaii Gazette*, Honolulu (July 2, 1901) 4.

55 "Paul Neumann is dead of Paralysis of the Brain," *Hawaii Gazette*, Honolulu (July 2, 1901)4; Gaylord C. Kubota, "The Lynching of Katsu Goto," *Hawaii's Chronicles: Island History from the Pages of Honolulu Magazine.* University of Hawaii Press: Honolulu (1996) 197–214; *Hawaii's Story by Hawaii's Queen*, 380.

56 The original précis has been lost. It was reprinted in full in "Liliuokalani's Brief," *New York World* (February 24, 1893) 2.

57 Dr. Rayford W. Logan, *The Betrayal of the American Negro, From Rutherford B. Hayes to Woodrow Wilson.* Collier Books: New York, Collier-Macmillan Ltd., London (1965 ed.) 3–47, 85–86, 115–118 (Supreme Court) 188.

58 Lorrin Thurston, *Memoirs of the Hawaiian Revolution.* Honolulu Advertiser Co., Ltd: Honolulu (1936) 143, 342.

59 *Hawaii's Story by Hawaii's Queen*, 296–297.

60 Richard Gambino, *Vendetta, The True Story of the Worst Lynching in America.* Doubleday & Company, Inc. Garden City, New York (1977) (Italian immigrants in New Orleans), and *Blood of My Blood, The Dilemma of the Italian-Americans.* Doubleday Anchor Book, New York (1974) 118–119.

61 James M. Goode, *Best Addresses, A Century of Washington's Distinguished Apartment Houses.* Smithsonian Books, Washington, D.C. (1988) 20–21; James M. Goode, *Capital Losses, A Cultural History of Washington's Destroyed.* Smithsonian Books: Washington, D.C. (2003) 120–121.

62 *Best Addresses, A Century of Washington's Distinguished Apartment Houses.* 20–21; *Capital Losses,* 120–121.

63 Ralph S. Kuykendall, "Negotiations of the Hawaiian Annexation Treaty of 1893." *Annual Report of the Hawaiian Historical Society for the Year 1942* (September 1943) 50.

64 Thomas J. Osborne, *Empire Can Wait.* The Kent State University Press: Kent, Ohio (1981) 91–92; *Thurston Memoirs,* 284–286 (contract labor; Liliuokalani offer); *Who Owns the Crown Lands?* 135 (Dole);

65 *Thurston Memoirs,* 284.

66 *Thurston Memoirs,* 282.

67 Sandord.B.Dole, "The Problems of Population." *The Pacific Commercial Advertiser,* (September 28, 1873)3. *Who Owns the Crown Lands?* 134–135 (Dole); Sanford Dole, "Evolution of Hawaiian Land Tenures." *Overland Monthly,* San Francisco (June 1895), Vol.25, Issue 150, 556–579. Cf. to *Na Kua'aina,* 23–40; *Betrayal of Liliuokalani,* 319.

68 James McLaughlin, *My Friend The Indian.* Houghton Mifflin Company: Boston (1910) 272.

69 *Hawaii's Story by Hawaii's Queen,* 369.

70 *Thurston Memoirs,* 340; Liliuokalani's notes (undated) to her attorney, Clarence DeKnight, written subsequent to the congressional hearing in 1902 in Honolulu and referenced by DeKnight in a reply letter to her (October 2, 1902), Hawaii Archives, Liliuokalani Collection, nos. 159, 160; *Thurston Memoirs,* 286; "Negotiations of the Hawaiian Annexation Treaty of 1893," 60.

71 *Thurston Memoirs,* 287.

72 *Thurston Memoirs,* 288; "Negotiations of the Hawaiian Annexation Treaty of 1893," 30–31.

73 *Thurston Memoirs,* 288; "Negotiations of the Hawaiian Annexation Treaty of 1893," 30–31.

74 *Thurston Memoirs,* 288; "Negotiations of the Hawaiian Annexation Treaty of 1893," 30–34 (President Harrison also sought to provide a lump sum for Princess Kaiulani, perhaps as an inducement to separate the family and to suggest Harrison was amenable — and the senate should know it — to demonstrating fairness).

75 *Thurston Memoirs,* 291.

76 Asa Thurston had been a scythe maker, with a "life as a party boy." He was asked by his brother to "carry on the pledge of mission service" that his brother was unable to fulfill. He also "won ... the respected title of Class Bully" during his training for the ministry. Thurston Twigg-Smith *Hawaiian Sovereignty: Do The Facts Matter?* Goodale Publishing: Honolulu (1998) 14; Thurston later purchased *The Advertiser* newspaper, was an investor in Oahu Railroad and Land Company, Hawaii Consolidated Railroad, the Honolulu Rapid transit Company, and "a number of sugar plantations." *Hawaiian Sovereignty: Do The Facts Matter?* 146.

77 Lorrin Thurston's farther, Asa Goodale Thurston graduated from Williams College in 1849. He married Sarah Andrews, whose parents were missionaries. Lorrin Thurston's first wife (she died giving birth to their second child) was the daughter of a missionary family. *Do The Facts Matter?* 138,144; Lucy Thurston, *Life and Times of Lucy G. Thurston.* Ann Arbor, Michigan (1882) 6 ; *Missionary Album,* 82,46,48,59; Dana Roberts, "Evangelist or

Homemaker," *North American Foreign Missions, 1810–1914,* 123, 116,123,127, n 32; Thomas Coffman, *Nation Within, The Story of America's Annexation of the Nation of Hawaii,* Honolulu: Epicenter (1998) 70; Francis John Halford, *9 Doctors & God.* Honolulu: University of Hawaii Press (1954) 180.

78 "Evangelist or Homemaker," 122.

79 "Evangelist or Homemaker," 123; *Life and Times of Lucy G. Thurston,* 102, 128, 148.

80 *Life and Times of Lucy G. Thurston,* 147; "Evangelist or Homemaker," 128.

81 *Life and Times of Mrs. Lucy G. Thurston,* 17.

82 *Life and Times of Lucy R. Thurston,* 17.

83 *Empire Can Wait,* 6, 79.

84 *For Whom Are the Stars?* 39.

85 Edmund L. Like and John K. Prendergast, *The Biography of Joseph K. Nawahi.* (1908), (translated by M. Puakea Nogelmeier), The Hawaiian Historical Society: Honolulu (1908) (1988 CD), 6–10, 154–161(Nawahi Biography).

86 *Nation Within,* 137; *Nawahi Biography,* 52–65; Miriam Michelson, "Many Thousands of Native Hawaiians Sign a Protest to the United States Government Against Annexation," *The San Francisco Call* (September 30, 1897). *Aloha Betrayed,* 130–131.

87 *Nawahi Biography,* 52–65; "Many Thousands of Native Hawaiians Sign a Protest to the United States Government Against Annexation;" The lehua blossom is a red flower that grows in the Ohia tree. The lehua, which is a sign of new birth and love, is the flower of the island of Hawaii. Hopoe was a large stone capable of movement while in place. The stone was named by native Hawaiians in honor of Hopoe, the graceful dancer of Puna who taught Hiiaka, the youngest sister of Pele, how to dance. Hopoe was transformed into this large stone.

88 "Many Thousands of Native Hawaiians Sign a Protest to the United States Government Against Annexation."

89 *Aloha Betrayed,* 131 and n. 33 (from the Blount Report).

90 *Nation Within,* 138, fn. omitted.

91 Father Reginald Yzendoorn, *History of the Catholic Mission in Hawaii,* Honolulu: Hawaii Star Bulletin: Honolulu (1927) 7; Robert Montcreiff, *Bart Giamatti, A Profile.* Yale University Press: New Haven (2007) 100; The demise of the Hawaiian people was attributed by some to "the mysterious will of God," and "hardly worth while..., when it is a given point that all means for the purpose [of stopping the demise] will be alike unavailing," (Reverend Titus Coan), *9, Doctors & God,* 189–190.

92 *Na Kua'aina,* 23, 27–29; Kame'eleihiwa, Lilikala. *Native Land and Foreign Desires.* Bishop Museum Press: Honolulu (1992) 25–29, 31, 48, 56; *Aloha Betrayed, Native Hawaiian Resistance To American Colonialism.* Duke University Press. (Durham & London, 2004) 7.

93 *Native Land and Foreign Desires,* 73; *Na Kua'aina, Living Hawaiian Culture,* 31; *History of Catholic Mission in Hawaii,* 72, 74, 79–80.

94 *Native Land and Foreign Desires,* 73; *Na Kua'aina,* 31; *History of Catholic Mission in Hawaii,* 72, 74, 79–80 (Bingham's critical concern was whether the expulsion would harm financial contributions from the United States) 30, 46–47 51, 66–88 88–96, 98–112.

95 *9 Doctors & God,* 125, 142 (emphasis in the original); *History of Catholic Mission in Hawaii,* 49.

96 William A. Kinney, Hawaii's *Capacity for Self-Government All But Destroyed*. Salt Lake City: Jensen Publisher (1927) 38–55, 159, 164–165. William Kinney was born in Hawaii in the 1860's. As described later in the text, Kinney supported the *coup*, led the prosecution against Liluokalani, and was a central advocate for annexation. Kinney's critique is unusually candid, harsh, and late. See also *9 Doctors*, 221–22 and William R. Castle, Jr., *The Life of Samuel Northrup Castle*, Samuel and Mary Castle Foundation and Hawaiian Historical Society: Honolulu (1960), 72–81, 98.

97 See, for example, *Aloha Betrayed*, 23–25.

98 *Aloha Betrayed*, 38–39.

99 *Aloha Betrayed*, 86; Paul Johnson, *The Intellectuals*. Harper & Row, New York (1988) 28–29.

100 Elbert and Mahoe, *Na Mele o Hawaii Nei, 101 Hawaiian Songs*, Collected by Samuel Elberty and Noelani Mahoe University of Hawaii Press (Honolulu: 1970) 14 (quoting Roberts). See also *The Betrayal of Liliuokalani*, 38, 46. *Missionary Album*, 24, 37, 47, 79 (transformation and religious use of the Hawaiian oral language in schools and churches); *Na Kua'aina*, 2.

101 See also *In the Hawaiian Kingdom, 1838–1917*, 404, n.4 (family history with music); *Hawaii's Story by Hawaii's Queen*, 53, 346–347 (first national anthem); *The Intellectuals*, 28. (Unlike Shelley, Hawaiians tended to live what they professed to believe).

102 *Aloha Betrayed*, 71

103 *Betrayal of Liliuokalani*, 85.

104 In *The Hawaiian Kingdom, 1874–1893*, 186–187, Ralph S. Kuykendall faulted native Hawaiians for "race antagonism," ignoring the condescension and racial denigration engaged in by missionary families in attitude and practice and the role race played in the imposition of the 1887 constitution on King Kalakaua by the all-Caucasian vigilante force. Kuykendall also accepted Caucasian pronouncements about an idyllic past in Hawaii that never existed. Kuykendall occasionally wrote like a state employee crafting his work to ensure he reflected the attitudes of Hawaii in the 1930s through the early 1960s.

105 *The Hawaiian Kingdom, 1874–1893*, 307, 312–314; Thomas Bokenkotter, *A Concise History of the Catholic Church*. Doubleday: New York (1966) 331–382.

106 *The Hawaiian Kingdom, 1874–1893*, 307, 312–314. Kalakaua had said he would elevate the Hawaiian culture, civic, and educational accomplishment into elements of Hawaii's governance. Kuykendall is so preoccupied with the Caucasian division of the world into American and British camps that he could not see the value of the Kalakaua's perspective on nationalism.

107 *Betrayal of Liliuokalani*, 111.

108 Agnes Quigg, "Kalakaua Hawaiian Studies Abroad Program." *Hawaiian Journal of History*, Vol. 22 (1988) 170.

109 Kristin Zambucka, *Kalakaua, Hawaii's Last King*. Mana Publishing Company (2002) 89.

110 *Betrayal of Liliuokalani* 161–162.

111 *Hawaii's Story by Hawaii's Queen*, 125–126.

112 *Hawaii's Story by Hawaii's Queen*, 125, 165, 166; *Betrayal of Liliuokalani*, 266; *Aloha Betrayed*, 129.

113 *First Great Triumph*, 176–177.

114 "A Forgotten Fighter Against Plutocracy," 53–57.

115 "A Forgotten Fighter Against Plutocracy," 53–57.

116 *Empire Can Wait*, 3.

117 *To Whom Are the Stars?* 41.

118 *To Whom Are the Stars?* 39.

119 George Hoar, *Autobiography of Seventy Years*. C.Scribner's Sons: New York (1903) 264–265; *San Francisco Examiner* (January 31, 1893) 1 (Pettigrew); *United States v. Kagama*, 118 U.S. 375(1886); "Comment, The Indian Battle for Self-Determination," 58 Cal. L. Rev. 4455 (1970).

120 *Empire Can Wait*, 7; *To Whom Are the Stars?* 41.

121 *Betrayal of Liliuokalani*, 120–121.

122 President's Message to Congress with attachments (December 18, 1893) 2, 4 (emphasis added).

123 *Betrayal of Liliuokalani*, 300–301.

124 Dolly Blount Lamar, *When All Is Said and Done*. The University of Georgia Press: Athens (1952) 3.

125 *When All Is Said and Done*, 2.

126 *When All Is Said and Done*, 41.

127 Clifton Jackson Phillips, *Protestant America and the Pagan World, The First Half Century of the American Board of Commissioners For Foreign Missions, 1810–1860*. Harvard East Asian Monographs, Harvard University Press, 1969 (reprint of Phillips' 1954 PhD dissertation) 227.

128 *Reminisces*, 54–55, 69–72; and *9 Doctors*, 160–164, 175.

129 Charles A. Maxfield, "The 1845 Organic Sin Debate: Slavery, Sin, and the American Board of Commissioners for Foreign Missions." *North American Foreign Missions, 1810–1914, Theology, Theory, and Policy* (2004) 87–88, 91.

130 "The 1845 Organic Sin Debate," 92, 95, 100.

131 "The 1845 Organic Sin Debate," 90, 109, 112–114; *Uncle Tom's Cabin*. Border's Classics Edition: Ann Arbor, Michigan (2006) 4, 12.

132 "God and Sugar: The Gulick Brothers' Fight Against King Kamehameha V and the Sugar Planters in Hawaii, 1864–1870." *The Hawaiian Journal of History*, Vol.37 (2003), 63–64, 80–81; Ronald Takaki, *Pau Hana, Plantation Life and Labor in Hawaii*. University of Hawaii Press: Honolulu (1983) 70–75.

133 *Pau Hana*, 74; Katherine Coman, *The History of Contract Labor*. Published for the American Economic Association: New York (August 1903), Third Series, Vol. IV, no.3 preface, 33; Eleanor C. Nordyke, "Blacks in Hawaii: A Demographic and Historic Perspective." *The Hawaiian Journal of History*: Honolulu, Vol. 22, 1989, 244; *The History of Contract Labor*, preface, 33, 498.

134 *Wood v. Afo*, 3 Haw.448 (1873); See also *J. Nott & Co. v. Kanahele*, 4 Haw. 14(1887); *C. Afong v. Kale*, 7 Haw. 594 (1894).

135 *King v. H.N. Greenwell*, 1 Haw. 85 (1853); see also *Hawaii's Capacity for Self Government*,

119–120.

136 Granville Allen Mawer, *Ahab's Tragedy, The Saga of South Seas Whaling*. St. Martin's Press: New York (1999) 264–269.

137 Ruth M. Tabrah, *Hawaii, A History*. W.W. Norton: New York (1980) 70–71; *Aloha Betrayed*, 47; *Sanford Ballard Dole and His Hawaii*, 44.

138 Louis Menand, *The Metaphysical Club, A Story of Ideas in America*. Farrar, Straus and Giroux: New York (2001) 61–65.

139 Hawaii Archives, Liliuokalani Collection (M-93, Box 91, Folder 90). These letters were brought to the author's attention by Corrine Chun-Fujimoto, curator, Washington Place.

140 *Sanford Ballard Dole and His Hawaii*, 44.

141 *The New South Faces the World*, 20; Tenant S. Williams, "James H. Blount, the South, and Hawaiian Annexation," *Pacific Historical Review*, (1988) 25.

142 *The New South Faces the World*, 19.

143 *When All Is Said and Done*, 97.

144 President's Message to Congress, Senate Report, 53rd Cong. 2nd Sess. No, 227, Blount Report, 19.

145 President's Message to Congress, Senate Report, 53rd Cong. 2nd Sess. No. 227, Blount Report, (Blount to Gresham, April 26, 1893 and various correspondence to Gresham) 13–24, et seq.

146 Morgan Report (Blount testimony) January 11, 1894, 750. Blount Report (Smith submission, No. 48) 489.

147 Blount Report, 545–546 (Robert Wilcox), 551–552 (Crown lands).

148 *Who Owns the Crown Lands?* 190.

149 *Na Kua'aina*, 31–40; *Who Owns the Crown Lands?* 25–29.

150 *In the Matter of Kamehameha IV*, 2 Haw. 715 (1864).

151 *Who Owns the Crown Lands?*, 100–110

152 *Liliuokalani v United States of America*, National Archives, RG 123 Records of the United States Court of Claims, general Jurisdiction Case Files, 1855–1939, 30559 thru 30577. Box no. 2200, Reply Brief of the United States, 12, 15, 18.

153 Tennant S. Williams, *The New South Faces the World*, Louisiana State University Press: Baton Rouge (1988) 31–32 (citing correspondence between Charles L. Carter and Sanford Dole).

154 *The New South Faces The World*, 28, 30; *When All Is Said and Done*, 96.

155 *The New South Faces the World*, 33; *Reminiscences*, 53.

156 President's Message to Congress, Blount Report, 231–234, and 938 ("no native is capable of carrying on business for himself, much less of carrying on government.")

157 President's Message to Congress, Blount Report, 354–355, 374.

158 President's Message to Congress, Blount Report, 83–89 (Blount to Gresham, July 6, 1893).

159 *The Betrayal of Liliuokalani*, 316.

160 Charles W. Calhoun, "Morality and Spite: Walter Q. Gresham and the U.S. Relations With Hawaii." *Pacific Historical Review* (1983) 292.

161 "Morality and Spite: Walter Q. Gresham and the U.S. Relations With Hawaii," 292; Kenneth J. Grieb, "A badger *general*'s foray into diplomacy: *General Edward S. Bragg* in Mexico." *Wisconsin Magazine of History*, Vol. 1 (autumn 1969) 21.

162 "A New Minister to Hawaii." *The New York Times*, (September 9, 1893).

163 *The New South Faces the World*, 39–40; See also Minister Stevens' retort to Blount of November 19, 1893 reprinted in *Memoirs of the Hawaiian Revolution*, (Thurston) 233.

164 Blount Report, 4–6, 21.

165 Blount Report, 9–13.

166 Blount Report, 17.

167 Blount Report, 29–39.

168 Joseph A. Fry, *John Tyler Morgan and the Search for Southern Autonomy*. University of Tennessee Press (1992) 16–17.

169 Claude L. Chilton, "Memorial Address on John T. Morgan." Delivered before the Woman's Auxiliary of the Southern Commercial Congress, Mobile, Alabama (October 28, 1913)1.

170 *John Tyler Morgan and the Search for Southern Autonomy*, 19; see also Drew Gilpin Faust, *This Republic of Suffering, Death and the Civil War*. Alfred A. Knopf: New York (2008) 193 ("The cult of the Lost Cause and the celebration of Confederate memory that emerged in the ensuing decades were in no small part an effort to affirm that the hundreds of thousands of young southern lives had not, in fact, been given in vain.") 193–194 (Oliver Wendell Holmes) and 237 (the accounting and recognition of the dead was, at first, confined only to Union soldiers).

171 *John Tyler Morgan and the Search for Southern Autonomy*, 20–24; Ezra J. Warner, *Generals in Gray, Lives of Confederate Commanders*. Baton Rouge: Louisiana State University (1959) 221–222.

172 *John Tyler Morgan and the Search for Southern Autonomy*, 19; *This Republic of Suffering, Death and the Civil War*, 237 (the accounting and recognition of the dead at first was confined only to Union soldiers).

173 "Memorial Address on John T. Morgan," 6.

174 *The Betrayal of Liliuokalani*, 306–308; *Hawaii's Story by Hawaii's Queen*, 244–251.

175 *The Betrayal of Liliuokalani*, 306–308; *Hawaii's Story by Hawaii's Queen*, 244–251; *Memoirs of the Hawaiian Revolution* (Thurston) 274.

176 *The Betrayal of Liliuokalani*, 306–308; *Hawaii's Story by Hawaii's Queen*, 244–251.

177 *For Whom Are the Stars?* 80.

178 President's Message Relating to the Hawaiian Islands (December 18, 1893), 53rd Con. 2nd Sess., Ex. Doc No. 47, iii.

179 President's Message Relating to the Hawaiian Islands (December 18, 1893), 53rd Con. 2nd Sess., Ex. Doc No. 47, v, xvi.

180 President's Message Relating to the Hawaiian Islands (December 18, 1893), 53rd Con. 2nd Sess., Ex. Doc No. 47, iii–xvi.

181 Morgan Report, 363.

182 Joseph A. Fry, "Strange Expansionist Bedfellows, Newlands, Morgan, and Hawaii." *Halcyon*, Vol. II, 108.

183 Thomas Adams Upchurch, "Senator John Tyler Morgan and the Genesis of Jim Crow Ideology, 1889–1891." *Alabama Review* (2004) 2–7.

184 *John Tyler Morgan and the Search for Southern Autonomy*, 164–170; "Strange Expansionist Bedfellows, Newlands, Morgan, and Hawaii," 113–116; Joseph O. Baylen and John Hammon Moore, "Senator John Tyler Morgan and Negro Colonization in the Philippines, 1901to 1902." *Phylon*, Vol. 29 (Spring 1968) 65–75; *Memoirs of the Hawaiian Revolution*, (Thurston) 287.

185 *Memoirs of the Hawaiian Revolution* (Dole) 120–121, 142–143.

186 *Memoirs of the Hawaiian Revolution*, (Dole) 106, 126.

187 *The Betrayal of Liliuokalani*, 309; *For Whom Are the Stars?* 87.

188 *Memoirs of the Hawaiian Revolution* (Thurston) 287.

189 Morgan Report (Emerson), December 27, 1893, 539–540.

190 Morgan Report (Stalker), January 26, 1894, 1010–1024; (Simpson), February 5, 1894, 1128; P.W. Reeder (January 30, 1894, 1036; (Francis Day), January 31, 1894, 1085.

191 Morgan Report (Coffman), January 20, 1894, 1002–1003; (Coffman), January 26, 1894, 999, 1000–1003.

192 Morgan Report (Swinburne), January 17, 1894, 830,846.

193 *Empire Can Wait*, 75.

194 Morgan Report, (Alexander), January 17, 1894, 674, 683–685; Morgan Report, January 17, 1894, (Alexander) 653, (Morgan) 662.

195 Morgan Report, cf. Stevens' testimony (912–922) with, for example, Castle (947).

196 Morgan Report, (Macarthur), January 26, 1894, 1064; (Bowen), January 29, 1894, 1026.

197 Morgan Report (Belknap) January 31, 1894, 1070; (Jewell); January 11, 1894, 791. See also, 441 (Lecture by Dutton); 475 (article by Mahan).

198 Morgan Report (Morgan) 364.

199 Morgan Report (Morgan) 364–365; (Mass Meeting), 400–401; 384–385.

200 Morgan Report (dissent) 397–398.

201 *Missionary Album*, 49. *Reminisces*, 10 (Thurston Foreword).

202 *Aloha Betrayed*, 173–178; *The Betrayal of Liliuokalani*, 343.

203 *President's Message Relating to the Hawaiian Islands*, 68 (Blount to Gresham, May 9, 1893).

204 *Missionary Album*, 49. Sereno Edwards Bishop, *Reminisces of Old Hawaii*. Hawaiian Gazette Co., Ltd: Honolulu(1916) 10 (Thurston Foreword).

205 William Saunders Scarborough, "The Ethics of the Hawaiian Question." *The Christian Recorder* (1894), reproduced at http://www.blackpast.com.

206 William M. Springer, "Our Present Duty." *North American Law Review*, Vol. 157, No. 445 (1894) 745,749; "Outlook for Hawaiians," *New York Times* (December 4, 1893) (quoting Stevens' article); John Stevens, "A Plea for Annexation." *North American Law Review*, Vol.

157, No.445 (1894) 736. See also Eugene Tyler Chamberlain, "The Invasion of Hawaii." *North American Law Review*, Vol. 157, No.445 (1894) 731.

207 *For Whom Are the Stars?* 88–89; Edward Towse, *Rebellion of 1895, A Complete History of the Insurrection Against the Republic of Hawaii*. Royal Designs: Hawaii (published in 1895; edition relied upon published in 2004 by F.W. Grantham: Hawaii) 65; *Honolulu, 100 Years in the Making*, (DVD), Bishop Museum, Mountain Apple Company: Hawaii (2006); *A Hawaiian Reader*. Edited by G. Grove Day and Carl Stroven. Mutual Publishing Company: Hawaii (1959), 150,192; see also History of Hawaiian Electric Company, http://www.funderuniverse.com/company-histories/Hawaiian-Electric-Industries-Inc-Company-History.html (2008).

208 Don Hibbard and David Franzen, *The View From Diamond Head, Royal Residence to Urban Resort*. Editions Limited Book: Hawaii, 33, 20–36.

209 *For Whom Are the Stars?* 89.

210 *For Whom Are the Stars?* 90; *Betrayal of Liliuokalani*, 320–323.; *Rebellion of 1895*, 5 (use of the tug Elue).

211 Alfred L. Castle, "Advice for Hawaii: The Dole–Burgess Letters." *Hawaiian Journal of History*, Vol. 15(1981) 24–30.

212 *Who Owns the Crown Lands?* 174–175.

213 *Who Owns the Crown Lands?* 172–182; *Aloha Betrayed*, 136–138; *The Betrayal of Liliuokalani*, 319.

214 *For Whom Are the Stars?* 87; *The Betrayal of Liliuokalani*, 313.

215 *Who Owns the Crown Lands?* 172–182; *Aloha Betrayed*, 136–138.

216 *Aloha Betrayed*, 136–145; *Autobiography of Seventy Years*, 264–265.

217 *The Course of Empire, An Official Record by Richard F. Pettigrew of South Dakota*. Boni & Liveright: New York (1920) 3.

218 "The American League: Minister Thurston's Speech Friday Night." *Hawaii Star* (June 16, 1894) 3.

219 "The American League: Minister Thurston's Speech Friday Night."

220 "The American League: Minister Thurston's Speech Friday Night."

221 *Hawaii's Story by Hawaii's Queen*, 258–259.

222 *For Whom Are the Stars?* 104.

223 *For Whom Are the Stars?* 104.

224 Hawaii Archives (Kennedy to Widemann, May 8, 1895) ("I have given considerable thought to the question of the ex-Queen's claim against the United States for the part taken by United States' Minister Stevens and Captain Wiltse"); David W. Forbes, *Hawaiian National Bibliography, 1780–1900*. University of Hawaii Press: Honolulu (2003) (refers to 2nd edition of Kennedy's book published in 1897).

225 See, generally, *This Republic of Suffering*, 15–27 (Dying).

226 "The Boy Preacher — Crammond Kennedy," *New York Times* (December 27, 1862); "The "Mora Claim Paid At Last," *New York Times* (October 19, 1895); "The Mora Claim Settled," *New York Times* (August 21, 1895).

227 *Empire Can Wait*, 82, fn.39; *Hawaii's Story by Hawaii's Queen*, 258–260.

228 "Four Alleged Conspirators Arrested," *The Pacific Commercial Advertiser* (December 10,

1894); *Aloha Betrayed*, 138–142; *For Whom Are the Stars?* 112–113.

229 *For Whom Are the Stars?* 13–170; *Unconquerable Rebel*, 149–166.

230 "Exiled from Honolulu, An American Citizen Forcibly Ejected," *New York Times* (February 11, 1895); *Unconquerable Rebel*, 150–161; *Rebellion of 1895*, 59, 60; *Trial of A Queen: 1895 Military Tribunal*. Judicial History Center, Hawaii State Judiciary (1995; revised 1996)18, 59; "Uprising in Hawaii," *New York Times* (January 19, 1895).

231 "Exiled from Honolulu, An American Citizen Forcibly Ejected," *New York Times* (February 11, 1895); *Unconquerable Rebel*, 150–161; *Rebellion of 1895*, 59, 60; *Trial of A Queen: 1895 Military Tribunal*. 18; *I Knew Liliuokalani*, Bernice Pilani Irwin, Native Books, Inc.: Hawaii (2006), 51–52 (Reign of Terror).

232 "Exiled from Honolulu, An American Citizen Forcibly Ejected," *New York Times* (February 11, 1895); *Unconquerable Rebel*, 150–161; *Rebellion of 1895*, 59, 60; *Trial of A Queen: 1895 Military Tribunal*. 18.

233 Roberta Strauss Feuerlicht, *Justice Crucified, The Story of Sacco and Vanzetti*, McGraw-Hill: New York (1977) 63–64, 68, 106–138; Upton Sinclair, *Boston*, Albert and Charles Boni: New York, 1928, 156; *Colyer, et al. v. Skeffington*, 265 F. 17, 18(D. Mass.1920); *I Knew Liliuokalani*, 51–52 (Reign of Terror).

234 *Trial of a Queen: 1895 Military Tribunal*, 1 (Introduction); *Rebellion of 1895*, 17–18 (jurisdiction).

235 *To Whom Are the Stars?* 196 (Smith, Hatch).

236 *The Betrayal of Liliuokalani*, 326; *Hawaii's Story by Hawaii's Queen*, 267.

237 *The Betrayal of Liliuokalani*, 326–327; *For Whom Are the Stars?* 191, 210, (Neumann's challenge to the court's jurisdiction and his contemplation of civil suits would have required review by Hawaii's judiciary) 211, (challenge that no statutory offense existed titled misprision of treason); *Trial of A Queen: Military Tribunal*, 1 (Van Dyke on the United States' judicial precedents).

238 *Native Lands and Foreign Desires*, 175 (see chart of organization).

239 "Negotiations of the Hawaiian Annexation Treaty of 1893," 5, 30; see also *Who Owns The Crown Lands?* 84–88.

240 See J. Madison, *Debates to the Federalist Convention* (Int'l ed. 1920) 48–51 (Debates of June 2, 1787) and 527 (Debates of September 7, 1787); 1 J. Elliot, *Debates on the Federal Constitution*, 379 (Luther Martin's Letter), 250 (Debates of August 20, 1787), 257 (Debates of August 22, 1787) 293(Debates of September 7, 1787)(2d ed. 1836); *The Federalist No. 70* (Alexander Hamilton). See also Proto, Neil Thomas, "The Opinion Clause and Presidential Decision Making,"44 *Missouri Law Review* 185 (Spring 1979).

241 *In Re J.C. Kalanianaole*, 10 Haw. 29 (1895).

242 *Hawaii's Story by Hawaii's Queen*, 31–32, 289–292; *Aloha Betrayed*, 186, 180–191.

243 "Mr. Thurston Returns," *New York Times*, January 9, 1895; *Rebellion of 1895*, 19–25; *For Whom Are the Stars?* 195.

244 *Rebellion of 1895*, 19–25; *For Whom Are the Stars?* 195.

245 *Betrayal of Liliuokalani*, 256, 285–289; 331–332; *The Hawaiian Kingdom*, 588; *Hawaii's Story by Hawaii's Queen*, 273–277; *Aloha Betrayed*, 180–191

246 *Betrayal of Liliuokalani*, 331.

247 *For Whom Are the Stars?* 207.

248 *Hawaii's Story by Hawaii's Queen,* 281–286

249 *Hawaii's Story by Hawaii's Queen,* 281–284; "Hawaii Trade May Be Ours," *Los Angeles Time* (December 20, 1908) 15.

250 *For Whom Are the Stars?* 209; *Hawaii's Story by Hawaii's Queen,* 281–284.

251 Hawaii Archives, Kennedy to Widemann, (May 8, 1895)

252 *Who Owns The Crown Lands?,* 198–199.

253 *Hawaii's Story by Hawaii's Queen,* 295–296.

254 *Biography of Joseph Nawahi,* 22, 250; *Hawaii's Story by Hawaii's Queen,* 300.

255 *Aloha Betrayed,* 194

256 "A Concession to Liliuokalani," *New York Times* (February 17, 1896).

257 "Exporting Christian Transcendentalism, Importing Hawaiian Sugar," *American Literature,* Vol. 72, Number 3, Duke University Press (September 2000) 521.

258 Mayor James P. Phelan, "The Ideal City." *San Francisco News Letter* (1897); "Women in the Police Department," *San Francisco News Letter* (November 29, 1896); Witold Rybczynski, *The Clearing In The Distance.* Scribner: New York (1988) 275 *; "Golden Rule First In City," *The San Francisco News Letter* (October 14, 1935).

259 See generally Jean Pfaelzer, *Driven Out, The Forgotten war Against Chinese Americans.* Random House: New York (2008).

260 *Hawaii's Story by Hawaii's Queen,* 61–62; John E. Baur, "When Royalty came to California." *California History* (December 1988) 244–264.

261 *Hawaii's Story by Hawaii's Queen,* 309–311.

262 "Hawaii, The Queen's Book, Pleading the Cause of Her People," *New York Times* (January 22, 1898); *Hawaii's Story by Hawaii's Queen,* 310.

263 Hawaii Archives, Nawahi to Liliuokalani (December 16, 25, 1896, February 22, 1897, March 22, 1897). The English translation is provided by the Hawaii archives and accompanied each letter.

264 "Liliuokalani in a Sleigh, She enjoys the first ride of her life." *New York Times* (December 28, 1896); "Ex-Queen to see 'Captain Cook,'" *New York Times* (July 12, 1897); *Hawaii's Story by Hawaii's Queen,* 315–316.

265 *First Great Triumph,* 149.

266 *First Great Triumph,* 150–151.

267 *First Great Triumph,* 154.

268 *First Great Triumph,* 187 ('dauntless intolerance'); Michael Klarman, *From Jim Crow To Civil Rights, The Supreme Court and the Struggle for Racial Equality.* Oxford University Press: New York (2004) 12–13.

269 *From Jim Crow To Civil Rights, The Supreme Court and the Struggle for Racial Equality,* 3; *Plessy v. Ferguson,* 163 U.S. 537 (1896); Peter Vellon, "Black, White or In Between." *Ambassador,* No. 46(Summer 2000) 10; *Vendetta,* 97.

270 *First Great Triumph,* 179.

271 *I Would Live It Again,* 185, 191.

272 *I Would Live It Again*, 187–188.

273 "Liliuokalani Not Afraid," *New York Times* (February 23, 1897); *Hawaii Story by Hawaii's Queen*, 340–343,348; *Autobiography of Seventy Years*, 265.; Declaration of Principles of Anti-Imperialist League (1899).

274 "Liliuokalani Not Afraid," New York Times (February 23, 1897); *Hawaii Story by Hawaii's Queen*, 340–343,348; Autobiography of Seventy Years, 265; Declaration of Principles of Anti-Imperialist League (1899).

275 HABS, 81, n.252.

276 The treaty, including Article II (land transfer), and VI (commission), is reproduced in *Hawaii's Story by Hawaii's Queen*, 397–398(Appendix D); see also *Who Owns the Crown Lands?* 312–314.

277 *Hawaii's Story by Hawaii's Queen*, 358–360, Appendix E, F, and G; "Our Treaty With Hawaii," *New York Times* (June 28, 1897).

278 *Hawaii's Story by Hawaii's Queen*, 358–360, Appendix E, F, and G; "Our Treaty With Hawaii," *New York Times* (June 28, 1897).

279 "Many Thousands Sign a Protest to the United States Against Annexation,"

280 *Who Owns The Crown Lands?* 210; *Aloha Betrayed*, 136–163.

281 Hawaii Archives, Liliuokalani to J.O. Carter (October 24, 1897; December 11, 1897).See also *Aloha Betrayed*, 136–163.

282 *Hawaii's Story by Hawaii's Queen*, 373–374; *Aloha Betrayed*, 164–172, 178–179; "Hawaii, The Queen's Book Pleading the Cause of Her People," *New York Times* (January 22, 1898); Lydia Kualapai, "The Queen Writes Back." *Studies In Indian Literature*, Vol. 17, No.2 (Summer 2005).

283 *Hawaii's Story by Hawaii's Queen*, 373–374; *Aloha Betrayed*,164–172, 178–179; "Hawaii, The Queen's Book Pleading the Cause of Her People," *New York Times* (January 22, 1898); "The Queen Writes Back."

284 *From Jim Crow To Civil Rights, The Supreme Court and the Struggle for Racial Equality*, 12–13.

285 Hon. Harry Bingham, "The Annexation of Hawaii: A Right and A Duty," delivered before the Grafton and Coos Bar Association, Woodsville, New Hampshire (January 28, 1898); Bumford Press: Concord, New Hampshire (1898).

286 Hawaii Archives, Liliuokalani to J.O. Carter (September 8, 1897).

287 I *Would Live It Again*, 218–219.

288 *Who Owns the Crown Lands?* 212; Hawaii Archives, Liliuokalani to J.O. Carter (June 8, 1898); "Strange Expansionist Bedfellows," 119–120.

289 *Who Owns the Crown Lands?* 211. *The Betrayal of Liliuokalani*, 362; Hawaii Archives, Liliuokalani to J.O. Carter (June 8, 1898).

290 "Queen to Claim Crown Lands," *New York Times* (July 24, 1898).

291 *Betrayal of Liliuokalani*, 361–363; a photograph of the event that included Emma Nawahi was shared with the author by Corinne Chun-Fujimoto, curator, Washington Place.

292 "Queen Liliuokalani Has A Cancer," *New York Times* (July 28, 1898); Ruby Haseqaua Lowe, *Liliuokalani*. Kamehameha Schools: Honolulu (1993) 79–89.*Unconquerable Hero*, 178–180.

293 "The Dewey Monument," *The San Francisco Call* (July 3, 1899).

294 Hawaii Archives, Liliuokalani to J.O Carter (November 24, 1898; March 24, 1899; April 5, 1899), Macfarlane to Wundenberg (January 25, 1899). Neither agreement was located. "Lilienthal" is referenced only in Macfarlane's letter. At the time Macfarlane was dealing with the Anglo-California Bank. Macfarlane made no reference to Lilienthal's first name.

295 *Capital Losses*, 51.

296 *Betrayal of Liliuokalani*, 366.

297 HABS 18, n 286; Hawaii Archives, Liliuokalani to J.O. Carter (November 24, 1898; March 24, 1899); *Betrayal of Liliuokalani*, 366.

298 Hawaii Archives, Liliuokalani to Macfarlane (June 9, 1899) attachment.

299 Hawaii Archives, Liliuokalani to Wundenberg (January 3, 1899).

300 Hawaii Archives, Macfarlane to Wundenberg (January 26, 1899); Wundenberg to Liliuokalani (February 15, 1899); Macfarlane to Wundenberg (February 1, 1899).

301 Hawaii Archives, Ashford to Liliuokalani (March 11, 1899); Liliuokalani to Ashford (April 5, 1899).

302 Hawaii Archives, Macfarlane to Liliuokalani (April 5, 1899, April 15, 1899).

303 Hawaii Archives, Macfarlane to Liliuokalani (April 15, 1899).

304 Hawaii Archives, Liliuokalani to Carter, July 21, 1899; August 3, 1899); Hawaii Archives Liliuokalani to Macfarlane (August 29, 1899); Department of Justice, Opin. of Attorney Gen. (John W. Griggs) (November 21, 1899); Hawaii Archives, Liliuokalani to Carter (undated, post November 21, 1899).

305 Hawaii Archives, Liliuokalani to Carter, July 21, 1899; August 3, 1899); Hawaii Archives, Liliuokalani to Macfarlane (August 29, 1899); Department of Justice, Opin. of Attorney Gen. (John W. Griggs), (November 21, 1899); Hawaii Archives, Liliuokalani to Carter (undated, post November 21, 1899).

306 *Capital Loses*, 215–217.

307 Hawaii Archives, W.O. Smith Collection M-33, Smith to Lodge (February 17, 1900); Smith to Swanzy (March 15, 1900).

308 Hawaii Archives, Smith to an unspecified group, signed (a common practice of Smith's) (January 15, 1900); W.O. Smith to Hartwell (December 21, 1899); W.O. Smith to DeKnight (January 31, 1900).

309 *Unconquerable Hero*, 188; Hawaii Archives, Smith to unspecified group, signed (March 1, 1900).

310 Hawaii Archives, Smith to unspecified group, signed (March 1, 1900); Hawaii Archives, Smith to unnamed member of congress, signed and noted (February 14, 1900).

311 Hawaii Archives, Liliuokalani to J.O. Carter (undated, signed 1899).

312 Hawaii Archives, Charles M. Pepper to W.O. Smith (April 10, 1900) 1, 6.

313 Hawaii Archives, Smith to unspecified group, signed (March 1, 1900).

314 "Hawaii Bill Is Passed," *New York Times* (March 2, 1900); Hawaii Investigation, Report of Subcommittee of the Pacific Island and Porto Rico [sic], United States Senate (1903) 97; "Topics of the Times," *New York Times* (November 8, 1900). The *Philadelphia Press*, opposed any recognition of the queen's right to compensation because, in part,

"the ex-queen has a rich husband."

315 "Liliuokalani Will Receive No Pension." *New York Times* (March 11, 1900); *Betrayal of Liliuokalani*, 369; *Autobiography of Seventy Years*, 264–265; Hawaii Investigation, Report, Part I, 97.

316 "Ex-Queen of Hawaii in San Francisco," *New York Times* (November 18, 1901).

317 *Unconquerable Hero*, 200–201; "Paul Neumann Dead of Paralysis of the Brian," *Hawaiian Gazette* (July 2, 1901) 4.

318 David Howard Bain, *Sitting In Darkness*, Houghton Mifflin (Penguin Books): Boston: (1984) 361–393; *Unconquerable Hero*, 200–201; "Ex-Queen of Hawaii in San Francisco," *New York Times* (November 18, 1901); Hawaiian Investigation, Report, Part 1, 28.

319 "Dewey Curbed the Poet," *New York Times* (October 31, 1899); "Praises Dewey in Verse, *The New York Times* (October 29, 1899); *Sitting In Darkness*, 361–393.

320 Paul Kramer, "The Water Cure," *The New Yorker* (February 25, 2008) 38, 42–43; *First Great Triumph*, 386–417; "Sorrow in Massachusetts," *New York Times* (October 1, 1904).

321 "Danced for Charity," *Washington Post* (January 17, 1895) 3; "C.W. DeKnight, Attorney, Dies in Hospital Here," *Washington Post* (November 24, 1936)8.

322 Bishop Museum, Liliuokalani Diary (June 5, 1902).

323 George F. Henshall, "What is the Matter with Hawaii? *World Today* (July–December, 1902) 1949.

324 Hawaiian, Investigation, Report, Part 1, 3.

325 *Islands in Transition*, ed. Thomas Kemper Hitch and Robert M. Kamins, University of Hawaii (1993) 123; *Who's Who In America* (1902) 1931–1932.

326 Hawaii Archives, DeKnight to Liliuokalani (June 29, 1902 and July 3, 1902).

327 "Hawaii Officer in Hot Water," *Chicago Daily Tribune*, (May 24, 1899); "Charges Against A Judge," *Washington Post* (August 8, 1901) 7. The total amount of the fee was not discernable from the archival records. The queen did authorize a payment of one thousand five hundred dollars as the last installment. Hawaii Archives, Liliuokalani to J. O. Carter (August 8, 1902).

328 Hawaii Archives, Macfarlane to Liliuokalani (August 23, 1902). The queen's meeting with the Burtons is implicit in her diary entry of September 20, 1902; Bishop Museum, Diary (September 17, 20, 1902); *Yale Shingle*, Yale University: New Haven (1904)54 (Aluli class photograph).

329 Investigation, Report, Part 1, 6.

330 Investigation, Testimony, Part 2, 38–48, (Dole) 237, 205–213.

331 Investigation, Testimony, Part 2, (Humphreys) 205–213, (Gear) 55–61; (Little) 349–350.

332 Investigation, Testimony, Part 2, (Smith) 495–499.

333 Investigation, Testimony, Part 2, (Sanford Dole) 435–439.

334 Investigation, Testimony, Part 2, (Kuhio) 315, 326–328.

335 Investigation, Testimony, Part 2, (Kuhio) 326–327; *Betrayal of Liliuokalani*, 371.

336 Investigation, Testimony, Part 2, (Kuhio) 326–327.

337 Investigation, Testimony, Part 2, (Kuhio) 326–327.

338 Investigation, Testimony, Part2, (Little) 367–389.

339 Investigation, Testimony, Part 2, (Mitchell) 452.

340 Bishop Museum, Smith to "Everybody"(signed September 29, 1902).

341 Investigation, Testimony, Part 2, 453–488, et al.

342 Investigation, Part 2, 474–475, 542.

343 Investigation, Part 2, 475 (Dole), 467 (Smith), 461 (Thurston), 459 (Damon), 460 (Cooper).

344 Investigation, Testimony, Part 2, 486–487, 550–551, (Loebenstein), 585(Iaukea).

345 Bishop Museum, Liliuokalani Diary (September 20, 1902).

346 Hawaii Archives, DeKnight to Liliuokalani (October 7, 1902).

347 Hawaii Archives, DeKnight to Liliuokalani (October 7, 1902).

348 *Unconquerable Hero*, 222–227.

349 Hawaii Archives, DeKnight to Liliuokalani (October 7, 1902); Liliuokalani to DeKnight (October 24, 1902, attached list of debts, bond, and property sales); Liliuokalani personal notes (undated) No.183d; *Unconquerable Hero*, 244–246.

350 "Liliuokalani in Washington," *New York Times* (November 24, 1902).

351 Charles Suddarth Kelly, *Washington, D.C., Then and Now*. Dover Publications, Inc: New York (1984), 56, 60.

352 Bishop Museum, Liliuokalani Diary (November 23, 26, 27, 1902); Bishop Museum, Liliuokalani Diary (December 1, December 18, and January 18, 1903).

353 Investigation, Report, Part 1, 8–9, 15, 18, 30, 32.

354 Investigation, Report, Part 1, 87.

355 Investigation, Report, Part 1, 83–86, 87–88, 93, 99.

356 Investigation, Report, Part 1, 93, 99.

357 Cong. Record 57th Con; 2nd Sess. Senate (February 9, 1903) 1929; Bishop Museum, Liliuokalani Diary (January 23, 24, 26, February 8, 12, 1903).

358 James Parker, "Paternalism and Racism: Senator John C. Spooner and American Minorities, 1892–1907." *Dictionary of Wisconsin History*, Vol. 57 (1974) 195; "Proceedings in Congress," *New York Times* (February 25, 1903) 3; Cong. Rec. 57th Cong 2nd Sess. Senate (February 25, 1903) 2616; Bishop Museum, Liliuokalani Diary (February 26, 28, 1903).

359 James Parker, "Paternalism and Racism: Senator John C. Spooner and American Minorities, 1892–1907." *Dictionary of Wisconsin History*, Vol. 57 (1974) 195; "Proceedings in Congress," *New York Times* (February 25, 1903) 3; Cong. Rec. 57th Cong. 2nd Sess. Senate (February 25, 1903) 2616; Bishop Museum, Liliuokalani Diary (February 26, 28, 1903).

360 Bishop Museum, Liliuokalani Diary, March 3, 5, 8, 1902) "Liliuokalani's Claims," *Los Angeles Times* (February 26, 1903) 1; "No Money for the Ex-Queen," *Boston Daily Globe* (March 3, 1903).

361 *When All Is Said and Done*, 92–100; "Death List of a Day," *New York Times* (March 9, 1903);

"Colonel Blount Goes to Reward," *Atlanta Constitution* (March 9, 1903) 1.

362 "Liliuokalani in Washington, D.C." *Washington Post* (November 24, 1903); Cong. Rec. Senate, 58th Cong.1st Sess. (November 20, 1903) 398; Hawaii Archives, Liliuokalani to J.O. Carter (May 4, June 1, 1902).

363 Cong. Rec., 58th Cong. 2nd Sess. House (January 18, 1904) 854, Senate (January 15, 1904) 791.

364 Cong. Rec., 58th Cong. 2nd Sess. (February 12, 1904) 1922–1928.

365 Cong. Rec., 58th Cong. 2nd Sess. (February 12, 1904) 1922–1928.

366 Cong. Rec., 58th Cong.2nd Sess. Senate, 1009, 1928, 1977, 1981–1982. In 1906, Senator Foraker engaged in a battle with the president over the fate of black members of the military he believed unfairly accused of wrongdoing in Brownsville, Texas.

367 Hawaii Archives, Liliuokalani to Hoar (February 1904, day not specified. She refers to his letter of February 16 and the prospect of the vote for reconsideration, which occurred on February 19); 58th Cong. 2nd Sess. Senate, 2014; *The Independent* (February 25, 1904), 56; "Sorrow in Massachusetts, Senator Hoar Death Announced in Worcester by Tolling of the Bells," *New York Times* (October 1, 1904).

368 Hawaii Archives, Liliuokalani to J.O. Carter (February 5, March 18, 1904).

369 See, generally, Jose D. Fermin, *The 1904 World's Fair, The Philippines Experience*. UP Press (2004)"; Flashes from the Wires," *Los Angeles Times*(May 12, 1904); "Liliuokalani is Ill," *New York Times* (May 12, 1904); see also "The World's Greatest Fair, Saint Louis," a film by Scott Huegerich and Bob Maino, Civil Pictures (2004), part 11,"A Women's View," part 13, "Savagery on Display."(DVD).

370 "Cannon Again Nominated," *New York Times* (March 16, 1904)1;Fenton Whitlock Booth, *To Whom It May Concern* (1926)43–45, personally published autobiography available through the Indiana Historical Society, Indianapolis, Indiana; Booth Tarkington, *Gentleman From Indiana*, S.S. McClure: New York (1899). Tarkinton's stories in *Penrod and Sam*, Grossett & Dunlap: New York (1916) were drawn largely from his childhood pranks and adventures with Fenton Booth during Tarkinton's visits to his maternal grandparents in Marshall. Tarkington also was the author of the widely acclaimed movie drawn from his novel, *The Magnificent Ambersons*, directed by Orson Wells.

371 *Sixth Annual Report of the Anti-Imperialist League* (1904) 9–15; Democratic Party Platform, 1904 in K.H. Porter, *National Party Platforms*, 246 (Democrat), 260(Republican); *To Whom It May Concern*,46; "Booth for Claims Bench," *The Washington Post* (March 15, 1905)4; Marion T. Bennett, *The United States Court of Claims, Part I, The Judges*. The Committee on the Bicentennial of Independence and the Constitution of the Judicial Conference of the United States, Washington, D.C. (1976)103.

372 "Wide Ranging Debate," *Washington Post* (February 12, 1904)4; "Liliuokalani En Route to Washington," *Wall Street Journal* (November 23, 1904)7.

373 Hawaii Archives, Liliuokalani to J.O. Carter (February 4, 1905); Dodge to Liliuokalani, (April 19, 1905). Con. Rec. 53rd Con. 3rd Sess. (January 13, 1905) 773; Hawaii Archives, Liliuokalani to J.O. Carter (January 23, 1905, March 14, 1905); Accounting Record by J.O. Carter (October 1905).

374 Hawaii Archives, Liliuokalani to J.O. Cater (March 14, 18, 27, 1905; April 1, 22, 1905); Hawaii Archives, Liliuokalani to J.O. Carter, February 13, 1905); Chamberlin to Liliuokalani (April 19, 1905).

375 Carol Highsmith and Fred Lardphair, *Embassies of Washington*. Preservation Press: Washington, D.C. (1992)97; Margaret MacMillan, *Paris 1919*. Random House: New York (2001) 366.

376 Hawaii Archives, Schoenfeld to Liliuokalani (April 28, 1905).

377 Hawaii Archives, Joseph Aea to Schoenfeld (May 1, 1905); Liliuokalani to John Boyd and Clarence DeKnight (May 3, 1905).

378 Hawaii Archives, Schoenfeld to Liliuokalani (July 9, 1905).

379 Hawaii Archives, Schoenfeld to Liliuokalani (July 28, 2005); Accounting Record (September 1905–December 1905).

380 Hawaii Archives, Liliuokalani Collection, Draft Petitions, 1905 (one in Hawaiian, with a translation done in 1928, to Congress and President Roosevelt) and draft and final letters to the vice president and congress (November 27, 1905).

381 Hawaii Archives, Liliuokalani Collection, Draft Petitions, 1905 (one in Hawaiian, with a translation done in 1928) to Congress and President Roosevelt) and draft and final letters to vice president and congress (November 27, 1905); "Ex-Queen Asks $10,000,000," *New York Times* (December 13, 1905).

382 Hawaii Archives, Kaipo to Liliuokalani (December 16, 1905); Liliuokalani to Kaipo (reply, undated, 1905 referring to December 16, 1905 letter).

383 *Na Kua'aina* (McGregor), 44; Davianna Pomaikai McGregor, Prince Kuhio," An Introduction to His Life,"1, and Noenoe K. Silva, "The First Election of Ke Keikialii Kuhio Kalanianaole," 4, *Biography Hawaii: Five Lives*, University of Hawaii: Manoa (2006); Wilcox died on October 23, 1903, *Unconquerable Hero*, 252–254.

384 Bishop Museum, Liliuokalani to Kuhio, (March 7, 1906); Hawaii Archives, Prince Kuhio to Liliuokalani (March 23, 1906).

385 Hawaii Archives, Liliuokalani to Fred Chamberline (May 1908); Hawaii Archives, Aimoku to Liliuokalani, (February 12, June 14, 1907); HABS, 63 (repairs at Washington Place).

386 Hawaii Archives, Kuhio to Liliuokalani (April 24, 1908).

387 "Senator Morgan Dies Suddenly," *New York Times*, July 12, 1907; "John Morgan is dead, but his name will ever be a precious heritage in Alabama." *Birmingham Age Herald*, (June 13, 1907) 4.

388 Hawaii Archives, Harden to Liliuokalani (June 29, 1908).

389 "Hawaii Trade May Be Ours," *Los Angeles Times* (December 20, 1908) V15; Alfred S. Hartwell, "The Organization of a Territorial Government for Hawaii." *Yale Law Journal*, Vol. IX no.3 (December 1899)112; In the United States Court of Claims, *Liliuokalani v. United States of America*, No. 30,577, Brief for Petitioner Upon Demurrer, 12, 20; Constitution of the Republic of Hawaii, Article 95 (1894.); *Who Owns the Crown Lands?* 229.

390 "Sidney Miller Ballou Dies: Ex-Judge of Hawaii," *New York Times* (October 2, 1929)2; "The Organization of a Territorial Government,"3; *Territory of Hawaii v. Kapiolani Estate, Limited.* 18 Haw. 640 (1908); In the Court of Claims, *Liliuokalani v. United States of America*, No. 30,577, Brief for Petitioner Upon Demurrer, 12, 20; *Hawaii's Story by Hawaii's Queen*, 280; E. Laurence Gay, "Nineteenth Century Law Practice And The Genesis of a Honolulu Law Firm," *Hawaii Bar Journal*, Vol VII(2004) 74,75;Carol A. Eblen,"Goodsill Anderson Quinn & Stifel," *Hawaii Bar Journal* (October 1999)91,92; *Hawaii's Story by*

Hawaii's Queen, 354–357, 358–360; See, for example, Ballou argued in *Carter v. Territory of Hawaii*, 200 U.S. 255(1906); *Kawananankoa v. Polyblank*, 205 U.S. 348(1907); and *Notley v. Brown* 208 U.S. 429(1908).

391 "Sidney Miller Ballou Dies: Ex-Judge of Hawaii," *New York Times* (October 2, 1929) 2; "The Organization of a Territorial Government,"3; *Territory of Hawaii v. Kapiolani Estate, Limited.* 18 Haw. 640 (1908).

392 *Territory of Hawaii v. Kapiolani Estate, Limited*, 18 Haw. 640, at 644–645 (1908).

393 *Territory of Hawaii v. Kapiolani Estate Limited*, 18 Haw. 640 at 645. For example, in *Luther v. Borden*, 48 U.S. 1, 39–40 (1849), the merits of the case were decided effectively by the Rhode Island Supreme Court, which gave comfort to the United States Supreme Court. In *Jones v. United States*,137 U.S. 202(1890), a trial on the merits was held. The question before the United States Supreme Court was the degree of deference that should be shown to the opinions of the Secretary of State and Treasury about the meaning of the law. The Supreme Court upheld the duty of the trial court to hear and decide the merits of the case.

394 *To Whom It May Concern*, 50–51 (Booth admired Taft's tenure as chief justice of the United States Supreme Court. Taft also nominated Booth to be chief justice of the court of claims but without success and later recommended him to President Calvin Coolidge). "Significance of Taft Toast, Washington Talks of Brilliant Predictions of Col. Hopkins, Bard," *New York Times* (January 31, 1904) (Hopkins' toast, read by Secretary Eliu Root, included the following: "It needs no prophet's eye to read his fate; His time will surely come to head the State...."); Kenneth Wimmel, *Roosevelt and the Great White Fleet, America Sea Power Comes of Age.* Washington, DC: Brassey's (1998).

395 Bishop Museum, Petition by Liliuokalani to William Howard Taft (November 8, 1908).

396 "Queen Liliuokalani Borrows $70,000," *New York Times* (November 12, 1908)1; see also Answer in *Liliuokalani and her next friend Jonah Kuhio Kalanianole v. Iaukea, Smith, Damon, and others*, Hawaii, Civil No. 2009 (March 9, 1916), 29, Para. XVIII; "Liliuokalani Arrives," *New York Times* (November 23, 1908) 1.

397 "Hawaii Trade May Be Ours," *Los Angeles Times* (December 20, 1908) 15.

398 "Hawaii's Queen Writing Book," *Honolulu Semi-Weekly Star* (December 4, 1908) 6. To the author's knowledge a manuscript of the book has never been located or disclosed publicly. Perhaps the manuscript, if done in the manner the reporter described (the queen was not quoted in the article about this subject), was submitted to the publisher; *Dictionary of American Biography*, Vol. XVII, p. 502. New York: Charles Scribner's Sons (1935) 502 (Jane Stanford).

399 "Liliuokalani Asks $200,000," *New York Times* (November 30, 1908); "Payne Makes Speed at Tariff Hearings," *New York Times* (November 20, 1908); "Seek Changes for Hawaii," *Washington Post* (January 25, 1908) 4 (McClellan was from Oklahoma and Kansas); Hatch, originally from Portsmouth, New Hampshire arrived in Honolulu in 1878 at twenty-five years old. "Nineteenth Century Law Practice and the Genesis of a Honolulu Law Firm," E. Laurence Gay, *Hawaii Bar Journal*, Vol. II, No. 13, 1.

400 *Damon v. Territory of Hawaii*, 194 U.S. 154(1904), opinion by Justice Oliver Wendell Holmes.

401 "Ex-Queen Before Committee," *New York Times* (January 15, 1909) 4; "Ex-Queen Appears

at Capitol," Boston *Daily Globe* (January 15, 1909) 2; "Plea of the Queen," *Honolulu Semi-Weekly Star* (January 26, 1909) 7.

402 "Current Topics," *The Youth Companion* (December 24, 1908) 654.

403 "Claim of Liliuokalani, Evidence before the Committee on Claims of the House of Representatives," House Bill 7094, 60th Cong.: 1st Sess., January 14 and 21, 1909. Government Printing Office (1909) 4–7.

404 Committee on Claims, 5–6.

405 Committee on Claims, 6–7.

406 Committee on Claims, 7, 14.

407 Committee on Claims, 8

408 Committee on Claims, 11–13.

409 Committee on Claims, 11–13.

410 Committee on Claims,15, 17. "Liliuokalani Asks $200, 000," *New York Times* (November 30, 1908)1(She was "forced to mortgage her home for funds with which to finance her trip here." The *Times* also reported that her income was $4000 a year provided by the Hawaii legislature. See Committee on Claims, 21; See also "Queen Liliuokalani Borrows $70, 000," *New York Times*, (November 12, 1908)1.

411 Committee on Claims, 17.

412 Committee on Claims, 17–19.

413 Committee on Claims, 19–20.

414 Committee on Claims, 20–21.

415 Committee on Claims, 20–21.

416 Committee on Claims, 20–22.

417 "Ex-Queen Appears At Capitol," *Boston Daily Globe* (January 15, 1909) 2.

418 Committee on Claims, 22–34.

419 "Fair Treatment for Liliuokalani," *Christian Science Monitor* (January 23, 1909) 1; "Ex-Queen before Committee," *New York Times* (January 15, 1909) 4; "Ex-Queen Seeks the Restoration of Fortune," *Los Angeles Times* (January 15, 1909) 1; "Pathetic Appeal By Ex-Queen Lil," *Chicago Daily Tribune* (January 15, 1909) 1; "A Queen's Mistake," *Washington Post* (January 25, 1909) 6.

420 "Ex-Queen Appears At Capitol," *Boston Daily Globe* (January 15, 1909) 2; "Liliuokalani Tells Story of Her Life," *Boston Daily Globe* (February 14, 1909) 1.

421 "Callers at the White House," *Washington Post* (March 3, 1909) 4; "Liliuokalani says Farewell To Roosevelt," *Honolulu Semi-Weekly Star* (March 19, 1909) 3; "The Queen Returns," *Honolulu Semi-Weekly Star* (April 2, 1909) 1.

422 "The Queen Returns," *Honolulu Semi-Weekly Star* (April 2, 1909)1; Hawaii Archives, Hatch to Iaukea (November 27, 1911); "Justice Ballou Complimented" *Honolulu Semi-Weekly Star* (May 4, 1909) 4.

423 *Hawaii's Story by Hawaii's Queen*, 142; Curtis Iaukea and Lorna Watson, *By Royal Command*, Thompson Shore: Dexter, Michigan (1988) 59–127. *By Royal Command* was defined by its authors as "biographical notes" published well after Iaukea's death. The book's characterization of events is not necessarily attributable to Iaukea. See *By Royal*

Command, History of Manuscript, i; Hawaii Archives, Power of Attorney, Liliuokalani to Iaukea (May 4, 1909, notarized May 19, 1909). A previous power of attorney was revoked twice by the Queen. Iaukea assumed responsibility for her property and finances on November 13; "Iaukea After Jonah, Hawaiian Colonel Will Go to Washington and Endeavor to Have the Prince Unseated," *Los Angeles Times* (December 13, 1904).

424 "Nineteenth Century Law Practice and the Genesis of a Honolulu Law Firm,"74 (Hatch's relationship to Kinney, Ballou, Prosser, and Anderson); "Justice Ballou Complimented," *Honolulu Semi-Weekly Star* (May 4, 1909) 4; *Who Owns the Crown Lands?* 229, n.18; *Men of Hawaii*, 1930 (Mason Prosser), 401 and 1935 (Robbins Anderson), 25; 25 *Hawaiian Almanac and Annual*, 1899. Thomas G. Strum: Hawaii (1899) 136; Hawaii Archives, Accounting Statement, Aea to Liliuokalani (July 1 through July 31, 1909).

425 *Liliuokalani v. United States of America*, Petition No. 30577, (typed version), at 10.

426 *The Betrayal of Liliuokalani*, 372.

427 *Liliuokalani by her Next Friend, Jonah Kuhio vs. Iaukea, Smith and others*, Equity Division No. 2009, Circuit Court of First Judicial Circuit. Answer of Respondents (March 9, 1916) 7 par. VIII.

428 Hawaiian Archives, Queen Liliuokalani Deed of Trust (December 2, 1909); "Ex-Queen to Endow Orphans," *New York Times* (December 4, 1909) 7.

429 *Hawaii's Story by Hawaii's Queen*, 111.

430 Hawaii Archives, Iaukea to Liliuokalani (December 4, 1909).

431 Smith's law firm did not represent Liliuokalani during the law suit filed by Kuhio in 1915 to have the Queen's decisions, beginning in late 1909, declared null and void because she lacked the competence to make them. Smith's firm represented the Trust. The Queen was represented by former Hawaii Supreme Court justice Antonio Perry and, for a period of time, by a court appointed lawyer, Lorrin Andrews. " Kuhio Institutes Suit to Break Trust Which Controls Property of Queen Liliuokalani," *Pacific Commercial Advertiser*(December 1, 1915)1,7,9; See also *Liliuokalani by her Next Friend, Jonah Kuhio vs. Iaukea, Smith and others*, Equity Division No. 2009, Circuit Court of First Judicial Circuit. Answer of Respondents (March 9, 1916), 16–36 par. XII. Unresolved disagreement existed among the parties as to the precise facts extant in 1910, especially as they related to the Crown lands claim; "Liliuokalani To Oppose Breaking Her Trust Deed," *Pacific Commercial Advertiser* (December 17,1915)19; "Queen Asks To Dismiss Action Over Property," *Pacific Commercial Advertiser*(December 31,1915) 1,7;See also *Jonah Kuhio Kalanianaole v. Liliuokalani*, 23 Haw. 457(1916) (list of counsel); Hawaii Archives, Iaukea to Liliuokalani (December 8, 1909).

432 Hawaii Archives, Cleghorn to Liliuokalani (December 18, 1909).

433 Hawaii Archives, Iaukea to Liliuokalani (January 14, 1910).

434 Hawaii Archives, Cleghorn to Liliuokalani (January 26, 1910).

435 *The United States Court of Claims, A History. Part II, Origin–Development–Jurisdiction*, 1855–1978, The Committee on the Bicentennial: Washington, D.C. (1976) 7–13.

436 *Court of Claims History. Part II*, 1, 7, 9–13, 16, 23(note 14) 38, 41–45; See, for example, *Mahin v. United States*, 41 Ct.Cl. 1(1905); *Blacklock v. United States*, 41 Ct.Cl. 89(1906); *Herbert v. United States*, 41 Ct.Cl. 378(1906) (arguments based on the submission of evidence).

437 See generally *Court of Claims History*, Part II, 20–21 (procedures), 36–37 (appearance); "The Corcoran Gallery of Art," *The Aldine, The Art Journal of America*, Vol. II, No. 6, James Sutton Company: New York (June 1874) 120. The physical composition of the court room also was described in cryptic references in untitled documents provided to the author by a diligent archivist at the Renwick Art Gallery.

438 *Liliuokalani v United States of America*, No. 30577. United States Court of Claims. Petition (January 20, 1910), National Archives, Printed Copy (January 24, 1910). Allegation 1, 2, 3, 4, 5, 6, 7, 8, 9.

439 *Liliuokalani v United States of America*, Petition, Allegation 1, 2, 3, 4, 5, 6, 7, 8, 9.

440 *Liliuokalani v. United States of America*, Petition, Allegation 10, 11, 12, 13, 14.

441 *Liliuokalani v. United States of America*, Petition, Allegation 12, 13, 14, 15, 16.

442 *Liliuokalani v. United States of America*, Petition, Allegation 19.

443 *History of the Court of Claims, A History, Part II*, 1, 9, 16, 23(note 14) 38; Rules of the Court of Claims of the United States. Government Printing Office: Washington, D.C. (1907) (1907) Rules 19–23 (Statutes of Limitations).

444 See Rules of the Court of Claims of the United States. Rule 32 (Amendments as of right with and without objection by defendant). It also would have been helpful to have some facts about Hawaii's origins and the use and meaning of land within the Hawaiian cultural experience. Given the narrow perspective of the missionary historians and their children and the absence of any meaningful reliance on Hawaiian language documents such an undertaking would have required a radical departure from the prevailing methods and perspective that was well beyond Ballou's willingness or, probably, his ideological interest or cultural perspective.

445 *Liliuokalani v. United States of America*, Demurrer and Brief for the Defendants, 4–5.

446 *Liliuokalani v. United States of America*, Demurrer and Brief, 4–5; Reply Brief of the Defendants, 12.

447 Liliuokalani v United States of America, Demurrer and Brief, 4–5.

448 *Liliuokalani v. United States of America*, Demurrer and Brief for the Defendants,4; See Rules of the Court of Claims of the United States(1907) Rule 32 (Amendments as of right with and without objection by defendant).

449 "Liliuokalani in Boston," *Boston Daily Globe* (January 31, 1910) 12; "Harvard Visited By Liliuokalani," *Christian Science Monitor*,"(February 1, 1910)4; "Queen Lil Now A Poor Women," *Los Angeles Times* (February 10, 1910)18; "Waterfront Events," *Honolulu Semi-Weekly Star* (March 25, 1910)7.On March 28, 1910 the committee on claims issued an Adverse Report, with a recommendation that the bill providing Liliuokalani compensation "do lie on the table, for the reason that the claim is now pending in the Court of Claims." U.S. Congressional Record, 61st Cong. 2nd Sess. 2(March 28,1910), Vol. 45, 3876; "Liliuokalani, Adverse Report," Report No. 880, 61st Con.2nd Sess. to accompany H.R. 7414.

450 "Views of Visitors In Washington," *Washington Post* (March 17, 1910) 6.

451 "Views of Visitors In Washington," *Washington Post*, (March 17, 1910) 6.

452 *History of the Court of Claims*, Part I, The Judges 1855–1976, 86–90,92–96, 104, 111.

453 *For Whom It May Concern*, 46, 54–55; *Damon v. Territory of Hawaii* 194 U.S. 154(1904) opinion by Justice Oliver Wendell Holmes. In examining the existence of certain fishing rights,

Holmes wrote that "A right of this sort is somewhat different...but it seems to be well known to Hawaii, and, if it is established...the plaintiff's claim is not to be approached as if it were anomalous or monstrous."; *Hamilton v. United States and Chickasaw Nation*, 42 Ct.Cl. 282(1907) (Booth in Indian case).

454 *Liliuokalani v. United States of America*, Brief for Petitioner Upon Demurrer (March 26,1910),4–9; See, for example, the thoughtful and thoroughly researched explanation of the political nature of the 1864 Hawaii Supreme Court decision done by Professor Jon M. Van Dyke. *Who Owns The Crown Lands?* 71–88.; Ballou's brief was filed on March 23. It is unclear how Ballou, sitting alone in Washington, D.C., produced a twenty-two page printed brief in three days. He may have made use of a local law firm or his own firm already had produced a memorandum or tentative brief for Ballou before he left Hawaii that he merely adapted *post haste* to the demurrer filed by the United States. The brief made no reference by name, date or quotation to the content of the demurrer except on the cover page and in the last paragraph. It was like two ships passing in the night.

455 *Liliuokalani v. United States of America*, Brief for Petitioner Upon Demurrer, 11.

456 *Liliuokalani v. United States of America*, Brief for Petitioner Upon Demurrer, 12–13, 22.

457 *Liliuokalani v. United States of America*, Brief for Petitioner Upon Demurrer, 18, 20–21.

458 *Liliuokalani v. United States of America*, Reply Brief of Defendant, 1, 2, 7.

459 *Liliuokalani v. United States*, Supplemental Brief, 21.

460 "S.S. Ashbaugh Dies of Paralysis," *Washington Post* (December 3, 1928)3.

461 There was no verbatim transcript of the oral argument. Common practice was for the clerk to transcribe the oral argument in short hand or summarize or recite from notes made by the lawyers. Absent as well was the colloquy between and among the judges and the lawyers. The clerk's recitation of the oral arguments was included at the beginning of cited case. *Liliuokalani v. United States of America*, 45 Ct.Cl. 418(1910).

462 *Liliuokalani v. United States of America*, 45 Ct.Cl. at 423.

463 *Liliuokalani v. United States of America*, 45 Ct.Cl. at 424.

464 *Liliuokalani v. United States of America*, 45 Ct.Cl. at 426–427.

465 *Liliuokalani v. United States of America*, 45 Ct.Cl. at 428.

466 *Liliuokalani v United States*, 45 Ct. Cl. at 428.

467 *Liliuokalani v United States*, 45 Ct. Cl. at 429; "Liliuokalani Loses her Case," *Hawaiian Gazette* (May 20, 1910)3; Editorial, "Sympathy for Liliuokalani," *Hawaiian Gazette* (May 20, 1910)4.

468 "About 'Queen Lil's' Claim," *Tucson Citizen*, reprinted in the *Honolulu Semi-Weekly Star* (January 21, 1910)7.

469 *Betrayal of Liliuokalani*, 372; David C. Farmer, "A Legal Legacy," *Biography of Hawaii: Five Lives, A Series of Public Remembrances*. Center for Biographical Research: University of Hawaii: Manoa, September 6, 2007(Sanford Dole); Smith, Warren & Hemenway, Smith's law firm, represented the Queen before the Hawaii legislature. Hawaii Archives, Invoice from Smith, Warren & Hemenway to Liliuokalani (April 28, 1911); Ballou and his wife Lucia moved actively into Washington's social fabric. He became a lobbyist for the Hawaii sugar corporations in Washington, D.C. and San Francisco, which included his involvement in the highly visible exposure and controversy

concerning the money he and others expended in pursuit of their craft. "Sugar Men Have Spent $100,000, Carter and Ballou Before Committee," *Boston Daily Globe* (June 11, 1913)18; "Secretary and Mrs. Lane are Quests of Judge and Mrs. Ballou at Luncheon," *Washington Post* (May 8, 1915) 7. "Sidney Ballou Dies — Ex Judge of Hawaii," *New York Times* (October 30, 1929) 20.

470 Jean Hobbs. Hawaii: *A Pageant of the Soil.* Stanford University Press, Palo Alto (1935), 123; *Who Owns The Crown Lands?* 274 (*Rice v. Cayetano*); Neil Thomas Proto, "Culture Into Law, The Conveyance of Kahoolawe Island," Symposium on Native Hawaiian Land Rights, Eminent Domain and Regulatory Takings (Honolulu, Hawaii), January 12, 1995, sponsored by the University of Hawaii Law School, the Native Hawaiian Bar Association, Pacific Law Institute and the Kamehameha Schools/Bernice Pauahi Bishop Estate (federal judiciary and native Hawaiian decisions).

471 *The Betrayal of Liliuokalani*, 392; "An American Queen," *Outlook* (May 30, 1917) 177. The original publication of this event at Washington Place was recited without the characterization of "reconciliation" later imposed in a reiteration of the event at the time of the queen's death in "The Queen is Dead," *Outlook* (November 21, 1917) 452, and then quoted again, perhaps in the biographer's need for closure of a kind, by Helena Allen in the *Betrayal of Liliuokalani.*

472 "Liliuokalani Near Death," *New York Times* (November 10, 1917); "The Queen is Dead," *The Outlook* (November 21, 1917) 452; *Betrayal of Liliuokalani*, 397–398.

473 William C. Hodges, Jr., *The Passing of Liliuokalani*, Honolulu Star-Bulletin Publishers (1918) 35, 39–40, 51–52, 55–58. The description of the funeral in the text is based on the eloquently crafted words from this source.

SELECTED BIBLIOGRAPHY

BOOKS AND PERIODICALS

Allen, Helena. *The Betrayal of Liliuokalani, Last Queen of Hawaii.* Mutual Publishing: Honolulu, 1982.

Allen, Helena. *Sanford Ballard Dole, Hawaii's Only President, 1844-1926.* Arthur Clark, Glendale, California, 1998.

Andrade, Ernest Jr. *The Unconquerable Rebel, Robert Wilcox and Hawaiian Politics, 1880-1903.* University Press of Colorado: Niwot, Colorado, 1996.

Beatty, Jack. *The Age of Betrayal, The Triumph of Money in America, 1865-1900.* Vintage: New York, 2008.

Booth, Fenton Whitlock. *To Whom It May Concern* (1924). Unpublished personal memoir available through the Indiana Historical Society (Indianapolis).

Castle, Alfred L. "Advice for Hawaii: The Dole–Burgess Letters." *Hawaiian Journal of History*, Vol. 15 (1981).

Castle, William R. Jr., *The Life of Samuel Northrup Castle.* Samuel and Mary Castle Foundation and Hawaiian Historical Society: Honolulu, 1960.

Coman, Katherine. *The History of Contract Labor.* Published for the American Economic Association: New York, Third Series, Vol. IV, No.3 (August, 1903).

Cook, Evelyn E. *100 Years of Healing, The Legacy of a Kauai Missionary Doctor.* Halewai Publishing: Kauai, 2003.

Coffman, Thomas. *Nation Within, The Story of America's Annexation of the Nation of Hawaii.* Epicenter Press: Hawaii, 2006.

Curti, Merle. *The Growth of American Though.* Harper & Row Publishers. New York, 1964(3rd edition).

Dole, Sanford. "The Problems of Population." *The Pacific Commercial Advertiser*, (September 28, 1873).

Dole, Sanford. "Evolution of Hawaiian Land Tenures." *Overland Monthly*, Vol.25, Issue 150 (June 1895).

Faust, Drew Gilpin. *This Republic of Suffering, Death and the Civil War*. Alfred A. Knopf: New York, 2008.

Gambino, Richard. *Vendetta, The True Story of the Worst Lynching In America*. Doubleday & Company, Inc. Garden City, New York, 1977.

Gambino, Richard. *Blood of My Blood, The Dilemma of the Italian-Americans*. Doubleday Anchor Book: New York, 1974.

"God and Sugar: The Gulick Brothers' Fight Against King Kamehameha V and the Sugar Planters in Hawaii, 1864-1870." *The Hawaiian Journal of History*, Vol.37 (2003).

Goode, James M. *Best Addresses, A Century of Washington's Distinguished Apartment Houses*. Smithsonian Books, Washington, D.C. Smithsonian Books: Washington, D.C., 1988.

Goode, James M. *Capital Losses, A Cultural History of Washington's Destroyed Places*. Smithsonian Books: Washington, D.C., 2003.

Halford, Francis John. *9 Doctors & God*. University of Hawaii Press: Honolulu, 1954.

Hibbard, Don and David Franzen. *The View from Diamond Head, Royal Residence to Urban Resort*. Editions Limited Book: Hawaii, 1986.

Hoar, George. *Autobiography of Seventy Years*. C. Scribner's Sons: New York, 1903.

Irwin, Bernice Pilani. *I Knew Liliuokalani*. Native Books, Inc: Hawaii, 2006.

Johnson, Paul. *The Intellectuals*. Harper & Row, New York, 1988.

Kameeleihiwa, Lilikala. *Native Land and Foreign Desires*. Bishop Museum Press: Honolulu, 1992.

Kling, David W. "The New Divinity and the Origins of the American Board of Commissioners for Foreign Missions, 1810-1914," *North American Foreign Missions, 1810-1914, Theology, Theory, and Policy Studies in the History of Christian Missionaries*. William B. Eerdmans Publishing Co. Grand Rapids, Michigan, Cambridge, U.K., 2004.

Kinney, William A. *Hawaii's Capacity for Self Government All But Destroyed*. Frank L. Jensen, Publishers: Salt Lake City, Utah, 1927.

Kubota, Gaylord C. "The Lynching of Katsu Goto," *Hawaii Chronicles: Island History from the Pages of Honolulu Magazine*. University of Hawaii Press, Manoa (1996).

Kuykendall, Ralph S. "Negotiations of the Hawaiian Annexation Treaty of 1893." *Annual Report of the Hawaiian Historical Society for the Year 1942*, (September 1943).

Kuykendall, Ralph S. *The Hawaiian Kingdom, Vol. III, 1874-1893,The Kalakaua Dynasty*. University of Hawaii Press, 1967.

Lamar, Dolly Blount. *When All Is Said and Done*. The University of Georgia Press: Athens, 1952.

Lasch, Christopher. *The True and Only Heaven*. Norton: New York, 1991.

Like, Edmund L. and John K. Prendergast. *The Biography of Joseph K. Nawahi*. (Published in 1908; translated by M. Puakea Nogelmeier (CD)). The Hawaiian Historical Society: Honolulu, 1988 Ed.

Logan, Dr. Rayford W. *The Betrayal of the American Negro, From Rutherford B. Hayes to Woodrow Wilson*. Collier Books: New York, Collier-Macmillan Ltd., London. 1965.

Long, David F. *Gold Braids and Foreign Relations, Diplomatic Activities of U.S. Naval Officers 1798-1883*. Naval Institute Press: Annapolis, 1988.

Liholiho, Alexander. *The Journal of Prince Alexander Liholiho, The Voyages Made to the United States, England and France in 1849-1850.* University of Hawaii Press: Honolulu, 1967.

Liliuokalani. *Hawaii's Story By Hawaii's Queen.* Charles E. Tuttle Company, Inc.: Rutland, Vt., 1964 Ed.

MacMillan, Margaret. *Paris 1919.* Random House: New York ,2001.

Madison, James. *Debates to the Federalist Convention* (Int'l Ed.) 1920.

Mahan, Alfred Thayer. *The Interest of America in Sea Power, Present and Future.* Boston, Little, Brown & Company, 1897.

Mawer, Granville Allen. *Ahab's Tragedy, The Saga of South Seas Whaling.* St. Martin's Press: New York, 1999.

Maxfield, Charles A. "The 1845 Organic Sin Debate: Slavery, Sin, and the American Board of Commissioners for Foreign Missions," *North American Foreign Missions, 1810-1914, Theology, Theory, and Policy Studies in the History of Christian Missionaries.* William B. Eerdmans Publishing Co. Grand Rapids, Michigan, Cambridge, U.K., 2004.

McGregor, Davianna Pomaika'i. *Na Kua'aina, Living Hawaiian Culture.* University of Hawaii Press: Honolulu, 2007.

McLaughlin, James. *My Friend The Indian.* Houghton Mifflin Company: Boston (1910).

Menand, Louis. *The Metaphysical Club, A Story of Ideas in America.* Farrar, Straus and Giroux: New York, 2001.

Missionary Album, Sesquicentennial Edition 1820-1970. Hawaiian Mission Children's Society, Honolulu, Hawaii, 1969.

Montcreiff, Robert. *Bart Giamatti, A Profile.* Yale University Press: New Haven, 2007.

Nordyke, Eleanor C. "Blacks in Hawaii: A Demographic and Historic Perspective." *The Hawaiian Journal of History*: Honolulu, Vol.22, (1989).

Osborne, Thomas J. *Empire Can Wait, American Opposition To Hawaiian Annexation, 1893-1898.* The Kent State University Press, Kent, Ohio, 1981.

Parrington, Vernon. *Main Currents in American Thought, An Interpretation of American Literature From the Beginnings to 1920.* Harcourt, Brace and Company, New York, 1930.

Pettigrew, Richard. *The Course of Empire, An Official Record by Richard F. Pettigrew of South Dakota.* Boni & Liveright: New York ,1920.

Philips, Clifton Jackson. "Protestant America and the Pagan World, The First Half Century of the American Board of Commissioners for Foreign Missions, 1810-1860." *Harvard East Asian Monographs,* Harvard University Press: Cambridge, 1969 (reprint of Philips' 1954 PhD. dissertation).

Price, Virginia B. *Washington Place, Historic American Buildings Survey,* National Park Service: Washington, D.C., 2008.

Proto, Neil Thomas, "The Opinion Clause and Presidential Decision Making," 44 *Missouri Law Review* 185, (Spring 1979).

Quigg, Agnes. "Kalakaua Hawaiian Studies Abroad Program," *Hawaiian Journal of History,* Vol. 22, (1988).

Roberts, Dana. "Evangelist or Homemaker," *North American Foreign Missions, 1810-1914, Theology, Theory, and Policy Studies in the History of Christian Missionaries.* William B. Eerdmans Publishing Co. Grand Rapids, Michigan, Cambridge, U.K., 2004.

Silva, Noenoe K. *Aloha Betrayed, Native Hawaiian Resistance To American Colonialism.* Duke University Press: Durham, 2004.

Sinclair, Upton. *Boston*, Albert and Charles Boni: New York, 1928.

Strauss, Roberta Feuerlicht. *Justice Crucified, The Story of Sacco and Vanzetti.* McGraw-Hill: New York, 1977.

Stowe, Harriet Beecher. *Uncle Tom's Cabin.* Border's Classics Edition: Ann Arbor, Michigan, 2006.

Strum, Philippa. *Louis D. Brandeis.* Cambridge: Harvard University Press, 1984.

Tabrah, Ruth M. *Hawaii, A History.* W.W. Norton: New York, 1980.

Takaki, Ronald. *Pau Hana, Plantation Life and Labor in Hawaii.* University of Hawaii Press: Honolulu, 1983.

Tayman, John. *The Colony.* Scribner: New York, 2006.

Thurston, Lucy. *Life and Times of Mrs. Lucy G. Thurston.* S.C. Andrews: Ann Arbor, Michigan, (2nd Ed.) 1921.

Thurston Twigg-Smith. *Hawaiian Sovereignty: Do The Facts Matter?* Goodale Publishing: Honolulu, 1998.

Towse, Edward. *Rebellion of 1895, A Complete History of the Insurrection Against the Republic of Hawaii*, Royal Designs: Hawaii, 1895 and F.W. Grantham: Hawaii, 2004 Ed.

The United States Court of Claims, A History. Part II, Origin-Development-Jurisdiction, 1855-1978, The Committee on the Bicentennial. Government Printing Office: Washington, D.C., 1976.

Trial of A Queen:1895 Military Tribunal. Judicial History Center, Hawaii State Judiciary, 1995; revised 1996.

Warde, William F. "A Forgotten Fighter Against Plutocracy," George Novak writing as William F. Warde. *Fourth International*, New York, Vol. 10, No.2. (February 1949).

Williams, Tennant S. *The New South Faces the World.* Louisiana State University Press: Baton Rouge,1988.

Williams, Tenant S. "James H. Blount, the South, and Hawaiian Annexation," Pacific Historical Review (1988).

Upchurch, Thomas Adams. "Senator John Tyler Morgan and the Genesis of Jim Crow Ideology, 1889-1891." *Alabama Review* (2004).

Van Dyke, Jon. *Who Owns the Crown Lands?* University of Hawaii Press, Honolulu, 2008.

Yzendoorn, Father Reginald, SS.CC. *History of the Catholic Mission in Hawaii.* Hawaii Star Bulletin: Honolulu,1927.

Zambucka, Kristin. *Kalakaua, Hawaii's Last King.* Mana Publishing Company: Honolulu, 2002.

Zimmerman, Warren. *First Great Triumph, How Five American's Made Their Country A World Power.* New York: Farrar, Straus and Giroux, 2004.

JUDICIAL DECISIONS

C. Afong v. Kale, 7 Haw. 594 (1894).

Colyer, et al. v. Skeffington, 265 F.17 (D. Mass.1920).

Damon v. Territory of Hawaii, 194 U.S.154 (1904).

J. Nott & Co. v. Kanahele, 4 Haw. 14 (1887).

In the Matter of the Estate of His Majesty Kamehameha IV, 2 Haw. 715(1864).

King v. H.N. Greenwell, 1 Haw. 85 (1853).

Kuhio v. Liliuokalani, 23 Haw. 457(1916).

Liliuokalani v United States of America (1910), National Archives, RG 123 Records of the United States Court of Claims, general Jurisdiction Case Files, 1855-1939, 30559 thru 30577. Box no. 2200.

Liliuokalani by Her Next Friend, Jonah Kuhio v. Iaukea, Smith, Damon, et al., Equity Division No. 2009, Circuit Court of First Circuit, Hawaii (1915).

L. Ahlo v. Henry Smith et al, 8 Haw. 420 (1892).

Luther v. Borden, 48 U.S. 1(1849).

Territory of Hawaii v. Kapiolani Estate, Limited, 18 Haw. 640 (1908).

Wood v. Afo, 3 Haw. 448 (1873).

Newspaper Articles

"A Concession to Liliuokalani." *New York Times* (February 17, 1896).

"Archibald Hopkins Dies In Washington." *New York Times* (June 19, 1926).

"Exiled from Honolulu, An American Citizen Forcibly Ejected." *New York Times* (February 11, 1895).

"Fair Treatment for Liliuokalani. *Christian Science Monitor* (January 23, 1909).

"Four Alleged Conspirators Arrested." *The Pacific Commercial Advertiser* (December 10, 1894).

"Harvard Visited By Liliuokalani." *Christian Science Monitor* (February 1, 1910).

"Hawaii Trade May Be Ours." *Los Angeles Time* (December 20, 1908).

"Liliuokalani's Brief." *New York World* (February 24, 1893).

Miriam Michelson, "Many Thousands of Native Hawaiians Sign a Protest to the United States Government Against Annexation." *The San Francisco Call* (September 30, 1897).

"Paul Neumann is Dead of Paralysis of the Brain." *Hawaii Gazette*, Honolulu (July 2, 1901).

"The American League: Minister Thurston's Speech Friday Night." *Hawaii Star* (June 16, 1894).

"The Boy Preacher — Crammond Kennedy." *New York Times* (December 27, 1862).

"The Mora Claim Paid At Last." *New York Times* (October 19, 1895).

"Queen Lil Now A Poor Woman." *Los Angeles Times* (February 10, 1910).

INDEX

Bank of America, 115
Barney, Samuel Stebbins, 199
Bate, William Brimage, 167
Beals, Jesse Tarbox, 163
Bey, Minister, 168
Bierce, Ambrose, 30
Bingham, Harry, 127, 227
Bingham, Hiram, 47, 127
Bishop, Charles, 129, 188
Bishop, Sereno, 72, 89-90, 118, 126, 223
Blackburn, Joseph, 144
Blaine, James, 9
Blount, James, 57, 61, 67, 75, 79-80, 100, 119, 122-123, 159-160, 179, 184, 197, 221, 242
Blount, James, Jr., 122
Bohemian Club, 30
Booth, Fenton Whitlock, 4, 165-166, 175, 199, 201-202, 231, 239
Boston, 3, 13-14, 16, 27-28, 31, 40, 47, 55, 64, 67-68, 78, 103, 112, 117-120, 160, 172, 185, 189, 198, 210, 213, 215, 217, 225, 229-230, 234, 236, 238, 241-242
Boston Globe, 118, 160, 185, 213, 230, 234, 236, 238
Boyd, John, 143, 166, 168, 232
Bragg, Edward S., 76, 222
Breckinridge, John C., 79
Brumindi, Constantine, 57
Bryan, William Jennings, 55, 58, 175
Burnham, Daniel, 163, 186
Burton, Joseph, 144
Bush, John, 101

C

Cairo Hotel, 33
California Hotel, 131, 153
Calvin, John, 37
Calvinists, 2, 13-14, 21, 46-47, 49, 53, 102, 210
Campbell, Abigail Kuaihelani Maipinepine, 44
Campbell, Joseph, 45
Cannon, Joseph, 165, 169-171
Cape May, New Jersey, 118
Capitol, 27, 33, 57, 121, 170, 179, 184, 194, 198, 234
Captain Cook, 118, 206, 226
Carlisle, John, 60, 75
Carter, Joseph Owen (J.O.), 23
Castle, Samuel, 48, 219, 239

Caucasians, 16, 33, 53, 63, 65, 69-70, 77, 82, 84, 94, 96-97, 101, 104, 110, 116, 140, 144
Cavour, Camille de, 53
Chamber of Commerce, 136, 178
Chapin, Dr. Alonzo, 47
Cherokee Indians, 36
Chicago, 30-31, 36, 39, 120, 160, 163, 165, 172, 185-186, 190, 198, 229, 234
Chicago Daily Tribune, 185, 229, 234
Chicago Exposition, 39
Chickahominy River, 62
Chickamauga Creek, 79
China, 18, 52, 116, 145, 166
Chinese, 28, 38, 116, 122, 147, 226
Christian Science Monitor, 185, 234, 236, 243
Christians, 4, 14, 37, 40, 46-47, 53, 73, 77, 85, 90, 100, 118, 122, 127, 139, 185, 214, 223, 226, 234, 236, 240-241, 243
Civil War, 3, 17, 19, 21, 29, 31, 33, 35, 55, 57, 66-67, 75-76, 83, 119, 121, 136, 142, 193, 198, 210, 222, 240
Clark, Clarence D., 138
Claudine, SS, 28-29, 148
Cleghorn, Archibald, 23, 32, 134, 188
Cleveland, Grover, 9, 28, 31, 63, 75
Coffman, Lieutenant Dewitt, 86, 215, 218, 223, 239
Columbia Law School, 39
Committee of Safety, 78, 82
Committee on Foreign Affairs, House: Committee on Foreign Affairs, 61
Committee on the Pacific Islands and Porto Rico, Senate, 144-145, 162
Confederacy, 17, 35, 57, 66
Congo, 84
Contract labor, 11, 15, 38, 48, 65-66, 77, 86, 90, 94, 105, 122, 137, 141, 147, 215, 217, 220, 239
Cooke, Amos, 48
Cooper, Henry, 22
Corcoran, William, 1
Corcoran Gallery, 1, 213, 236
Corcoran House, 33
Cosmos Club, 121
Costaggini, Filippo, 57
counter coup (1895), 101, 110, 118
coup d'état (1893), 1-4, 9, 11-13, 15-17, 19-20, 22-23, 28-32, 38-39, 44-45, 51, 55-56, 58, 60-61, 69-70, 77-78, 84-86, 88, 90, 95, 99, 101-102, 104, 107-110, 116, 118, 132, 139, 142,